To Chuck –

With the hope that you find in Ellacuría's life & his theological vision food for your own passionate journey of faith.

Kevin Burke, S.J.
July 11, 2000

# The Ground Beneath the Cross

*The Theology of Ignacio Ellacuría*

✝
# The Ground Beneath the Cross

## The Theology of Ignacio Ellacuría

Kevin F. Burke, S.J.

Georgetown University Press, Washington, D.C.
© 2000 by Georgetown University Press. All rights reserved
Printed in the United States of America
10  9  8  7  6  5  4  3  2  1      2000
This volume is printed on acid-free offset book paper.

**Library of Congress Cataloging-in-Publication Data**

Burke, Kevin F.
  The ground beneath the cross : the theology of Ignacio Ellacuría /
Kevin F. Burke.
      p.   cm.
  Includes bibliographical references and index.
  ISBN 0-87840-761-8 (cloth : alk. paper)
    1. Ellacuría, Ignacio.    I. Title.
BX4705.E46B87   2000
230'.2'092—dc21                                      99-38855
                                                          CIP

 *Dedication*

For my brothers, Larry Burke (1947–1969)
and Dan Burke (1946–1991)

# Contents

# *Abbreviations*

**Collections, Books, and Periodicals**

CIRD       Ellacuría, *Conversión de la Iglesia al Reino de Dios* (1984)

ECA        *Estudios Centroamericanos* (periodical, El Salvador)

EF         Ellacuría, *Escritos filosóficos*, Vol. 1 (1996)

ESTE       Ellacuría et al., *El Salvador: Entre el terror y la esperanza* (1982)

ETM        Ellacuría, *Ignacio Ellacuría: Teólogo mártir por la liberación del pueblo* (1990)

FMF        Ellacuría, *Freedom Made Flesh* (1976)

FRH        Ellacuría, *Filosofía de la realidad histórica* (1990)

IPOP       Ellacuría, *Iglesia de los pobres y organizaciones populares* (1979)

ML/ MLT    Sobrino and Ellacuría, *Mysterium Liberationis* (1990/ English trans., 1994)

RLT        *Revista Latinoamericana de Teología* (periodical, El Salvador)

SPP        Ellacuría, *Seis pistas para la paz* (1994)

ST         *Sal Terrae* (periodical, Spain)

TP         Ellacuría, *Teología política* (1973)

TSSP       Hassett and Lacey, *Towards a Society That Serves Its People* (1991)

VA         Ellacuría, *Veinte años de historia en El Salvador (1969–1989)* (1991)

Zubiri, IS   *Inteligencia sentiente: Inteligencia y realidad*

Zubiri, IL   *Inteligencia y logos*

Zubiri, IR   *Inteligencia y razón*

Zubiri, HD   *El Hombre y Dios*

Zubiri, NHG  *Nature, History, God* (English trans.)

Zubiri, OE   *On Essence* (English trans.)

Zubiri, SE   *Sobre la esencia*

Zubiri, SH   *Sobre el Hombre*

## Frequently Cited Articles by Ellacuría

| | |
|---|---|
| 1975 "Antropología" | "La antropología filosófica de Xavier Zubiri" |
| 1975 "Hacia" | "Hacia una fundamentación filosófica del método teológico latinoamericano" |
| 1975 "Tesis sobre teología" | "Tesis sobre la posibilidad, necesidad y sentido de una teología latinoamericana" |
| 1976 "Propiedad" | "La historización del concepto de propiedad como principio de desideologización" |
| 1977 "Sacramento histórico" | "Iglesia de los pobres, sacramento histórico de la liberación" |
| 1978 "Bien común" | "Historización del bien común y de los derechos humanos en una sociedad dividida" |
| 1978 "Por qué muere Jesús" | "Por qué muere Jesús y por qué le matan" |
| 1978 "Teología como praxis" | "La teología como momento ideológico de la praxis eclesial" |
| 1979 "Fundamentación biológica" | "Fundamentación biológica de la ética" |
| 1981 "Lugar teológico" | "Los pobres, 'lugar teológico' en America Latina" |
| 1981 "Nueva obra" | "La nueva obra de Zubiri: 'Inteligencia Sentiente' " |
| 1981 "Verdadero pueblo" | "El verdadero pueblo de Dios según Monseñor Romero" |
| 1983 "Aproximación" | "Aproximación a la obra completa de Xavier Zubiri" |
| 1985 "Función liberadora" | "Función liberadora de la filosofía" |
| 1987 "Religiones abrahámicas" | "Aporte de la teología de la liberación a las religiones abrahámicas en la superación del individualismo y del positivismo" |
| 1987 "Teología frente al cambio" | "La teología de la liberación frente al cambio socio-histórico de América Latina" |
| 1988 "Reduccionismo" | "La superación del reduccionismo idealista en Zubiri" |
| 1989 "Derechos humanos" | "Historización de los derechos humanos desde los pueblos oprimidos y las mayorías populares" |

1989 "Utopía y profetismo"       "Utopía y profetismo desde América
                                 Latina: Un ensayo concreto de
                                 soteriología histórica"

# Preface

.

S hortly after midnight, on November 16, 1989, several units of
Salvadoran soldiers from the elite Atlacatl Battalion stole onto the
campus of the University of Central America (UCA) in San Salvador. One group burned and bombed the offices of the Monseñor Romero
Pastoral Center. Another entered the Jesuit residence compound and
massacred six Jesuit priests, a seminary cook, and her fifteen-year-old
daughter. Among the eight victims lay Ignacio Ellacuría. A scholar well-
grounded in the classical tradition of Western literature and philosophy,
Ellacuría possessed a piercing, creative intellect, an enormous capacity
for work, and a profound compassion for the victims of historical injustice.
At the time of his death, he was the rector (president) of the university,
a professor of philosophy and theology, the editor of various university
publications, and a vigorous participant in the public life of El Salvador.
Yet amidst the demands of this active life, he found time to produce
several books and over two hundred articles on a range of topics, exploring in depth the political implications of Christian faith and the philosophical foundations of Christian theology. Much has been written about
why he and his companions were killed, about the long years of suffering
that led to this night of horror, and about those who ordered and executed
the UCA massacre.[1] Less is known, especially in the United States, about
the actual content of Ellacuría's thought and its bearing on the way he
lived and died.[2] I write this book to investigate and interpret his thought
and to assess his relevance for the future of Roman Catholic theology.
In short, I want to explore the distinctive way he approaches the Christian
gospel of salvation from the ground of a rigorous, prophetic-utopian
realism.

Investigating the theology of Ignacio Ellacuría presents challenges and offers rewards. On the one hand, while a profound unity permeates all his works, his only truly systematic text, *Filosofía de la realidad histórica*, was unfinished at the time of his death and was published posthumously. It has not yet been translated into English. Most of his writings were first published as essays, including all of his theological reflections and everything that has appeared in English translation. Yet these can seem obscure, especially when read as isolated works separated from the philosophical vision and theological method that undergird them. On the other hand, I am convinced that Ellacuría's writings represent an untapped treasure for contemporary Catholic theology. They reveal an affinity with the timbre of our age, an attentiveness to the oppressed, and an openness to the new, while they remain anchored in the deep waters of the Western philosophical and Christian theological traditions. His interests span a variety of disciplines as he shifts attention back and forth from local affairs to questions of universal import. Various debates within twentieth-century thought, serious questions regarding change within Roman Catholicism, and passionate conflicts emanating from the political turmoil in Latin America hover in the background of his essays. Evidence abounds of his scholastic training, his encounters with Marxism, his grounding in the *Spiritual Exercises* of St. Ignatius Loyola. He often averts to the thought of his philosophical mentor, Xavier Zubiri, but also leaves traces of his debt to Karl Rahner, while implicitly retracing steps taken by the pioneers of liberation theology. Amidst all these influences and overtones, one hears a strikingly original voice in Ellacuría. One encounters a distinctive harmonization of political involvement and scholarly detachment, action and passion, rationality and compassion. What grounds and integrates all this? What source generates his enormous moral weight? Where in his thought can one locate the center of gravity? What contribution has he to offer to the situation of theology today? These broad concerns drive this investigation.

Personal reasons also prompt me to undertake this study. I learned about the UCA massacre the same morning the bodies were discovered. As a Jesuit working at a Jesuit school, Regis University in Denver, Colorado, I reacted to the news with a confusing blend of feelings—anger and sadness, pride and humility, fear and wonder. I recall the candlelight vigil we celebrated that evening in the *Sangre de Cristo* chapel. I can still hear the passionate homily that Vince O'Flaherty delivered a few days later at the enormous public Mass celebrated in St. Ignatius Loyola Church near Denver City Park. Although I never met Ignacio Ellacuría personally, I felt connected to him through fellow Jesuits and friends who had studied with him, whose stories of their time in El Salvador now echoed in memory. But two other events occurred within months of the UCA massacre which lit a fire in me and led more or less directly to an encounter with Ellacuría's thought.

The first event provided the firewood. In March 1990, Todd Waller, Stephen Belt, and I organized a spring break trip for a group of Regis students. We drove 1100 miles to a mining town in northern Mexico called Nueva Rosita. There we lived for a week with the people of San José Obrero parish, helping with some light construction work near one of their parish chapels. Blanca and Rito Martínez invited Stephen and me into their home. Their neighbors invited the others in our group into their homes. The people of Nueva Rosita treated us with kindness and respect. They welcomed us like their own children. At the same time, Padre Alejandro Castillo and his North American coworker Roberto Coogan introduced my students to a new way of seeing the world. For many, the simple experiences in Nueva Rosita turned them around, not only in terms of how they viewed their country in relation to its southern neighbors, but with regard to their Christian faith as well. In a way, I had expected or at least hoped this might happen. I just did not expect it to happen to me. "The people will break your heart," I heard Dean Brackley say during my second visit to El Salvador in 1996. The reality behind this saying had already caught up with me in Nueva Rosita.

The second event lit the match. It occurred in early May 1990 at the Regis graduation ceremony. The commencement speaker was Jon Sobrino, a member of the UCA community who had escaped the massacre only because he was out of the country when it took place. Sobrino's public remarks moved me deeply,[3] but a personal conversation with him over dinner that night affected the course my life and work would take. This was not the conversation in which he would urge me to consider focusing my doctoral studies on Ellacuría. That came during my first visit to El Salvador in 1993. But that conversation with Sobrino in the spring of 1990 tapped the questions that continue to animate my prayer and focus my theological reflection today. Who are my people? Through whom has God called me to hope? For whom do I write and teach theology?

Many people have contributed directly and indirectly to this book. I want to acknowledge and thank at least some of them. I am grateful to the people of Nueva Rosita and the students and staff who participated in the Mexico Project through the years. I am grateful for Chris and Lauri Pramuk, Mike McManus, and all those whose experiences in Mexico led them to help start Romero House in the Mexican-American neighborhood near Regis University. The hospitality of many other communities stirs my gratitude as well: the people of the Philippines; of Bagong Silong, a slum in metro Manila; of Dojoc Balite, a resettlement community near Mt. Pinatubo; and of the base communities scattered across Mindanao; the people of Limeras, Tapiquil, Los Encuentros, and other villages near Yoro, Honduras; and the people of Teocinte and Tremedal, two tiny resettlement communities in the highlands of El Salvador, where Holy Week, 1996, completely transfigured my resurrection faith. I want to recognize the kindness shown me by Doug Marcouiller, Dick Perl, Carlos Cabarrús, and many other Jesuits in Boston, Honduras, Guatemala, and Bolivia. I wish to thank the Jesuits and lay workers at the UCA in San Salvador, especially Jon Sobrino, Antonio González, Dean Brackley, Rafael Sivatte, and Martin Maier. I am deeply grateful to Adán Cuadra and the community of the Martyrs' Residence at the UCA, and to three friends in particular—Renzo Rosales, José Sols, and Gene Polumbo, whose generosity during my visits to El Salvador I can never repay.

Likewise, I have found enormous personal and professional support here in the United States. Matt Ashley, Bill Rehg, Bob Lassalle-Klein, Jim Keenan, Meg Guider, Steve Pope, Francis Schüssler Fiorenza, and David Tracy read my manuscript and helped me in various ways to deepen and clarify my thinking. Particular thanks go to Roger Haight, who encouraged me to undertake this project and then guided me in the research and writing of the first draft of this book. Likewise, I am deeply grateful to Cristina Stevens, who generously read the entire manuscript and suggested ways to decompress my prose, to Larry Yevenes, who corrected my Spanish translations and served as a consultant on Zubiri's philosophy, and to John Samples and the entire staff at Georgetown University Press. I also want to remember Ken Hughes, the community at Faber House, and my colleagues at Weston Jesuit School of Theology in Cambridge, Massachusetts; Fr. Jim Barry and the people of Our Lady of Grace parish in Chelsea, Massachusetts; the Jesuits of the Missouri Province; my students; my large and generous family living in Wyoming, Colorado, Iowa, Massachusetts, and places in between and beyond.

Finally, as Johann Baptist Metz reminds us, taking history seriously means remembering and keeping faith with those who have died. In this spirit, I wish to remember Ignacio Ellacuría and his companions, Ignacio Martín-Baró, Segundo Montes, Amando López, Juan Ramón Moreno, Juoquín López y López, Elba Ramos, and Celina Ramos. Likewise, I honor the memory of Oscar Romero, Rutilio Grande, Ita Ford,

Maura Clarke, Dorothy Kazel, Jean Donovan, and all the martyrs of El Salvador and other lands whose blood cries out to heaven. I remember, too, my friends and family: Sr. Ann Manganero, who worked as a medical doctor in El Salvador; photo-journalist Mev Puleo; Matt Klene, a student at Regis and enthusiastic participant in the Mexico Project; Fr. Vince O'Flaherty, S.J., the founder of Romero House; my uncle, Fr. Jim Burke, S.J.; my mother, Mary Josephine Burke, who died while I was finishing this manuscript, and my brothers, Dan and Larry Burke. In the course of my work on his theology, I often pictured Ignacio Ellacuría as an older brother who died too young. This association led to my dedication.

### Notes to Preface

1. For a partial biography of Ellacuría's life and an informative, balanced account of the events surrounding the UCA massacre, see Teresa Whitfield, *Paying the Price: Ignacio Ellacuría and the Murdered Jesuits of El Salvador* (Philadelphia: Temple University Press, 1994), hereafter cited as "Whitfield"; this book includes a sketch of Ellacuría's education, see Whitfield, 15–32, 41–45, 57–60, 203–229. Further biographical sources include "El P. Ignacio Ellacuría," in S. Carranza, ed., *Mártires de la UCA: 16 de noviembre de 1989* (San Salvador: UCA Editores, 1990) 351–362; Víctor Cordina, "Ignacio Ellacuría, teólogo y mártir," *RLT* (No. 21, 1990) 263–269; Jorge Alvarado Pisani, "Vida y pensamiento de Ignacio Ellacuría (1930–1989)" in A. González, ed., *Voluntad de vida* (Managua: UCA, 1993) 129–141; Juan José Tamayo, "Ignacio Ellacuría (1930–1989): Con los pobres de la tierra," in *Para comprender la teología de la liberación* (Navarra: Ed. Verbo Divino, 1991) 225–235; J. Sobrino, I. Ellacuría, et al., "Ignacio Ellacuría" in *Companions of Jesus: The Jesuit Martyrs of El Salvador* (Maryknoll: Orbis, 1990) 59–63; Phillip Berryman, "Ignacio Ellacuría: An Appreciation," *America* (July 7, 1990) 12–15. For a sense of Ellacuría's political importance in El Salvador, see Philip Berryman, *Stubborn Hope: Religion, Politics and Revolution in Central America* (Maryknoll: Orbis, 1994). An exhaustive study of the UCA massacre and the attempt to cover it up can be found in Martha Doggett, *Death Foretold: The Jesuit Murders in El Salvador* (Washington, D.C.: Georgetown University Press, 1993). For official documentation, see The United Nations, "From Madness to Hope: The 12-Year War in El Salvador," *Report of the Commission on the Truth for El Salvador*, April 1, 1993.

2. Until recently, not many secondary sources on Ellacuría have appeared in English. However, a new volume with articles by twelve authors, including Jon Sobrino, Gustavo Gutiérrez, Roger Haight, Martin Maier, and Maria Pilar Aquino, has begun to rectify this; see R. Lassalle-Klein and K. Burke, eds., *The Love That Produces Hope: The Thought of Ignacio Ellacuría* (Collegeville, Minn.: Liturgical Press, forthcoming); see also Robert Lassalle-Klein, "The Body of Christ: The Claim of the Crucified People on U.S. Theology and Ethics," *Journal of Hispanic/Latino Theology* (Vol. 5, No. 4, May 1998) 48–77, hereafter cited as "Lassalle-Klein, The Body of Christ"; Kevin Burke, "The Love That Produces Hope," *Budhi: A Journal of Ideas and Culture* (Vol. 1, No. 3, 1997) 71–80. Ellacuría also receives some attention in a few recent books; besides Whitfield, see Anselm Kyongsuk Min, *Dialectic of Salvation: Issues in Theology of Liberation* (Albany, NY: SUNY Press, 1989) 27–31, 84–91; Thomas L. Schubeck, *Liberation Ethics: Sources, Models, and Norms* (Minneapolis: Fortress Press, 1993) 116–126,

250–252; Dean Brackley, *Divine Revolution: Salvation and Liberation in Catholic Thought* (Maryknoll: Orbis, 1996) 100–102. Finally, see Robert Lassalle-Klein, *The Jesuit Martyrs of the University of Central America: An American Christian University and the Historical Reality of the Reign of God*, unpublished Ph.D. dissertation (Berkeley: Graduate Theological Union, July 26, 1995), hereafter cited as "Lassalle-Klein, *Jesuit Martyrs.*"

3. See Jon Sobrino, "The Salvadoran Martyrs and the Meaning of a Christian University," in M. McDonald, A. Reich, E. Stewart, and T. Steele, eds., *Adducere II: Regis University Faculty Lectures of the Year, 1987–1993* (Denver: Regis University, 1995) 11–17.

# Introduction

# Theology at the Dawn
# of the Twenty-First Century

*Christians, on pilgrimage toward the heavenly
city, should seek and savor the things which
are above. This duty in no way decreases, but
rather increases, the weight of their obligation to
work with all people in constructing a more
human world.*

Second Vatican Council[1]

The Second Vatican Council shifted the tectonic plates under the
Roman Catholic Church and created new horizons for all its devotional, theological, and institutional dynamics. Thirty-five years
after its conclusion, it stands as the event that has most forcefully shaped
Catholic life and thought during the twentieth century. It was a big event
in more ways than one. It took place on a scale previously unseen in
church history, with more active participants and longer final documents
than any previous council. But a number of other features also distinguish
it as a turning point in church history: the breadth of the issues it
considered; the sophistication of the theological resources placed at the
disposal of its participants; the representation of bishops and theologians
from lands beyond Western Europe; the invitation to Catholic women
and non-Catholic men to attend as observers; the decision to address
its documents to the whole human family; the presence and impact of
modern communications media.[2] Out of all this Vatican II inaugurated

1

a new ecclesial culture. Among other things it required and allowed the Roman Church to find new ways to articulate its self-understanding and mission. "Something happened at the council," Yves Congar later observed, "and the dominant values in our way of looking at the church were changed by the council."[3] In turn, these ecclesiological expeditions profoundly affected the church's evaluation of the world and understanding of salvation. How to evaluate the world and how to understand its salvation represent the two central concerns of this book.

At the dawn of the twenty-first century, the aftershocks of Vatican II continue and the mood within the church remains unsettled. These tremors profoundly affect Roman Catholic theologians, since rival interpretations of the council reflexively parallel different ways of conceiving the nature of theology, its role in the church, and the crisis presently besetting it. Indeed, the years following Vatican II spawned strikingly different interpretations of the council's vision, prompting German theologian Johann Baptist Metz to ask, "Will an aggressive or a defensive form of fidelity to this council and retrieval of the church's traditions prevail?"[4] It may not yet be possible to answer this question or fully assess the historical event and cultural impact of Vatican II. For one thing, the council is still too close and, insofar as it manifests the qualities of what North American theologian David Tracy calls "a classic event," it stands in need of constant reinterpretation.[5] Nevertheless, theology must attempt to appraise its present context and identify its own current tasks. These imperatives obtain even though, as a direct result of the atmosphere that has gripped the church in this postconciliar period, such attempts prove controversial and dangerous. Instinctively the question arises: where to now? Issues associated with the context of theology lie embedded here. What characterizes the situation of theology at the close of the century that Vatican II shaped? What are the signs of the times to which theology must respond as a new century dawns? What kind of theology will prove adequate to the needs of our present situation and the interpretation of these signs?

Such questions provide the proper context for an investigation of the theology of Ignacio Ellacuría. Before introducing that investigation, however, I wish to explore further the current situation of theology, following the leads provided by Tracy and Metz. It should be noted at the outset that the turmoil presently engulfing Catholic theology represents not only a "Catholic" or merely a "theological" phenomenon. Such turmoil betrays roots that reach beyond ecclesial soil into every aspect of what Tracy calls "an age that cannot name itself."[6] Hence, contemporary theological ambiguity represents one manifestation of an enormous "conflict of interpretations in that place which was once construed as the center of history—Western, including Western Christian theological, culture."[7] To map this conflict over how best to name the nameless present, Tracy identifies three general attitudes toward an earlier historical epoch that confidently and a bit triumphalistically named itself "the Age of Reason," "the Enlightenment." The first attitude aligns itself with and defends modernity. It assumes that a basic continuity runs from the eighteenth century to the present. At the same time it relies on increasingly refined notions of progress and evolution, presented in the patois of a scientific, technological rationality, to justify its confidence in a limitless future. Despite the tragedies of the twentieth century, defenders of modernity manifest an unquenchable optimism that stands in sharp contrast to the pessimism of a second approach, that of antimodernity. Whether in the guise of fundamentalism or postliberal neoconservativism, the various strands of this second approach share a conviction that the modern age has failed. Only the retrieval of some tradition, some version of the premodern past, can provide hope for the future. Tracy notes, however, that even in the case of honorable, nonfundamentalist versions of antimodernity, there appears a tendency to convoke an overly partial defense of tradition and an untroubled rejection of the legitimate gains of modernity. A third family of approaches appears under the rubric of postmodernity. Rejecting both the illusions of the moderns and the traditionalism of the antimoderns, postmodern thinkers seek hope for the future by embracing difference, by turning to "the other," especially those others marginalized in both traditional and modern cultures. However, even postmodern thinkers betray their own peculiar ambiguities, as Tracy is not alone in pointing out. "They wish to deconstruct the *status quo* in favor of the *fluxus quo*. And yet they cannot without further reflection on the ethical-political import of their own deconstructive exposures. There is an implied ethics of resistance in postmodern thought. But that ethic is one that is present often against the grain of postmodern reflections on the impossibility of any determinateness."[8]

Modern, antimodern, and postmodern namings of our present situation attempt in their own ways to serve as guides to Christian theology for the coming century. Tracy affirms that each shows promise in this task precisely in the measure that it mediates gospel values to our current situation. However, he concludes that each by itself proves incapable of providing theology with the radical grounding it needs. For one thing, "the Western center, however named—modern, antimodern, or postmodern—cannot and should not hold as the center."[9] For another, theological discourse now finds itself permanently disquieted by the irruption into history of history's victims, by the voices that cry out from history's crosses.

> Where, in all the discussions of otherness and difference of the postmoderns as well as the moderns and the antimoderns, are the poor and the oppressed? These are the concrete others whose difference should make a difference. For through them the full and interruptive memory of the gospel is alive again among us. In their prophetic speech and their liberating actions lies hope for the true time of the present before a judging and saving God. In their actions, historical subjects act and speak for all who have ears to hear.[10]

Tracy concludes that theology must direct its attention to the poor and oppressed to recover its own bearings. In this he does not stand alone. The irruption of the poor into history has indelibly marked contemporary theology and will affect the course of the theological conversation for the foreseeable future. But coming from a North American hermeneutical theologian engaged in a passionate dialogue with thinkers as diverse as Jürgen Habermas, Hans Urs von Balthasar, and Jean-Francois Lyotard, this suggestion seems at least a little strange. Significantly, however, Tracy links the irruption of the poor into history with the most urgent tasks facing both contemporary theology and philosophy. "The hope of reason must be defended in any philosophy worthy of the name. The great human questions of finitude, guilt, anxiety, and death must be clarified in any theology worthy of the name. But that hope and even those questions—in this modern situation—can only live if they become explicitly historical and political. In our theological context, the questions must become mystical-political."[11]

Tracy's provocative suggestion that intellectual honesty in the face of our nameless present requires theology to adopt a mystical-political framework explicitly echoes a central theme running through Metz's mature reflections.[12] An assiduous student of Rahner's transcendental method during the first part of his career, Metz later pioneered a new political theology as fundamental theology. Seeking to avoid abstract formulations of faith and ahistorical accounts of suffering, he focuses on a faith that is at once mystical and political, a faith in history and society.[13] Looking specifically at the situation of faith today and the demands inherent in our situation, Metz discerns three primary directions taken by contemporary Catholic theology: neoscholasticism, transcendental-idealism, and postidealism. The first manifests many of the characteristics which Tracy links with antimodernity, including a fundamental defensiveness in the face of modern suspicions of tradition. Although currently enjoying a "late summer" at the end of Christianity's second millennium, this route simply does not have the resources to face the complex challenges of the present. The second paradigm, developed perhaps most fully by Karl Rahner, represents "the attempt to use the church fathers and scholastics in a productive offensive confrontation with the challenges of modern Europe: the discovery of subjectivity as a crisis in classic metaphysics; the critico-productive confrontation with Kant, German idealism and existentialism on the one hand, and the social processes of secularization and scientific civilization on the other."[14] This is the theological route that led to the Second Vatican Council. But in Metz's view, theology at the end of the twentieth century faces challenges that even this paradigm lacks the capacity to meet. Hence, Metz argues for a third option, the postidealist paradigm. While he himself has not developed a complete postidealist systematic theology, he indicates the shape such a theology would assume by exploring three major challenges presented by our current situation which a postidealist approach could meet.

The first demand, which contemporary theology must address, comes from the Enlightenment, above all, from certain strands of Marxist and revisionist Marxist thought. The recognition of historical consciousness and the social interests that underlie every attempt to do theology have put an end to theology's cognitive innocence. Theology must reckon with the relationship between knowledge and interest. "If all empirical knowledge is determined by some interest, then not only the contents but also the subject and addressee of knowledge are significant for cognitive processes."[15] For this reason Metz argues passionately for a political theology of the *subject*, which addresses in a new and robust way "the question of the subjects and the audience of the theological enterprise."[16] However, the challenge does not stop there. A theology that does not wish to practice some form of intellectual hibernation must encounter the world as *history*, for the religious and metaphysical views of the world that formerly supplied the context for doing theology no longer prove convincing. In one sense, of course, the Jewish-Christian religious tradition has always focused on history. Its vision of God as the One who works salvation through mighty deeds in history stands in sharp contrast with other major religious and mythical world views. A postidealist theology exploits this vision. In view of the challenge posed by Marxism, it insists that salvation history cannot be separated from secular history or conceived dualistically.[17] However, in contrast with doctrinaire Marxist thought, it refuses to split off, project, or otherwise deny historical guilt.[18] Instead, postidealist theology focuses on the subjects of faith and their concrete praxis as the place where historical guilt is recognized and historical responsibility is exercised.

In Metz's view, the second challenge appears most forcefully at Auschwitz. This *tremendum*, along with other similarly incomprehensible historical catastrophes, brought theology to the end of its historical innocence. "There is no meaning which one could salvage by turning one's back on Auschwitz, and no truth which one could thereby defend. Theology therefore has to make an about-turn, a turn which will bring us face-to-face with the suffering and the victims."[19] After Auschwitz, theology can no longer idealistically turn its back on any historical suffering. Because a true theology in and of history must address the suffering of history, theology must likewise attend to the historical irruption of the poor. In short, theology must once again take up the question of theodicy, and must do so in terms of the victims of history. "It is precisely because Christians believe in an eschatological meaning for history that they can risk historical consciousness: looking into the abyss. Precisely because of this, they can risk a memory that recalls not only the successful but the ruined, not only that which has been realized but that which has been lost, a memory that in this way—as dangerous memory—resists identifying meaning and truth with the victory of what has come into being and continues to exist."[20]

Third, theology at the dawn of the twenty-first century must account for a church that is truly worldwide. Moreover, it must recognize that both the world and the church are socially divided and culturally polycentric. In sum, contemporary theology can no longer pretend one or other form of social innocence. For Metz, this means that "the social conflicts in the world move to the center of ecclesial and theological awareness. Conditions that are directly contradictory to the Gospel—like oppression, exploitation and racism—become challenges for theology. They demand the formulation of the faith in categories of transformation and of a resistance that is prepared to suffer. Consequently, theology, from its own logos, becomes political."[21] Metz rejects the suggestion that this new social awareness leads either to sheer relativism on the one hand or the enthronement of some new, non-European theological monocentrism on the other. Christianity cannot and should not alienate itself from its Western and European historical origins. However, fidelity to those very origins requires the Christian movement, both in its ecclesial practice and theology, to develop a profound capacity for reciprocity. Can the older churches learn from newer churches? Can the European center receive guidance from the margins of Asia, Africa, and the Americas? Have the little ones anything to say to the great ones?

I turn now to the central focus of this book. I have alluded to Tracy's attempt to name our nameless age and Metz's efforts to identify the crises facing contemporary theology in terms of a temporal symbol, "the dawn of the twenty-first century." There is nothing magical about this symbol, of course. But insofar as the coming of the twenty-first century augurs the passing of the twentieth, this symbol contains and evokes a tension inherent in Catholic theology, the tension between the new and the old. This tension appears clearly in the light of two themes of central importance at the Second Vatican Council, *ressourcement* and *aggiornamento*. What is required of a theology that seeks to do justice both to the demands of tradition and to the need for innovation? In particular, what is required after such a theology has been stripped of its cognitive, historical, and social innocence? I believe that a penetrating contemporary response to these questions appears in the thought of Ignacio Ellacuría, above all in the way he grounds liberation theology in a philosophy of historical reality. If I am correct and if the general validity of Metz's attempt to diagnose our present situation is granted, then Ellacuría deserves our attention not only as a martyr but as a thinker who has something important to contribute to our current theological conversation. Before concluding this introduction with a preview of the seven chapters that follow, I will briefly describe Ellacuría's achievement in terms of three points implicit in the claim that he has produced a genuinely postidealist theology.

First, Ellacuría has developed a critical theology. Initially this observation might appear unremarkable, for it applies in varying degrees to many strands of contemporary Catholic theology, including liberation theologies. For example, Latin American liberation theology is famous (or infamous) for responding to the challenge posed by Marxism. In Ellacuría, too, this challenge is basic, insofar as his philosophical realism depends on a careful description of the materiality of reality. However, his nuanced treatment of Marxism is interesting precisely for the way he balances "materiality" with the "openness" of reality. Another example further clarifies this point. Ellacuría details the extent to which interest and perspective condition theology. But virtually all liberation theologians attend explicitly to the relationship between knowledge and interest. Once again the point hardly appears novel. Yet a unique contribution appears in the way Ellacuría accounts for interest and perspective: the process he calls "historicization," where the critical apparatus implicit in his method comes to bear on concepts. A third example: since by definition liberation theology insists on encountering the world as history, this key theme in Ellacuría's thought might also seem unnoteworthy. Yet even here Ellacuría's approach is distinctive. He shifts away from an exclusive focus on history to a philosophy of historical reality. An appraisal of this latter concept supplies a basic component in the argument that his theology is genuinely postidealist.

Second, Ellacuría's theology is historically conscious and conscious of history's victims. The first part of this assertion reflects his understanding of historical reality along with his account of how historically conditioned human intelligence apprehends reality. With other important contemporary philosophical thinkers, Ellacuría contends that not only the knowledge of reality but reality itself appears as historically constructed. The novelty in Ellacuría's approach appears in the way he balances two elements inherent in this claim. On the one hand, the real can only be apprehended through situated, contextual realities. On the other, historical reality manifests a radical and total unity. In the course of my analysis of his philosophy of historical reality, I will describe how he aims to strike this balance. The second element in this assertion maintains that Ellacuría is not only historically conscious but conscious of historical victims. In this he draws attention to a crucial Christian theme that all liberation theologies emphasize: the truth of reality becomes most manifest where reality has been crucified. On the basis of his understanding of historical reality, Ellacuría contributes a distinctive account of how and where the option for the crucified victims of our world enters theological method.

Third, Ellacuría crafts a theology immediately concerned with social divisions and profoundly attentive to the particularity of cultural context. In the preceding point his concern with the victims of such divisions already begins to appear. Like others who recognize that no theory can be socially innocent, Ellacuría calls theological attention to historical realities such as poverty, oppression, and injustice. He also unmasks toxic forms of ideology that attempt to cover up these historical scandals. Likewise, his theology places special attention on the categories of transformative praxis and martyrdom. These categories not only appear as verifications of a given theological position, but also function in the very unfolding of theological method. In effect, Ellacuría develops a rigorous method for contextual theologies. He argues against all abstract or idealistic articulations of the unifying logos of theology, insisting instead that such a logos must be historical and can only be apprehended concretely in a particular context. He therefore seeks to articulate a specifically

Latin American theology. However, he does not eschew Christianity's European heritage or reject its Western philosophical and theological traditions. Neither does he dissolve theology into an erratic pluralism of incommensurable theologies. Rather, he construes a rich, philosophically nuanced account of historical context capable of grounding any contextual theology.

While historical reality forms the methodological center of gravity in Ellacuría's thought, salvation theory serves as his central theological concern. In this book I aim to show how this methodological center and theological concern relate to one another. My conclusion can be stated succinctly: Ellacuría grounds theological method in historical reality and praxis in order to show how Christian salvation is salvation in and of history. Several things should be noted. First, I place the primary emphasis on Ellacuría's theology. One could select other focusing concerns: his philosophy, his liberative praxis, his analysis of El Salvador in the throes of civil war, his theory of a Christian university, his death. All of these factor in this study. However, my aim is to uncover and interpret his distinctive contribution to contemporary theology. Second, for Ellacuría theology involves argument: it attempts to render Christian faith intelligible and relevant to human life. With this in mind, I implicitly attend to the apologetic significance of his thought throughout this study. Third, the overall structure of Ellacuría's argument appears in the metaphor of *the ground*, the first term in my title. This image captures his rhetorical strategy in relation to the methodological center of gravity, historical reality. While I do not attempt to exhaustively study Ellacuría's view of historical reality, I partially sketch it in order to shed light on its function in his theology. Finally, the last term in the title, *the cross*, evokes Ellacuría's primary theological concern with salvation theory. It should not be taken to suggest that his soteriology focuses exclusively on the death of Jesus. Rather, as will be evident, he draws attention to the fact that the cross emerges first of all as a historical reality. Thus, the overall sequence in *The Ground Beneath the Cross* is from Ellacuría's (1) philosophy to his (2) theological method and his (3) theology of salvation. After first introducing his life, I spend two chapters apiece on these three themes.

In chapter 1, "The Martyr As Theologian," I trace Ellacuría's biography and preview his bibliography to provide a context for interpreting his thought. I start with the story of his life, focusing primarily on his role during the Salvadoran civil war, which dominated his latter years. Panning back, I then scan six broad and important influences upon his intellectual development, Vatican II, the dialogue with Marxism, the rise of liberation theology, the influence of Archbishop Romero, the papacy of John Paul II, and Ellacuría's own Jesuit background. In the third section I turn to Ellacuría's relationship with the man who most profoundly influenced his thought, Xavier Zubiri. Because Zubiri himself is not particularly well known in the United States, I include a brief sketch of his life and philosophical peregrinations in order to more clearly delineate the nature of his impact on Ellacuría. In the final section of chapter 1, I provide a general map of Ellacuría's writings and introduce the framework that I employ throughout this interpretation.

Chapter 2 introduces Ellacuría's "Philosophy of Historical Reality" and explores this central philosophical concept within the larger compass of Zubiri's thought.[22] Attempting to explicate Zubiri's entire philosophical system or assess its coherence would go beyond the limits of this work. Thus, I aim simply to sketch it with enough detail to illuminate Ellacuría's use of historical reality as a theological category. Section one begins with the character of human intellection. Ellacuría underscores how Zubiri's theory of sentient intelligence both critiques reductionistic versions of philosophical idealism and grounds a philosophical realism that is open to transcendence. In section two I trace how Ellacuría argues on the basis of Zubiri's account of sentient intellection that historical reality is the object of philosophy. In section three I rehearse a series of five theses in which Ellacuría diagrams Zubiri's understanding of the structure of reality, noting how reality appears in its highest form as historical reality. Then in the final section, utilizing the metaphor of the *grounds* of history, I attend to the weight that Ellacuría's materialist realism lends to his understanding of history.

Ellacuría's philosophy of historical reality focuses both on his understanding of the human person and his view of the human task of history. I take up these themes in chapter 3, "The Human in Historical Reality." In the first section of the chapter I address three crucial dimensions of human reality—the personal, the social, and the historical. I analyze these dimensions under the rubric of the human as the reality animal. With their sentient intelligence, humans not only perceive and respond to a biological habitat, they apprehend reality. The intelligent apprehension of reality—not rationality viewed in isolation—serves as the defining feature of the human species and grounds the personal dimension of the human. I complement the discussion of the personal dimension with an analysis of the social dimension. I focus on Ellacuría's explication of the material grounds of this indispensable human sociality. Finally, I consider history as a dimension of the human. This discussion directly probes the impact of history on the human and the necessity of viewing human reality as constitutively historical. The second section of chapter

3 probes the impact of the human on historical reality. With Ellacuría's view of history as a human task, the dynamics of human freedom and the moral dimension of human reality come into focus, as does the material connection that Ellacuría discovers between history and liberation.

Chapter 4 focuses on Ellacuría's distinctive approach to the "Foundations of Theological Method." Here I explore his analysis of the threefold structure of human intellection, his assessment of the impact of historicity on these three dimensions, and his treatment of the factors that critically condition theology. On the basis of his inquiry into the historicity of human knowing, he argues for the necessity of doing theology from and for Latin America. This necessity reflects the intrinsic connection which exists between theological production and theological place. It also leads directly to a discussion of the critical constitutive conditions of theological method. These include the activities that comprise theological production and the areas of reality that theology examines, the manner in which theology deals with the social forces that influence it, the structure of theological hermeneutics, and the use of the social sciences in theological production.

In chapter 5 I focus explicitly on the "Operations of Theological Method." I begin with what Ellacuría calls the process of historicization and note how it affects theological concepts and his view of theological place and praxis. In section two I examine the impact of historicization for the Christian vision. I begin with his account of the dialectic of utopia and propheticism, assessing the demands that this dialectic makes on theological reflection. I then turn to Ellacuría's distinctive articulation of the relationship of theology and praxis, addressing both the role of praxis in his theology and the converse impact of his theology on historical praxis. These issues point, in turn, to the relationship between ecclesial praxis and the larger historical praxis, as well as the connection between historical praxis and the Reign of God. Finally, I return to the notion of theological place with attention to the place of historicization, the place of utopia and propheticism, and the place of ecclesial praxis. This theological vision of faith leads to the foot of the cross and, in the extreme, to persecution and martyrdom.

In the final two chapters I treat Ellacuría's most important theological writings. In chapter 6, "Salvation in History," his central theological concern receives direct attention through the examination of two crucial issues: the relationship of salvation to history and the manner in which this salvation manifests an explicitly transcendent dimension. In the first section I analyze Ellacuría's understanding of the historicity of salvation, noting two approaches that he rejects while developing his own position.

Then I explore what he means by the claim that salvation history is a salvation in and of history. In sections two and three I examine how Ellacuría's view of salvation in history corresponds to an understanding of transcendence as transcendence in history. I trace his reflections on historical transcendence in the Old and New Testaments in section two. In section three I note what transcendence in history implies for christology and for Ellacuría's understanding of an important biblical image utilized by Vatican II, the people of God.

The theme of chapter 7, "The Cross and the Church," extends the dialectic of historical transcendence into Ellacuría's salvation theory and ecclesiology. I first retrace his analysis of the death of Jesus, then I reflect on the symbol of the crucified people, one of his most original contributions to liberation theology and a key element in his soteriology. In the final section I investigate the implications of his salvation theory for the followers of Jesus in history. Here I explore his use of the pre-ecclesiological symbol of the people of God, then note the logic that allows him to speak of the church of the poor as a historical sacrament of liberation. With Ellacuría's understanding of theology as the ideological moment of ecclesial praxis, these ecclesiological reflections also bring to light the salvific function of theology.

In the conclusion of *The Ground Beneath the Cross* I situate Ellacuría within the larger current of Latin American liberation theology. I compare him to several other major figures in that movement and probe how and to what extent his thought can be considered Latin American. While noting some of the limitations of his project, I highlight its strengths and call attention to Ellacuría's distinctive contribution to contemporary Roman Catholic theology.

## Notes to Introduction

1. Second Vatican Council, "Gaudium et Spes," No. 57, in W. Abbott, ed., *The Documents of Vatican II* (New York: Guild Press, 1966) 262.

2. John O'Malley, *Tradition and Transition: Historical Perspectives on Vatican II* (Wilmington, Delaware: Michael Glazier, 1989) 13; hereafter cited as "O'Malley"; see also Joseph Komonchak, "Vatican Council II," in J. Komonchak, M. Collins, D. Lane, eds., *The New Dictionary of Theology* (Collegeville, Minn.: Liturgical Press, 1987) 1072–1077; Timothy O'Connell, "Vatican II: Setting, Themes, Future Agenda," in T. O'Connell, ed., *Vatican II and Its Documents: An American Reappraisal* (Wilmington, Delaware: Michael Glazier, 1986) 237–255. Regarding non-Catholic observers, O'Malley notes that some Lutherans were present at Trent, although that council embodied a different atmosphere and spirit; see O'Malley, 19–20 and n. 2.

3. Yves Congar, "Moving Towards a Pilgrim Church," in *Vatican II by Those Who Were There* (London: Geoffrey Chapman, 1986) 129. O'Malley persuasively refutes interpretations of Vatican II that attempt to minimize its uniqueness or significance;

see O'Malley, 19–31. However, both O'Malley and Congar carefully avoid overstating the degree to which the council breaks with the past. The latter writes, "Vatican II was intentionally in continuity with the previous councils of the church and with tradition. Paul VI himself insisted on its continuity with Vatican I. As every historian knows, everything is always changing and at the same time there is in many ways a deep continuity," Congar, 129. For an extensive analysis of this point, see O'Malley, 44–81.

4. Johann Baptist Metz, "Do We Miss Karl Rahner?" *A Passion for God: The Mystical-Political Dimension of Christianity* (New York: Paulist Press, 1998) 93. Metz himself has lobbied tirelessly for a commitment to the former type of fidelity rather than attempting to return to a preconciliar, a premodern Roman Catholic world. For this reason he undertakes an extensive analysis of the status of theology and ecclesial practice under the changing conditions of late modernity. For an outside assessment of this aspect of Metz's thought, see Jürgen Habermas, "Israel and Athens, or to Whom Does Anamnestic Reason Belong? On Unity in Multicultural Diversity," in D. Batstone, E. Mendieta, L.A. Lorentzen, and D. Hopkins, eds., *Liberation Theologies, Postmodernity, and the Americas* (London and New York: Routledge, 1997) 243–252.

5. Tracy's reflections on the necessity and difficulty of interpreting another classic event, the French Revolution, are germane here; see David Tracy, *Plurality and Ambiguity: Hermeneutics, Religion, Hope* (Chicago: University of Chicago Press, 1987).

6. David Tracy, "On Naming the Present," *On Naming the Present: God, Hermeneutics, and Church*, Concilium Series (Maryknoll: Orbis, 1994) 3.

7. Ibid., 3.

8. Ibid., 16–17.

9. Ibid., 20.

10. Ibid, 21. For an insightful reflection on the anthropological significance of history's victims, see Gil Bailie, *Violence Unveiled: Humanity at the Crossroads* (New York: Crossroad, 1995). In his concluding chapter, "The Voice from *La Cruz*," Bailie meditates on a stunning detail in Mark Danner's account of a massacre that took place in El Salvador in 1981. Before they were killed, some of the victims were raped on a hill just outside of the village. Amidst their cries for help one girl could be heard singing hymns all through the afternoon. The name of the hill was *La Cruz*. Ibid., 268–269; Mark Danner, *The Massacre at El Mozote* (New York: Vintage, 1994) 78–79.

11. David Tracy, "On Naming the Present," 10.

12. See Johann Baptist Metz, "On the Way to a Postidealist Theology," *A Passion for God*, op. cit., 30–53; "Theology in the New Paradigm: Political Theology," in H. Küng and D. Tracy, eds., *Paradigm Change in Theology* (New York: Crossroad, 1991) 355–366; "Theology in the Modern Age, and Before Its End," and "Theology in the Struggle for History and Society," in Johann Baptist Metz and Jürgen Moltmann, *Faith and the Future: Essays on Theology, Solidarity, and Modernity*, Concilium Series (Maryknoll: Orbis, 1995) 30–37, 49–56. For an excellent interpretation of Metz and Rahner, see J. Matthew Ashley, *Interruptions: Mysticism, Politics and Theology in the Work of Johann Baptist Metz* (Notre Dame, Ind.: Notre Dame Press, 1998).

13. See Johann Baptist Metz, *Faith in History and Society: Toward a Practical Fundamental Theology* (London: Burns & Oates, 1980).

14. "Theology in the Struggle for History and Society," 50.

15. "On the Way to a Postidealist Theology," 35–36.

16. Ibid., 36. In his most important work, *Faith in History and Society*, Metz sketches his own approach to such a political theology of the subject; see especially pp. 32–83.

17. "There really is no world history with a salvation history alongside or above it. Rather, the history of salvation of which theology speaks is world history that is marked by a continually threatened and contested yet indestructible hope for universal justice: justice for the dead and for their suffering. The history of salvation is that world history in which there is hope even for past suffering," "On the Way to a Postidealist Theology," 37.

18. "The denial of guilt is a deadly attack upon the dignity of freedom. And the acceptance of guilt before God does not prevent persons from becoming the full and responsible subjects of their histories. On the contrary: wherever guilt is denied as a primordial phenomenon, or is denounced as false consciousness, exculpation mechanisms arise in the face of the suffering and contradictions of historical life. Historical responsibility, or being a subject in history, is irrationally cut in half, and failure and catastrophe are projected one-sidedly onto the historical opponent," ibid., 38.

19. "Theology in the New Paradigm: Political Theology," 362; see also "Facing the Jews: Christian Theology after Auschwitz," *Faith and the Future*, op., cit., 38–48.

20. "On the Way to a Postidealist Theology," 40.

21. Ibid., 43.

22. Because Ellacuría takes his basic philosophical vision from Zubiri, this discussion of his philosophy of historical reality necessarily directs much of the attention back to Zubiri. However, as others have noted, this implies no minimization of the importance and originality of Ellacuría's contributions. "Although he confessed to always being a disciple of Zubiri, his philosophical work is very far from being a simple repetition of the thought of his master, or a mere application of Zubirian doctrines— those ideas already fully articulated by Zubiri—to the circumstances of Latin America," Manuel Domínguez, "Ignacio Ellacuría, filósofo de la realidad latinoamericana," *Revista Universitas Philosophica* (No. 13, 1989) 70, translation mine, hereafter cited as "Domínguez." As will be seen in later chapters, Ellacuría's philosophical originality dawns in the manner in which he converts Zubiri's anthropology into a political philosophy (chapter 3) and in his use of the Zubirian system to construct his theological method (chapters 4 and 5). In systematic theology, his originality appears most clearly in his interpretation of Christian salvation from the perspective of historical reality (chapters 6 and 7).

Chapter One

# The Martyr
# As Theologian

*The inmost depths of you, your guts and your heart, wrenched at the immense pain of this people. That's what never left you in peace.*

Jon Sobrino[1]

## ELLACURÍA'S STORY

Ignacio Ellacuría was born on November 9, 1930, in the Basque town of Portugalete near Bilbao. The fourth of six children and the fourth boy to join religious life, he entered the Jesuit novitiate in Loyola on September 14, 1947, at the age of sixteen. He spent the first year of his novitiate in Spain, and afterward moved to El Salvador to spend his second year there as part of a group assigned to the Central American mission. The following year he traveled to Quito, Ecuador, to begin five years of studies in the humanities and philosophy. He received a standard introduction to the Aristotelian-Thomistic philosophical tradition, but also began to explore the thought of José Ortega y Gasset and others. His world was further expanded during these years by his direct contact with an outstanding classicist, Aurelio Espinosa Pólit, under whose tutelage he excelled in both classical languages and literature.[2] Ellacuría returned to San Salvador for three years to teach in the diocesan seminary, which the Jesuits directed. During this time he published several articles on Thomas Aquinas and Ortega y Gasset. From 1958 to 1962 he studied theology in Innsbruck under Karl Rahner. He was ordained

15

a priest in 1961 and, while in Spain that same summer, he paid a visit to the Basque philosopher, Xavier Zubiri, to explore the possibility of studying philosophy with him. Ellacuría remained in Spain from 1962 until 1967. During that time he completed a three-volume dissertation on Zubiri's thought and under his direction.[3] After he received his degree from Complutense University in Madrid, he returned to Central America in 1967. His relationship with Zubiri did not end, however. Although he was assigned permanently to El Salvador, he returned annually to Madrid in order to continue his own philosophical research and to help his former mentor prepare various writings for publication.

On the surface El Salvador might have appeared unchanged from the land Ellacuría left nine years earlier. Both within the church and in the world at large, however, profound transformations were underway. As elsewhere in Latin America, the high expectations spawned by the Alliance for Progress were souring.[4] Rather than redistributing wealth and improving the actual situation of the poor, the Alliance in fact only furthered the deep divisions already inherent to the continent. The Cuban revolution in 1959 aroused hopes and fears of revolution elsewhere. Those hopes and fears fused with cold-war intrigue to produce revolutionary movements and reactionary military coups. Increased repression deepened the already profound sense of crisis and despair that gripped Latin America. In El Salvador the political situation grew increasingly unstable and repressive. Grossly inequitable land distribution produced a steady increase in the number of landless *campesinos* during the 1960s, while chronic unemployment, inadequate housing, poor sanitation, lack of health care, illiteracy, and infant mortality gradually reached epidemic proportions. Poverty and injustice bred a uniquely Salvadoran discontent that invited radical change and exacerbated political repression.

The Salvadoran Church and the Jesuit mission in Central America appeared backward and relatively unchanged when Ellacuría returned to work there. The events shaking Catholic Europe during the mid-1960s were distant and disconnected from the ordinary concerns of life in Central America. But Vatican II was altering the general landscape of Catholic thought and practice, and the conciliar winds of change were unleashed within the Society of Jesus by General Congregation XXXI, which met in 1965. Under the leadership of the new Basque superior general Pedro Arrupe, the daily practices of Jesuit religious life underwent significant revision. More importantly, a new sense of mission and a new conception of the relationship between the church and the world began to influence the composition and orientation of Jesuit institutions and internal government. The most definitive articulation of this shift appears in the documents of General Congregation XXXII, which met in 1975. However, seven years earlier the Jesuit provincials of Latin America held a key meeting in Rio de Janeiro at which they called attention to the social problems of the continent. The document produced at that meeting was one of the first to insist that those problems be given priority among the Society's apostolic endeavors.[5] Then came Medellín. The Second General Conference of the Latin American Bishops (CELAM) assembled in Medellín, Colombia, from August 24 to September 6, 1968. It produced a ground-breaking interpretation of Vatican II that took as its crucial point of reference the history, poverty, and crisis of life in Latin America. The resulting documents provided the Latin American Church with a new horizon for action, and in the milieu sparked by the conference, liberation theology was born.[6]

In December 1969, a year after the Medellín conference, Ellacuría and his former novice master Miguel Elizondo codirected the Central American Jesuits in a week-long meeting/retreat modeled after the *Spiritual Exercises* of St. Ignatius.[7] The retreat employed the Ignatian pedagogy aimed at deepening the conversion and commitment of the one making the retreat, in this case, the entire vice-province of Central America. It sought to nurture within the vice-province a new way of seeing and acting. The impact of the retreat for the Central American Jesuits was profound. It transformed their self understanding as well as their apostolic horizons. This transformation, by which the Society of Jesus in Central America aligned itself with the fundamental direction mandated by the Latin American Jesuit provincials and the Latin American Bishops' Conference, received explicit confirmation from Arrupe. The following year, Ellacuría was placed in charge of Jesuit formation for the vice-province of Central America.

During the decade of the 1970s, the transformations reshaping the Latin American Church and the Society of Jesus began affecting the University of Central America. Originally founded in 1965 to provide an alternative to the left-leaning National University, the UCA opened the following year to 357 students with few teachers and little money. Ellacuría joined the UCA faculty in 1967, and the following year he was appointed to the five-member board of directors responsible for steering the course of the university. After the vice-province retreat in 1969, the debate among Central American Jesuits regarding the nature and role of the UCA intensified. Ellacuría found himself in the center of the storm. Whitfield writes of Ellacuría:

He was clearly both extraordinarily gifted and a natural leader, yet there were aspects of his character that won him only opposition: his ideas were so radical, so seemingly coherent, the strength of his dialectic so impregnable and at times shot through with a streak of aggression, that his opponents found themselves unable to reply and were left with the impression that they had been objects of an assault. The other members of the UCA board of directors were nervous about where his ideas were leading and considered that his views were attracting undesirable attention: the preceding April the director of immigration had taken declarations made by Ellacuría to the ministry of the interior, accused him of interfering in politics, and called for his expulsion.[8]

Between 1970 and 1975, Ellacuría split his energies between his position at the UCA and his work as the director of formation for the Central American Jesuits. But in 1975, apparently in response to fears about polarization within the Central American Province and the perception that Ellacuría's influence exacerbated those tensions, he was asked to resign as director of formation and prevented from holding other leadership positions in the province. Although initially painful, this change actually freed Ellacuría to invest all his energies in the university. His focus as a theologian grew sharper, and he quickly developed extensive leverage as a commentator on the national reality of El Salvador. Thus, when the Molina government agreed to move forward with a modest land reform proposal in 1976, and the landed oligarchy responded with a howl of protest, Ellacuría assumed an active role in the crisis. He published a lengthy and important analysis of the concept of property in the UCA journal, *Estudios Centroamericanos (ECA)*.[9] Later, when the Molina government succumbed to right-wing pressures and scrapped the land-reform initiative, he satirized the decision in a scathing *ECA* editorial.[10] Shortly thereafter, UCA offices were bombed, an occurrence that would be repeated numerous times in the coming years.

On February 22, 1977, Ellacuría and several other foreign priests were denied reentry into the country. For Ellacuría, this precipitated an eighteen-month exile. That same day, Monseñor Oscar Romero became the Archbishop of San Salvador. Three weeks later, Rutilio Grande, the Jesuit pastor of Aguilares, an old sacristan, and an altar boy were assassinated by members of a death squad with close ties to the Salvadoran military. They were driving to El Paisnal to celebrate Mass.[11] The tense atmosphere grew even more difficult that summer when another death squad calling itself "the White Warriors Union" warned that every Jesuit who did not leave the country within thirty days would be executed.

So began the most extraordinary three years in modern Salvadoran history, a period of intense persecution of the church, during which a dozen priests, several religious women, and hundreds of catechists were murdered. So also began the brutal civil war that would rage throughout the coming decade and claim more than seventy-five thousand lives in all. In October 1979, a bloodless military coup carried out by a group of younger officers represented the last futile efforts by the forces of moderation to achieve a peaceful solution to the mounting crisis. Román Mayorga, the president of the UCA since 1975, left the university to become one of the civilian members of the new ruling junta. Ellacuría, who had quietly reentered the country in August 1978, succeeded him as the rector of the UCA. The new government, besieged on all sides from its first day, imploded within a matter of weeks and the nation lurched into chaos. 1980 proved the blackest of years. The assassination of Archbishop Romero in March, the massacre of over three hundred *campesinos* at the Rio Sampul in May, and the brutal murder of four U.S. churchwomen by national guardsmen in early December headlined a year of horror in which over ten thousand Salvadorans died. Because of the threats on his life emanating from the Salvadoran military's high command, Ellacuría was once again forced into exile. He remained outside of El Salvador for another eighteen months, between November 1980, and April 1982.

Throughout the decade of the 1980s, the civil war in El Salvador dragged on. Although total revolution had seemed imminent early in the decade, massive transfusions of military aid from the United States kept the Salvadoran Army and a series of inept provisional governments in power. As the president of the UCA, Ellacuría remained deeply involved in the political dimension of the struggle. Along with Archbishop Arturo Rivera y Damas, he helped fill the leadership void caused by Monseñor Romero's death, becoming one of the few voices who could effectively oppose the policies of the government and denounce the conduct of the military. His manner and methods differed from those of both the martyred bishop and his episcopal successor, but Ellacuría exhibited a comparable capacity for moral authority and theological vision. He empathized with the majority of Salvadorans for whom the war caused terrible suffering, and he saw clearly the depth of the stalemate between the warring parties. Exerting all his influence, he implored the latter to negotiate a settlement to the conflict. But in 1989, with a peace agreement seemingly within reach, yet another round of talks between government and revolutionary leaders broke down. A long-threatened guerrilla offensive was launched. It did not lead to a military victory for either side, but it did give right-wing elements in the military high command a pretext for ordering the assassination of Ellacuría and his companions.

## MENTORS AND MOVEMENTS

The drama of Ellacuría's death is not incidental to an interpretation of his thought, nor did it occur in a vacuum. He died because of the way he lived.[12] He lived as he did in part because of the people who inspired him and the events that defined his times. The person who most powerfully animated his intellectual development was his mentor and friend, Xavier Zubiri. Because of his importance to an interpretation of Ellacuría, I introduce Zubiri at greater length in the following section. Before turning to their relationship, however, it is important to note several other significant influences in Ellacuría's life: (1) the ecclesial and theological culture inaugurated by Vatican II and exemplified by the thought of Karl Rahner; (2) the impact of Marxism on the revolutionary and counterrevolutionary forces seeking dominion in the countries of Latin America; (3) the meetings of the Latin American Bishops' Conference at Medellín, Colombia, in 1968 and Puebla, Mexico, in 1979, and the emergence of liberation theology; (4) the inspiration of Archbishop Romero and the poor of El Salvador; (5) the changing ecclesial atmosphere under Pope John Paul II and, in particular, the reaction of the Congregation for the Doctrine of the Faith (CDF) to liberation theology; (6) Ellacuría's own Jesuit background and roots, especially as these were nourished by the renewal of Ignatian spirituality under Pedro Arrupe. Ellacuría's relationship to each of these figures and historical currents could be studied in depth, both for how they directly affected his theology as well as for their impact on the larger social and ecclesial history of his times. The limits of this book preclude an in-depth study of all of these mentors and movements, but each appears explicity at various points in this investigation, and all of them remain in the background throughout.

**The Ecclesial Climate of Vatican II.** The historical earthquake of Vatican II directly and indirectly influenced the religious and theological development of Ignacio Ellacuría. To an unprecedented degree, the postconciliar church began to open itself to the modern world, a world imbued with a growing historical consciousness, a world fashioned largely by secular spheres of influence, yet a world burdened with intolerable suffering. While the council's documents themselves tentatively probed that suffering, the ecclesial climate generated by the council proved especially fertile for ongoing theological investigation into its causes, structures, and implications. So profound was the impact of Vatican II that one finds it difficult to imagine the emergence of liberation theology or the contributions of Ignacio Ellacuría apart from it.

The postconciliar ecclesial culture fostered a new atmosphere surrounding theological investigation. This shift affected Catholic theology's horizons, primary concerns, and method, and reconfigured the locus and organs of theological reflection. Of all those who helped shape the council and who symbolized the spirit of the postconciliar church, Karl Rahner was one of the most important.[13] Ellacuría studied directly under Rahner in Innsbruck during the years immediately preceding Vatican II. He considered Rahner an important influence in his own development, one who helped him move into the emerging theological world. In the secularized climate of post-war Europe, Rahner produced a compelling apologetic for doing theology in a new way. He also crafted a method to match his vision. Ellacuría recognized the enormous importance of Rahner's anthropological turn. He judged that it gave the church a new voice with which to engage the secular world in conversation. Nevertheless, he did not directly adopt Rahner's transcendental method in theology. He followed instead a path opened initially by Zubiri. Even though important differences appear between their respective theologies, he never criticized Rahner publicly. On the contrary, he never wavered in his admiration for Rahner as a person, nor in his appreciation for Rahner's enormous contribution to contemporary theology.

**Marxism and Leftist Revolutionary Ferment.** Following the Cuban revolution in 1959, and bolstered by such figures as Che Guevara and Camilo Torres, interest in and fear of revolution spread throughout Latin America. Ultimately stemming from the abysmal poverty that shackled the vast majority of the continent's population, this ferment captured the popular imagination and led to the formation of revolutionary groups, many of which were Marxist in orientation. Not surprisingly, many Christians committed to social change began to study Marx and such revisionist Marxists as Gramsci, Bloch, Girardi, Garaudy, and Berdyaev.[14] Likewise, in the ecclesial atmosphere that encouraged dialogue with the world, a number of Latin American theologians began using tools of social analysis derived from Marxism to help them explain their social situation. As a student of Western literature and philosophy, and with a keen interest in the philosophy of history, Ellacuría also became interested in these currents and developed his own distinctive dialogue with Marxist thought. In fact, he was commonly accused of being a Marxist.

In an interview he gave in Spain during his second exile from El Salvador, he responded to that charge.

> They can accuse me of being a communist, although I am not one. They can accuse me of being a Marxist. I know Marx, as I know Hegel, Aristotle, or Zubiri. Yet I am not a Marxist. When they accuse me, I reply, "I am a Christian." And a Christian is much more radical than any "red" or communist. Christianity understood in its purity is so radical that it is almost impracticable. St. Paul already said as much. Christianity was madness for the Greeks, the intellectuals of that time, and it was blasphemy and heresy for the Jews. So yes, they burden me with this accusation. But does that make it true?[15]

In concert with Marx, Ellacuría affirms the basic importance of philosophical praxis as well as the critical function of social-economic theory. However, he parts company with Marx and other revisionist Marxists on a number of crucial points, above all, on the open nature of reality (or the presence of God to reality) and the necessity and character of an adequate ground for one's social-historical critique. He also repudiated many of the political tactics espoused by leading Latin American Marxists. While he manifested a broad sympathy with the revolutionary movements in El Salvador, Nicaragua, and other parts of Central America, he was not afraid to criticize them and did so forcefully on numerous occasions. In short, his primary inspiration as a philosopher was Zubiri, not Marx, whereas in political matters he was not beholden to any ideology. Rather, his way of engaging historical reality gives preferential attention to the cry of the poor.

**Medellín, Puebla, and Liberation Theology.** The impact of the Latin American Bishops' Conference at Medellín rumbled through the 1970s and beyond like a Latin American aftershock of Vatican II. Together with the Third General Conference at Puebla eleven years later, Medellín exerted a powerful influence throughout this enormously complex and poor continent. It changed the thinking and praxis of many prominent bishops, theologians, and pastoral workers, to say nothing of the poor themselves, their popular movements and base communities. Like Vatican II, it so profoundly shaped Ellacuría in his context that his life and death cannot be adequately understood apart from it. However, although Ellacuría often cites Medellín and Puebla, his writings do not directly indicate how these conferences molded his thought. In the same way, although he occasionally cites the works of other liberation theologians, including Gustavo Gutiérrez, José Míguez Bonino, Juan Luis Segundo,

Enrique Dussel, Leonardo Boff, and Clodovis Boff, there are few explicit references in his writings to the way they influenced him. Yet his solidarity with these thinkers remains unmistakable, as does his deep sympathy with the pastoral initiatives and popular movements spawned and supported by liberation theology. Medellín and Puebla helped shape Ellacuría's spirit and he remained committed to their ideals to the end of his life.

Perhaps the liberation theologian who stimulated Ellacuría most directly and immediately and who was, at the same time, clearly influenced by him in return, was his companion and close friend, Jon Sobrino. Sobrino readily acknowledges his debt to Ellacuría, not only intellectually but personally, and that line of dependence can be easily traced. For one thing, because it was Ellacuría who died and Sobrino who lived to tell the story, we have the latter's moving reflections on the life and death of his friend.[16] We don't have the articles Ellacuría would have surely written about Sobrino had their fates been reversed. Moreover, Ellacuría focused more on foundations and method, whereas Sobrino trained in systematic theology. The explicit reliance of the latter on the former manifests the usual relationship of these disciplines, and proves easier to trace than the other way around. Yet the influence between them flowed both ways. Working closely with Sobrino enabled Ellacuría to stay in touch with the main currents in theology. At the same time, Sobrino's expertise in systematic theology freed Ellacuría to focus on those issues, especially in the area of theological method, to which he was more naturally inclined. While the relationship between them has received some attention, and will undoubtedly receive more in the years ahead, I do not develop an explicit and detailed account of it here.[17] I do turn to Sobrino, however, as one of the most important and reliable secondary sources for understanding Ellacuría's thought. Sobrino's use of Ellacuría's method in his christology, for example, proves an excellent illustration of its logic and utility.[18]

**Archbishop Romero and the Church of the Poor.** Oscar Romero merits a unique place in Salvadoran history. He exerted a dramatic influence on the church and the Jesuits, not to mention the larger political reality of his country and the world beyond El Salvador's borders. Likewise, he touched Ellacuría's life in profound ways. His influence was more spiritual than intellectual. It emanated from the narrative of his life. Through his transformation from a shy ecclesiastic to a bold defender of the poor, with his humble but powerful ecclesial praxis and, above all, in his holiness and martyrdom, Romero incarnated the same theological vision that animated Ignacio Ellacuría. The latter's admiration for the archbishop reverberates in the words he spoke when the UCA posthumously awarded an honorary doctorate to Romero.

> With the arrival of Romero as archbishop, the university became more deeply and fully conscious of its mission. Some have said with ill intent that Monseñor Romero was manipulated by our university. Now is the moment to publicly and solemnly declare that it was not so. Certainly Monseñor Romero asked our collaboration on various occasions and this represented, and continues to represent, a great honor for us, both because of him who asked and because of the cause for which he asked. . . . But in all our collaboration there was no doubt about who was master and who the helper, about who was the pastor giving guidelines and who was implementing them, about who was the prophet unraveling the mystery and who was being guided, about who was the animator and who was animated, about who was the voice and who was the echo.[19]

What was it, above all, that Ellacuría took from Romero? Ellacuría's own anthropology does not allow for facile separations of head and heart, theory and praxis, theology and spirituality, but insofar as one can legitimately place the accent on one term in each of these polarities, the influence of Romero had to do with the latter: *maestro* of Ellacuría's heart, praxis and spirituality, his legacy to Ellacuría was the gift of his own faith. Sobrino writes, "I have no doubt that Ellacuría was really and existentially affected by Monseñor Romero, but in a way that differed from a Rahner or a Zubiri. Monseñor's prophecy and mercy, his sense of utopia and freedom, left clear footprints on him. But in my opinion, the deepest and most specific influence was something else: Monseñor Romero's profound faith in the mystery of God, about which he spoke unaffectedly and naturally, and which he embodied in his person."[20] Ellacuría turned instinctively to Romero as the preeminent example of how ecclesial leadership ought to be exercised. On the basis of that example, he wrote about the elements and structure of an ecclesial praxis that is true to the demands of historical reality. Looking at the church through the example of Romero enabled Ellacuría to glimpse the true people of God and the God of that people.[21]

**The Vatican Instructions on Liberation Theology.** From its inception liberation theology encountered various degrees of ecclesiastical resistance. By the time of the CELAM meeting at Puebla in 1979, although the vision of Vatican II and Medellín continued to dominate the ecclesial climate in Latin America, reaction against the emphasis on liberation could be detected within certain sectors of the Latin American Church.

At a meeting in Sucre, Bolivia, in 1972, Bishop Alfonso López Trujillo, an outspoken critic of liberation theology, was elected secretary general of CELAM.[22] Later in the decade he made a strong attempt to dictate the outcome of the Puebla conference by controlling the process leading up to it. He explicitly attempted to exclude most of the leading liberation theologians from the conference, forcing them to make their contributions from outside the walls of the seminary where the conference was held. In the final analysis, Puebla did not back away from the general course set by Medellín, but neither did it go as far as it might have with regard to adopting the theological perspectives and pastoral strategies germane to liberation theology.[23]

In the 1980s, under the leadership of Pope John Paul II, not only did the ecclesial climate shift in Latin America, but a whole new ecclesiastical-theological culture emerged in the Roman Catholic Church. Concern for the poor remained an expressed priority, but for a variety of reasons, Vatican concern with and opposition to liberation theology also grew. This could be detected in the appointments of new bishops, the investigation and disciplining of different liberation theologians and, perhaps most importantly, in the two Instructions aimed at liberation theology issued by the CDF.[24] This new culture represented a different kind of influence on Ellacuría's thought, one rich with ambiguity and not easily summarized. On the one hand, Ellacuría did not hesitate to express his support and admiration for Pope John Paul. On several occasions he wrote lengthy articles analyzing the pope's words and deeds, particularly as those related directly to the situation in El Salvador. His evaluations were by and large very positive.[25] On the other hand, he carefully responded to criticisms of liberation theology, even when those criticisms came directly from the Holy See, as in the case of the CDF Instructions.[26] More importantly, his very attempt to ground theological method in a philosophy of historical reality results in a theology that is radically historically conscious. To many elements within the church, especially those whose philosophical tendencies run along classicist and essentialist lines, such a shift appears terribly threatening. This book does not dwell on the broad range of issues at play in the tensions between the Vatican and liberation theology. However, in the course of my analysis of Ellacuría's theological method and historical soteriology, unmistakable differences appear between his approach and those adopted by liberation theology's strongest critics.

**Ignatian Spirituality and Religious Renewal.** Another formative influence in Ellacuría's life, one so basic it can be easily overlooked, emerges from the fact that he was a Jesuit. Moreover, he came of age in the Society of Jesus just as the order was undergoing the profound process of renewal mandated by Vatican II. Like the events of Vatican II and Medellín, this renewal concretely changed the way Ellacuría lived out his vocation. Neither his theology nor his historical praxis can be appreciated fully apart from its influence. Pedro Arrupe, the Basque superior general who guided the Jesuit order during this tumultuous time, left a clear mark on it and upon Ellacuría himself. He also earned the latter's highest praise. "I know only one other distinguished man to whom [Arrupe's] style of evangelical leadership could be compared . . . Oscar Arnulfo Romero."[27]

One of the great landmarks of the Jesuit renewal under Arrupe involved the revitalization of the *Spiritual Exercises* of St. Ignatius Loyola. Ellacuría's writings in spirituality, including his direct reflections on the *Exercises*, reveal from yet another angle the distinctive mark of his religious vision. For him, the renewal of the *Exercises* meant recovering their power to place the one making them in historical reality in an active, efficacious way.[28] This power was unleashed in Ellacuría's life and work. It also appears in his words, most dramatically in his meditation on the "crucified peoples." He arrived at this image through the colloquy at the foot of the cross from the First Week of the *Exercises*, where one kneels before the crucified and asks, "What have I done for Christ? What am I doing for Christ? What ought I to do for Christ?"[29] In Ellacuría's adaptation of this exercise, believers are urged to place their "eyes and hearts upon these peoples who are suffering so much, some from misery and hunger, others from oppression and repression, and then, before this people thus crucified, to make the colloquy . . . by asking, what have I done to crucify them? What am I doing in order to uncrucify them? What ought I to do so that this people will be raised?"[30] The concrete impact on Ellacuría of Ignatian spirituality and its renewal under Arrupe appears most dramatically in the manner of his death. The words of General Congregation XXXII that are engraved above his tomb echo this view. "What does it mean to be a Jesuit today? It is to engage, under the standard of the cross, in the crucial struggle of our time: the struggle for faith and the struggle for justice which that same faith demands."[31]

## THE INFLUENCE OF XAVIER ZUBIRI

Ellacuría takes his philosophical foundations and framework from Xavier Zubiri, as was noted above. These in turn shape his entire approach to theology. Hence, the analysis of Ellacuría's philosophy of historical reality benefits from a look at Zubiri's thought. I begin with a brief sketch of Zubiri's life, focusing especially on his relationship to Ellacuría.[32] This biographical sketch provides background for an initial understanding of Zubiri's philosophy and what it was that attracted Ellacuría to it. Besides noting the general extent to which Zubiri's thought influenced Ellacuría's life and thought, I situate the specific way Ellacuría makes use of his mentor's philosophy in his theological writings.

Xavier Zubiri was born into a Basque family in San Sebastián, Spain, on December 4, 1898, and died nearly eighty-five years later in Madrid, on September 21, 1983. In the intervening years an uncommon dedication to academic life in general and philosophy in particular unfolded. Zubiri entered the diocesan seminary in 1918 and was sent to Madrid to study philosophy. He spent the next three years between universities in Spain, Belgium, and Italy. In 1920 he received his licentiate in philosophy from Louvain University in Belgium with a thesis on the thought of Edmund Husserl, *Le problème de l'objectivité d'après Ed. Husserl: I, La logique pure*. The following year he obtained a doctorate in theology from the Gregorian University in Rome and, in the same year, completed a doctorate in philosophy in Madrid under the direction of José Ortega y Gasset with a dissertation entitled, *Ensayo de una teoría fenomenológica del juicio*. In 1921 Zubiri began teaching at the University of Madrid, where he accepted a chair in the history of philosophy in 1926. Two years later he took a leave of absence in order to continue his own studies. Jorge Alvarado's sketch of this period in Zubiri's life catches something of the range of his interests and the quality of his intellectual gifts.

[In 1928 Zubiri] left Madrid to undertake a long and intense journey of four years through various European cultural centers in search of a scientific knowledge sufficient to permit posing the problems of philosophy in a realistic form. His curiosity, versatility and scientific competence were proverbial. He came to have a good command of numerous languages, including Basque, Spanish, German, French, Italian, Latin, Greek, Hebrew, Aramaic, Sumerian, Iranian, Acadian, and Sanskrit. During those years he studied classical philology with Werner Jaeger in Berlin, and continued, with De la Vallée-Poussin in Paris and Ernst Zermelo in Freiburg, the studies in mathematics he had begun with Rey-Pastor in Madrid. He studied biology with Van Gehuchten in Louvain, with Spemann in Freiburg, and with Goldschmidt and Mangolt in Berlin. He studied theoretical physics with Louis de Broglie in Paris and with Erwin Schrödinger in Berlin. He met Max Planck, Werner Heisenberg and Albert Einstein, and he lived with Einstein in the Professor's Residence called "Harnack

House." He also participated in the final lectures of Husserl and the earliest of Heidegger in Freiburg im Breisgau.[33]

In 1931 Zubiri returned to teach in Madrid. Although he had been ordained a priest earlier, he was released from his ordination by Pope Pius XI and he married Carmen Castro in 1936.[34] When the Spanish Civil War broke out later that year Zubiri was in Rome. He spent the next three years in Paris, teaching philosophy and theology at the Catholic Institute while studying ancient history and oriental languages at the Sorbonne. As the Civil War was ending and World War II was erupting, he returned to Spain and his position at the University of Madrid. But the repressive atmosphere of Franco's Spain pervaded the academy and strangled his university career. After one year he left Madrid for the University of Barcelona. In May 1942, he delivered a paper entitled "Our Intellectual Situation" in which the depth of his distress with university life can be detected. Disheartened by the state of the academy, saddened by the shambles that war was making of Europe, and fearful for Western civilization's very future, he ended on this poignant note.

> When human beings and human reason believed they were everything, they lost themselves; they were left, in certain respects, annihilated. Thus the person of the 20th century finds himself even more alone; this time without the world, without God, and without himself. A singular historical condition. . . . Whence the anguishing coefficient of provisionality which threatens to dissolve contemporary life. But if, by a supreme effort, the human being is able to fall back upon himself, he will sense the ultimate questions of existence pass by his unfathomable depth like *umbrae silentes*. The questions of being, of the world, and of truth echo in the depths of his person. Imprisoned in this new sonorous solitude, we find ourselves situated beyond the totality of what merely is, in a type of transreal situation, a situation which is strictly transphysical; it is in fact metaphysical. Its intellectual formula is precisely the problem of contemporary philosophy.[35]

Within weeks of delivering this address, Zubiri abandoned the university. He never returned to it. He did return to Madrid to gather some of his earliest articles, including "Our Intellectual Situation," for publication as a book. *Naturaleza, Historia, Dios* first appeared in 1944.

The decision to leave the university proved pivotal for Zubiri. It marked, in Ellacuría's view, the end of the first epoch in his career and the beginning of the second, during which he began giving private *cursos* in philosophy to small groups of select students. Robert Caponigri, a participant in various of these *cursos*, describes them and assesses their significance.

> The *cursos*, even more than the treatise or essay, must be recognized as Zubiri's personal and original mode of expression and communication. In them, even more than in his books and publications in learned journals, is to be found the living movement, the vital rhythm as well as the weighty insights of his thought. . . . Their texture is dense, but lucid. Above all it is the sense of direct participation in the quest of truth, in the immediate communication with the deep personal quest of a powerful intellect informing a personality of unshakable devotion and integrity that most impresses one; this and the particular didactic style, in which the auditor is not passive, but rather drawn directly into the active intellectual enterprise[*sic*] in which the lecturer is so manifestly absorbed.[36]

Ellacuría, too, participated in a number of Zubiri's *cursos* over the years. In 1962, as Zubiri moved into his final epoch, one marked by a further clarifying of his own philosophy and inaugurated by the publication of *Sobre la esencia*, Ellacuría came to study with him.[37] Because Zubiri had no official connections with any university, Ellacuría had to make special arrangements to have him direct his doctoral studies. For his part, Zubiri, who was not taking students, also made an exception, a decision he never regretted. Ellacuría proved a gifted student and valuable assistant. Even while he was writing his own 1,100-page dissertation on Zubiri's theory of reality, he took time to prepare a detailed and useful companion work to *Sobre la esencia*.[38] Zubiri highly valued these contributions and in 1968 he wrote a letter to Ellacuría's superior general, Fr. Arrupe, asking that Ellacuría be released from his obligation to the UCA in El Salvador so that he might come to work full-time with him in Madrid. After a careful discernment, a compromise was reached whereby Ellacuría would return to Spain and help Zubiri during school vacations, while retaining as his primary assignments teaching at the UCA and participating in the mission of the Central American Province to El Salvador.[39]

When Zubiri was nearly seventy years old, Ellacuría, along with Diego Gracia and Pedro Lain Entralgo, prevailed on him to write a major work detailing his theory of intelligence. The project proved massive. Zubiri was unwilling to publish anything before Ellacuría had carefully read it and they had discussed his comments. Ellacuría himself was caught up in the dramatic events of the years preceding and following the assassination of Archbishop Romero. Nevertheless, he contributed valuable time to the project, aided inadvertently by the two periods of exile from El Salvador. The venture came to fruition with the appearance of

Zubiri's magisterial three-volume work, *Inteligencia sentiente*, between the years 1980 and 1983.[40] Zubiri died in 1983 while Ellacuría was in Rome serving as a delegate to the Jesuits' General Congregation XXXIII. At the time of his death Zubiri was reworking another of his important *cursos* for publication. Ellacuría finished editing it and composed the introduction; *El hombre y Dios* appeared in 1984.[41] In a similar way he prepared *Sobre el hombre* for publication in 1986.[42] In order to make other writings by Zubiri available, the Xavier Zubiri Foundation was founded in Madrid, with Ellacuría serving as its first director.[43] Thus, during this last and greatest epoch of Zubiri's academic career, during the very years in which he guided Ellacuría's development, neither the benefits of their friendship nor even the direct intellectual influence flowed in only one direction. Ellacuría contributed mightily and in various ways to Zubiri's philosophical endeavor. In the final analysis he proved to be a key who unlocked the older man's reserve. If not for his protégé's encouragement and help, Zubiri's great but previously unpublished treasures might well have remained inaccessible to all but a small circle of philosophers.

Ellacuría came under Zubiri's guidance during the 1960s. He wanted to study with someone who was profoundly in touch with the times and that is what he found. In a letter to his superior written shortly after he began this final phase of his studies, he described Zubiri as "a juncture between the classical and the modern, between the essential and the existential."[44] He would soon adopt Zubiri's passion for pure philosophy, but like Zubiri he never understood this as a way to domesticate or flee from reality, to build an ivory tower, or to construct a self-contained conceptual system. Rather, Ellacuría had found a mentor who saw philosophy as a way to engage reality and to commit oneself to the demands of reality.

> Philosophy today needs an immense contact with reality. . . . Zubiri has attempted to apprehend, affirm and think about the totality of real things as real; in this sense he has created a special kind of pure philosophy. . . . But in having done so, he has enabled us to transcend the strictly philosophical sphere. And this not only because he offers us a *knowledge* that is close to things, a *direction* for the world and for life, and even a *form of life*, but rather because he equips us materially and formally to interpret the world and even to transform it, serving as an ultimate light to other modes of knowing and acting.[45]

In Ellacuría's estimation, philosophy was Zubiri's vocation. "The obligation of his life, the sweet and costly obligation, was to pour himself

out investigating the truth of those things that appear to be the funda-
mentals of human life."[46] Like Socrates whom he so admired, Zubiri
wanted to convert philosophy itself into an authentic way of life, to
make of theory a true mode of ethical existence. Concretely, this involved
finding an intellectually honest way through the ancient *aporia* of realism
and idealism. He felt compelled to articulate a philosophical realism that
caught reality as it actually is, but without lapsing into naïve realism
or sidestepping the challenges of idealism. This predilection for reality
inclined him toward the practical. In this he was not alone. Similar
tendencies can be detected in his own teachers, Ortega y Gasset and
Heidegger.[47] Zubiri lived the questions of ontology, but did not live in the
realm of the abstract. For him, philosophy was never merely academic, for
it touched the very body of human existence.

Along with his intellectual integrity, passion, and realism, Ellacuría
admired Zubiri for his philosophical openness to divine reality. When
Zubiri was awarded an honorary doctorate in theology by the University
of Deusto in Bilbao, Spain, in 1980, Ellacuría called attention to this
feature of his life and thought. Zubiri had authored erudite reflections
on such themes as eucharist, trinity, incarnation, creation, and the development of doctrine. Nevertheless, he advanced theology not so much
through these specifically *theological* reflections as through what Ellacuría
calls the *theologal* dimension of all his thought.[48]

> [The theologal] is the dimension in which the person, because he is
> connected to reality, is more than himself, even while, at every minute,
> he is a pilgrim utterly awed by the power of the real. . . . Zubiri is a
> theologal philosopher whose own philosophy of the human person
> brought him to a *living* encounter with the realm of the divine, which is
> implicated in the most personal dimension of a human being, but also
> in society and history. There is a theologal dimension of things and from
> this dimension a religious encounter with God is possible, a theological
> as well as a philosophical encounter.[49]

The concern with this implicit connectedness to the divine represents
another area in which the Zubirian influence on Ellacuría can be clearly
detected. For one thing, due both to his European and philosophical
roots, Ellacuría encountered and reflected deeply on the challenges posed
by modernity in general and atheism in particular. He faced the need
to engage a secularized world on its terms, but in such a way that the
door remained open to the realm of the divine. More importantly, from
1975 until his death, Ellacuría battled the idols of a practical atheism
that wrapped their brutality and their violent repression of El Salvador's

poor in theological justifications. In a manner that appears in some ways more reminiscent of Marx than Zubiri, Ellacuría developed a political consciousness and critical method so as to name and confront the violence operative in such rationalizations. However, like Zubiri and unlike Marx, Ellacuría confronted the idols with a theologal critique. For Zubiri, Ellacuría tells us, "the question of the human being, the question of history, and the question of the salvation of the human being and history could not be conceived adequately if the theologal dimension were not taken into account."[50] On this important point, as on so many others, the master and the disciple were of one mind.

Ellacuría worked on and off with Zubiri for over twenty years. During that time, he came to share in his teacher's vision of reality. But in many practical respects they could not have chosen more dissimilar lifestyles within which to express and embody that shared vision. While Zubiri formulated a philosophy that tended toward the practical, Ellacuría's orientation shifted from practical philosophy to *praxis*, from a theory about action to action informed by theory. While Zubiri lived the life of a contemplative, almost ascetical, philosophical recluse, Ellacuría took up an active life in the *polis*. The philosophy of historical reality becomes, in his hands, a philosophy of liberation. After he returned to El Salvador, he began to deploy Zubiri's philosophy of reality in ways that concretely and directly influenced that society. Citizen, social critic, teacher, writer, editor, television personage, university president, priest, he, too, exhibited an asceticism, but the properly Ignatian asceticism of a contemplative-in-action.[51] With profound consistency and controlled intensity, Ellacuría exercised his call to work for liberation. Philosophy served as one of his standard tools in that work. The same philosophical unity that undergirded his theological vision penetrated his analyses of social-political realities, his ministry as a Jesuit priest, his praxis as a university president. Thus, besides serving as a foundation for his intellectual labor, philosophy formed an important part of his life. It informed and tempered his praxis. He was, in many respects, philosophical to the core. But philosophy did not constitute his core. This important nuance is perhaps best summed up in the words of Jesuit philosopher, Antonio González, a disciple of Ellacuría.

> Ellacuría was a *philosopher* in the full sense of the word, although perhaps not in the usual sense. . . . His originality was rather in having converted philosophy itself into a style of authentic human life, in having made of theory a true mode of ethical existence. Perhaps the Socratic form of philosophizing and of being a philosopher should serve as the first key

in our assessment of the work of Ignacio Ellacuría. To paraphrase Zubiri, we might attempt a parallel with Socrates, saying that *the intellectual labor of Ignacio Ellacuría was characterized not so much by his having placed the historical praxis of liberation at the center of his philosophical reflections, but rather in his having made of philosophy a constitutive element of an existence dedicated to liberation.*[52]

## ELLACURÍA'S WRITINGS

Ellacuría's academic career unfolded in the dramatic context of his life. Significantly, as was noted above, despite the pressures he faced and the demands placed on his time and energy, he never stopped writing and publishing. He wrote out of multiple concerns, in different genres, for diverse audiences, and with varying degrees of editing and polish. For this reason one must exercise care when categorizing his writings.[53] Although his books and published articles can be generally grouped in one of three areas, philosophy, theology and political analysis, the lines dividing these areas admit a certain degree of fluidity. Some works, especially among his earlier published and unpublished writings, fall outside these classifications altogether. Moreover, while he clearly developed as a thinker, a certain unity permeates the writings he produced over a span of some thirty-three years.

Ellacuría's intellectual development falls into three relatively distinct stages. His early phase (1956–1964) coincided with the years of his academic and religious formation, continuing into his doctoral studies in Madrid. The second phase (1964–1975) dawned with the writing of his dissertation and served as a time of philosophical consolidation. Along with his dissertation (1965) and *Indices de "Sobre la esencia" de Xavier Zubiri* (1965), he produced several lengthy, technical articles dealing with philosophical concerns from the perspective mapped out by Zubiri.[54] During this middle period he also began publishing articles analyzing social, economic, and political concerns from within a philosophically informed framework. In 1972 he delivered a paper at a conference in Madrid entitled "Philosophy and Politics."[55] In the early 1970s he also began contributing essays to the nascent movement of liberation theology. He collected and published the most important of these in a book entitled *Teología política* in 1973.[56]

Ellacuría's mature phase (1975–1989) unveils the full breadth of his concerns, the intensity of his passion, and the concrete urgency of his historical commitments. Although he continued to write on explicitly philosophical themes, he devoted increasing attention to theology and social-political analysis, and to themes which lie at the intersection of philosophy, theology, and political theory. In 1975 he produced several articles in which the philosophical foundations, theological horizons, and social-historical concerns characteristic of his later thought are in full evidence. Two, in particular, stand out: a paper on the philosophical foundations of theological method that he gave at an important conference of liberation theologians in Mexico City,[57] and a series of theses on the possibility, necessity, and meaning of a Latin American theology that he contributed to a festschrift in honor of Karl Rahner's seventieth birthday.[58] Many of his later essays, although devoted to theological or political concerns, make explicit use of the philosophical framework sketched in these two articles.

Despite the interdisciplinary complexity of Ellacuría's mature phase, it is still possible to distinguish and review his later writings in terms of the categories of Zubirian philosophy, Salvadoran politics, and liberation theology. (1) In the late 1970s and early 1980s, while helping Zubiri prepare *Inteligencia sentiente* for publication, he wrote the rough draft for his own philosophical textbook, *Filosofía de la realidad histórica*.[59] This work, although clearly dependent on Zubirian foundations, represents the emergence of his own distinctive interpretation of Zubiri. Later, in what proved to be the last years of his own life, Ellacuría evaluated Zubiri's overall project in one major article and several short pieces.[60] He also wrote articles on the nature of philosophy and the link between philosophy and social analysis.[61] (2) It was noted above that the political situation in El Salvador demanded the lion's share of Ellacuría's attention during the last phase of his life. Together with Segundo Montes, Ignacio Martín-Baró, and their other colleagues at the UCA, he wrote extensively on the national reality of El Salvador, as the three-volume collection of his social-political essays testifies.[62] (3) However, Ellacuría also wrote the majority of his theological articles during this period. Many of these articles, especially those written between 1977 and 1984, deal with the relation of the church to the political realities of El Salvador, reflecting the intensity of the Romero years and the tragedy of the deepening political crisis. A number of these were gathered into a second book, *Conversión de la Iglesia al Reino de Dios*.[63] Several others were included in a volume on the church and the popular movements in El Salvador.[64] All of his theological essays appeared in one or more journals. The articles written during and after 1984 reflect the changing ecclesial climate in which liberation theology was regarded more and more with suspicion.[65] Increasingly conscious of the need to establish liberation theology's credibility, Ellacuría and Jon Sobrino made plans to edit a theological dictionary from a liberation perspective, along the lines of Rahner's *Sacramentum Mundi*. The final work, published as *Mysterium Liberationis*, appeared after Ellacuría's death and included four of his key theological articles.[66]

Besides these more formal works, many other writings can be located in the Ignacio Ellacuría Archive at the UCA and in the Archives of the Central American Province of the Society of Jesus in San Salvador. These include letters, interviews, class notes, retreat notes, unpublished drafts of various early articles, outlines for future essays and other projects, several volumes of notebooks detailing meetings with various public figures, and thousands of one- and two-page editorials, many of which he delivered on a daily basis over the UCA radio station YSAX between 1975 and 1989, or published in less formal UCA publications such as *Proceso*. The UCA is in the process of publishing a multivolume collection of his philosophical and theological writings that will include some of these previously unpublished short works. However, the dense body of Ellacuría's writings that he himself published or that were published shortly after his death form the primary medium through which I attempt to interpret his philosophy of historical reality and his contributions to liberation theology.

## Notes to Chapter 1

1. Jon Sobrino, "A Letter to Ignacio Ellacuría," *The Principle of Mercy* (Maryknoll: Orbis, 1994) 188.

2. See Ignacio Ellacuría, "El P. Aurelio Espinosa Pólit, S.J.," *ECA* (No. 178, 1963) 205–212; Whitfield, 25. Whitfield contends that five people profoundly influenced Ellacuría's intellectual and spiritual development. Along with Espinosa Pólit, they include Miguel Elizondo (his novice master), Karl Rahner and Xavier Zubiri (his theology and philosophy teachers), and Archbishop Oscar Romero; see Whitfield, 21–32, 213–217. Along with these five, I would add a sixth, Pedro Arrupe, the superior general of the Jesuits from 1965 to 1981. His influence on Ellacuría was less direct than the others, but was similarly definitive.

3. Ignacio Ellacuría, "La principialidad de la esencia en Xavier Zubiri" (Ph.D. Diss., Universidad Complutense, Madrid, 1965).

4. Whitfield, 32–37; see also Christian Smith, *The Emergence of Liberation Theology: Radical Religion and Social Movement Theory* (Chicago: University of Chicago Press, 1991) 111–115, hereafter cited as "Smith"; Penny Lernoux, *Cry of the People* (New York: Penguin Books, 1980, 1982) Part Two. For the recent history of El Salvador, see Tommie Sue Montgomery, *Revolution in El Salvador: From Civil Strife to Civil Peace* (Boulder, Co: Westview Press, 1995); Scott Wright, *Promised Land: Death and Life in El Salvador* (Maryknoll: Orbis, 1994).

5. Provincials of the Society of Jesus in Latin America, "Between Honesty and Hope," in A. Hennelly, ed., *Liberation Theology: A Documentary History* (Maryknoll: Orbis, 1990) 77–83.

6. CELAM, Second General Conference of Latin American Bishops in Medellín, Colombia, 1968, *The Church in the Present-Day Transformation of Latin America in the Light of the Council*, 2 Vols., (Washington, D.C.: United States Catholic Conference, 1970); see also Whitfield, 35–40; Smith, 150–164; Roberto Oliveros, "History of the Theology of Liberation," *MLT*, 14–16.

7. Whitfield, 44. On the significance of the retreat, see Lassalle-Klein, *Jesuit Martyrs*, 55–72.

8. Whitfield, 46.

9. Ignacio Ellacuría, "La historización del concepto de propiedad como principio de desideologización," *VA*, Vol. 1, 587–626, hereafter cited as "Propiedad"; first published in *ECA* (No. 335–336, 1976) 425–450; "The Historicization of the Concept of Property," *TSSP* (1991) 105–137, trans. by Phillip Berryman.

10. Ignacio Ellacuría, "¡A sus órdenes, mi capital!" *ECA* (No. 337, 1976) 637–643.

11. James Brockman, *Romero: A Life* (Maryknoll: Orbis, 1989) 9; see William O'Malley, *The Voice of Blood: Five Christian Martyrs of Our Time* (Maryknoll: Orbis, 1981) 3–63.

12. Ellacuría observes a similar connection between the life and death of Jesus; see Ignacio Ellacuría, "Por qué muere Jesús y por qué le matan," *Diakonía* (No. 8, 1978) 73; first published in *Misión Abierta* (No. 70, 1977); hereafter cited as "Por qué muere Jesús."

13. Martin Maier, a German theologian who studied with both Rahner and Ellacuría, has written extensively on their relationship; see "Karl Rahner: The Teacher of Ignacio Ellacuría," in R. Lassalle-Klein and K. Burke, eds. *The Love That Produces Hope*, op. cit.; "La influencia de Karl Rahner en la teología de Ignacio Ellacuría" *RLT*, Part I (No. 39, 1996) 233–255; Part 2 (No. 44, 1998) 163–187. The bibliography of secondary literature on Rahner is enormous. Excellent introductions to his life and thought include Herbert Vorgrimler, *Understanding Karl Rahner*, trans. by John Bowden (New York: Crossroad, 1986); Anne Carr, *The Theological Method of Karl Rahner* (Missoula, Mont.: Scholars Press, 1977); W. Kelly, ed., *Theology and Discovery: Essays in Honor of Karl Rahner* (Milwaukee: Marquette University Press, 1980). From the perspective of liberation theology, see Jon Sobrino, "Características generales del pensamiento de Karl Rahner" *ECA* (No. 262, 1970) 346–361; Because of Rahner's influence on the scope and nature of theology, his achievement has evoked comparisons to that of Thomas Aquinas; for example, see Gerald McCool, "Karl Rahner and the Christian Philosophy of St. Thomas Aquinas," in *Theology and Discovery*, op. cit., 63–93; George Vandervelde, "The Grammar of Grace: Karl Rahner as a Watershed in Contemporary Theology," *Theological Studies* (Vol. 49, No. 3: 1988) 445–459. Vandervelde provides a representative assessment of Rahner's importance to contemporary theology. "Rahner's stature is beyond dispute. Given his stature and brilliance, and given the profound way in which he has addressed the core of theology, i.e. the meaning of grace, any theologian worth the name must come to grips with his thought. In that sense it functions as a watershed in contemporary theology," ibid., 445.

14. The interest in a Christian-Marxist dialogue was not limited to Latin America, of course, but it evolved in a distinctive way there. Several important works from the side of Marxists interested in this dialogue include Roger Garaudy, *From Anathema to Dialogue: A Marxist Challenge to the Christian Churches*, trans. by Luke O'Neill (New York: Herder & Herder, 1966); *The Alternative Future: A Vision of Christian Marxism*, trans. by Leonard Mayhew (New York: Simon & Schuster, 1974); Giulio Girardi, *Marxism and Christianity*, trans. by Kevin Traynor (New York: Macmillan,

1968); for an assessment from the perspective of Christian theologians, see René Coste, *Marxist Analysis and Christian Faith*, trans. by Roger Couture and John Cort (Maryknoll: Orbis, 1985); Arthur McGovern, *Marxism: An American Christian Perspective* (Maryknoll: Orbis, 1980); Anselm Kyongsuk Min, *Dialectic of Salvation*, op. cit. For a criticism of liberation theology from a contemporary Marxist perspective, see Alistair Kee, *Marx and the Failure of Liberation Theology* (London: SCM Press; Philadelphia: Trinity Press International, 1990).

15. Josefina Martínez del Alamo, "El volcán jesuita: Entrevista con el padre Ellacuría, rector de la Universidad Centroamericana," *ABC* (March 28, 1982) 19, trans. mine; quoted in Whitfield, 217.

16. See Jon Sobrino, "Companions of Jesus," in J. Sobrino, et al., *Companions of Jesus* (Maryknoll: Orbis, 1990) trans. by Dinah Livingstone, 3–56; "Ignacio Ellacuría, el hombre y el cristiano: Bajar de la cruz al pueblo crucificado," *RLT*, Part 1 (No. 32, 1994) 131–161; Part 2 (No. 33, 1994) 215–244, hereafter cited as "Sobrino, Ignacio Ellacuría"; "La comunión eclesial alrededor del pueblo crucificado: A la memoria de Ignacio Ellacuría," *RLT* (No. 20, 1990) 137–162; "The Cost of Speaking the Truth: The Martyrs of Central America, El Salvador," *The Journal for Peace and Justice Studies* (Vol. 3, 1991) 1–11; "The Legacy of the Martyrs of the Central American University," in *The Principle of Mercy*, op. cit., 173–185.

17. For a detailed study of the theological collaboration between Ellacuría and Sobrino, one in which the relationship of both to Rahner is also examined, see Martin Maier, *Theologie des Gekreuzigten Volkes: Der Entwurf einer Theologie der Befreiung von Ignacio Ellacuría und Jon Sobrino* (Ph.D. dissertation, University of Innsbruck, 1992).

18. See Jon Sobrino, *Jesus the Liberator: A Historical-Theological View* (Maryknoll: Orbis, 1994); hereafter cited as Sobrino, *Liberator*.

19. Ignacio Ellacuría, "La UCA ante el doctorado concedido a Monseñor Romero," *ECA* (No. 437, 1985) 168, trans. mine; quoted by Sobrino, "Ignacio Ellacuría," 228, and Whitfield, 215.

20. Sobrino, "Ignacio Ellacuría," 229, trans. mine; see also Whitfield, 214.

21. See Ignacio Ellacuría, "El verdadero pueblo de Dios, según Monseñor Romero," *ECA* (No. 392, 1981) 529–554, hereafter cited as "Verdadero pueblo"; "Monseñor Romero, un enviado de Dios para salvar a su pueblo," *ST* (No. 811, 1980) 825–832; "Pueblo de Dios," in C. Floristan and J.J. Tamayo, eds., *Conceptos fundamentales de pastoral* (1983) 840–859; "Esquema de interpretación de la Iglesia en Centroamérica," *RLT* (No. 31, 1994) 3–29.

22. See Arthur F. McGovern, *Liberation Theology and Its Critics: Toward an Assessment* (Maryknoll: Orbis, 1989) 11–14, 47–50.

23. Ibid., 14–15; Smith, chapters 8–9; Penny Lernoux, "The Long Path to Puebla," and Moisés Sandoval, "Report from the Conference," in J. Eagleson and P. Scharper, eds., *Puebla and Beyond* (Maryknoll: Orbis, 1979) 3–43.

24. Congregation for the Doctrine of the Faith, "Instruction of Certain Aspects of the 'Theology of Liberation' " (Vatican City, August 6, 1984) in *Liberation Theology: A Documentary History*, op. cit., 393–414; "Instruction on Christian Freedom and Liberation" (March 22, 1986), ibid., 461–497. For a sharp critique of these developments in general and of the CDF's interventions in particular, see Penny Lernoux, *People of God: The Struggle for World Catholicism* (New York: Penguin Books, 1989).

25. In 1982 Pope John Paul II wrote an important letter to the Salvadoran bishops about the conflict. Ellacuría gratefully called attention to the way the pope addressed El Salvador's "concrete historical reality, about which he rendered an explicit and global

judgment, and to which he sought to address a solution and remedy," Ignacio Ellacuría, "Juan Pablo II y el conflicto salvadoreño," *ECA* (No. 405, 1982) 635, trans. mine. See also "Conflicto entre trabajo y capital en la presente fase histórica: Un análisis de la encíclica de Juan Pablo II sobre el trabajo humano," *ECA* (No. 409, 1982) 1008–1024; "El viaje del Papa a Centroamérica," *ECA* (No. 423–424, 1983) 255–272; "Mensaje ético-político de Juan Pablo II al pueblo de Centro América," *ECA* (No. 413–414, 1983) 255–272.

26. Ignacio Ellacuría, "Estudio teológico-pastoral de la 'Instrucción sobre algunos aspectos de la teología de la liberación,' " *RLT* (No. 2, 1984) 145–178; "Teología de la liberación y marxismo," *RLT* (No. 20, 1990) 109–136; "El desafío cristiano de la teología de la liberación," *Carta a las Iglesias*, Part 1 (No. 263, 1992) 12–15; Part 2 (No. 264, 1992) 11–13; Part 3 (No. 265, 1992) 14–16.

27. Ignacio Ellacuría, "Pedro Arrupe, renovador de la vida religiosa," *RLT* (No. 22, 1991) 7; first published in M. Alcala, ed., *Pedro Arrupe: Así lo vieron* (Santander: Sal Terrae, 1986).

28. See Ignacio Ellacuría, "Fe y justicia," *Christus*, Part 1 (August, 1977) 26–33; Part 2 (October, 1977) 19–34; partially resubmitted as "La contemplación en la acción de la justicia," *Diakonía* (No. 2, 1977) 7–14. See also "Espiritualidad," in *Conceptos fundamentales de pastoral* (1983) 304–309; "Lectura latinoamericana de los Ejercicios Espirituales de San Ignacio," *RLT* (No. 23, 1991) 111–147; "Misión actual de la Compañía de Jesús," *RLT* (No. 29, 1993) 115–126.

29. Ignatius Loyola, *The Spiritual Exercises of Saint Ignatius*, No. 53, trans. and ed. by G. Ganss (St. Louis: Institute of Jesuit Sources, 1992), hereafter cited as *Spiritual Exercises*.

30. Ellacuría, "Las Iglesias latinoamericanas interpelan a la Iglesia de España," *ST* (No. 826, 1982) trans. mine, 230.

31. This is my translation from the inscription above the six Jesuits' tomb. The official English translation of this text slightly softens it. "What is it to be a companion of Jesus today? It is to engage, under the standard of the Cross, in the crucial struggle of our time: the struggle for faith and that struggle for justice which it includes," *Documents of the 31st and 32nd General Congregations of the Society of Jesus* (St Louis: Institute of Jesuit Sources, 1977) 401.

32. For background on Zubiri's life and thought, see Robert Caponigri, "Introduction" to Xavier Zubiri, *On Essence* (Washington, D.C.: The Catholic University of America Press, 1980) 13–37, book hereafter cited as Zubiri, *OE*; Diego Gracia, "Zubiri, Xavier," in R. Latourelle and R. Fisichella, eds., *Dictionary of Fundamental Theology* (New York: Crossroad, 1995) 1165–1169; Jorge Alvarado Pisani, "Vida y pensamiento de Xavier Zubiri (1898–1983)" in A. González, ed., *Voluntad de Vida: Ensayos Filosóficos*, Seminario Zubiri-Ellacuría, Vol. 1 (Managua: UCA, 1993) 117–128; Javier Muguerza, "El lugar de Zubiri en la filosofía española contemporánea," in J. Gimbernat & C. Gómez, eds., *La pasión por la libertad: Homenaje a Ignacio Ellacuría* (Navarra: Editorial Verbo Divino, 1994) 289–306.

33. Jorge Alvarado Pisani, "Vida y pensamiento de Xavier Zubiri (1898–1983)" 118, trans. mine.

34. I learned these details in an informal interview with Jon Sobrino (San Salvador: May, 1996).

35. Xavier Zubiri, *Nature, History, God* (Washington, D.C.: The Catholic University of America Press, 1980) 29; trans. by Thomas Fowler from *Naturaleza, Historia, Dios* (Madrid: Editora Nacional, 1963, 1981); hereafter cited as Zubiri, *NHG*.

36. Caponigri, "Introduction" to Zubiri, *OE*, 18.

37. Xavier Zubiri, *Sobre la esencia* (Madrid: Gráficas Cóndor, 1962, 1980), hereafter cited as Zubiri, *SE*; trans. by Robert Caponigri as *On Essence*, op. cit.
38. Ignacio Ellacuría, *Indices de "Sobre la esencia" de Xavier Zubiri* (Madrid: Sociedad de Estudios y Publicaciones, 1965).
39. Whitfield, 42; see also ibid., nn. 4 and 5, 422. A similar request would be made a few years later by some of Zubiri's other disciples who recognized that Ellacuría's assistance to Zubiri was irreplaceable and feared for his safety in Central America.
40. Xavier Zubiri, *Inteligencia sentiente: Inteligencia y realidad*, Vol. 1 (Madrid: Alianza Editorial, 1980); *Inteligencia y logos*, Vol. 2 (Madrid: Alianza Editorial, 1982); *Inteligencia y razón*, Vol. 3 (Madrid: Alianza Editorial, 1983), hereafter cited respectively as Zubiri, *IS*, *IL*, *IR*.
41. Xavier Zubiri, *El Hombre y Dios* (Madrid: Alianza Editorial, Sociedad de Estudios y Publicaciones, 1984), hereafter cited as Zubiri, *HD*.
42. Xavier Zubiri, *Sobre el Hombre* (Madrid: Alianza Editorial, Sociedad de Estudios y Publicaciones, 1986), hereafter cited as Zubiri, *SH*.
43. Other posthumous works by Zubiri have been edited by Antonio González and Diego Gracia, the latter in his role as the current director of the Zubiri Foundation; see Xavier Zubiri, *Estructura dinámica de la realidad* (Madrid: Alianza Editorial, Sociedad de Estudios y Publicaciones, 1989); *Sobre el sentimiento y la volición* (Madrid: Alianza Editorial, 1992); *El problema filosófico de la historia de las religiones* (Madrid: Alianza Editorial, Sociedad de Estudios y Publicaciones, 1993); *Los problemas fundamentales de la metafísica occidental* (Madrid: Alianza Editorial, Fundación Xavier Zubiri, 1994).
44. Ignacio Ellacuría, letter to Luis Achaerandio, October 3, 1963, cited by Whitfield, 31. In an essay written shortly after his mentor's death, Ellacuría notes that Zubiri had considered being "relevant" less important than "being at the height of the times." The Spanish terms used are *actual* ("current, relevant") and *estar a la altura de los tiempos* (a common phrase often translated as "being abreast of the times"). Zubiri attaches his own special meaning to the latter phrase, taking it to denote a particular epoch, a part in the whole of history. One's times are unique: they cannot be repeated, revised, or interchanged with other times. This has significant ramifications. It means that each distinct historical epoch corresponds to a specific and distinct historical reality. One can only get at the whole of history from the part within which one lives, and the task of mediating between *la altura de los tiempos* and *historia* falls to philosophy. All this is at play when Ellacuría calls Zubiri a thinker who lived *a la altura de los tiempos*. See Ignacio Ellacuría, "Aproximación a la obra completa de Xavier Zubiri," *ECA* (No. 421–422, 1983) 966; hereafter cited as "Aproximación"; see also *FRH*, 442–460.
45. "Aproximación" (1983) 967–968, author's emphasis.
46. Ignacio Ellacuría, "Zubiri sigue vivo," *Vida Nueva* (No. 1396, 1983) 55, trans. mine. The cost of this struggle and the sacrifice demanded by this vocation remained hidden from all but a few. Ellacuría gives a hint of how exacting it could be. "I remember how, after he had written more that 600 pages of the book on intelligence, one day he told me that he had not been able to sleep. He had spent the night suppressing his tears so as not to awaken Carmen, his wife. 'For,' he told me, 'if what I wrote yesterday is true, then all the other pages are useless because they do not speak about things as they are, and I have to tear up the work of three years.' Only when he saw how to reconcile the truth he had just come across with what he had previously written could he recover his peace," ibid, 55.

47. Zubiri's early comments on Blondel also reveal this practical resonance. "Action is something practical. Here I treat not of theory, nor of practice, nor of thought, nor of life, but rather of the being of man [*sic*]. That splendid and redoubtable book of Blondel, *L'Action*, would not achieve its marvelous intellectual efficacy otherwise than by translating the problem to the sphere of ontology," Zubiri, *NHG*, 332.

48. The *theologal* is related to but distinct from the *theological*. The latter deals with the study, formulation, and explication of the divine, while the former attempts to express the implicit "God dimension" of reality. Compare this explanation with that of Edward Schillebeeckx in *Christ the Sacrament of the Encounter with God* (New York: Sheed & Ward, 1963) 16. The concept of the theologal dimension of reality is closely related to another neologism, *religación*, by means of which Zubiri evokes what he calls "the power of the real"; see below, chapter 2, n. 19.

49. Ignacio Ellacuría, "Zubiri, filósofo teologal," *Vida Nueva* (No. 1249, 1980) 45, trans. mine, author's emphasis.

50. Ibid., 45.

51. See "Fe y justicia," Part 2 (1977) 33–34.

52. Antonio González, "Aproximación a la obra filosófica de Ignacio Ellacuría," *ECA* (No. 505–506, 1990) 980, trans. mine, author's emphasis; hereafter cited as "González"; quoted in Whitfield, 203–204, 207.

53. Several bibliographies of Ellacuría have been published. The most extensive in English can be found in J. Hassett, and H. Lacey, eds., *Towards a Society That Serves Its People: The Intellectual Contribution of El Salvador's Murdered Jesuits* (Washington, D.C.: Georgetown University Press, 1991) 373–382; cited throughout as *TSSP*. This bibliography contains some minor inaccuracies.

54. "Antropología de Xavier Zubiri," *Revista de Psiquiatría y Psicología Médica de Europa y América Latina*, Part 1 (No. 6, 1964) 403–430; Part 2 (No. 7, 1964) 483–508; "Cinco lecciones de filosofía," *Crisis* (No. 45, 1965) 109–125; "La historicidad del hombre en Xavier Zubiri," *Estudios de Deusto* (Vol. 40, No. 14, 1966) 245–285, 523–547; "La religación, actitud radical del hombre: Apuntes para un estudio de la antropología de Zubiri," *Asclepio: Archivo iberoamericano de historia de la medicina y antropología médica* (Madrid, Vol. 16, 1966) 97–155; "La idea de filosofía en Xavier Zubiri," in A. Teulon, I. Ellacuría, et al., *Homenaje a Zubiri II* (Madrid: Editorial Moneda y Crédito, 1970) 477–485; "La idea de estructura en la filosofía de Xavier Zubiri" in *Realitas I. Seminario Xavier Zubiri* (Madrid: Editorial Moneda y Crédito, 1974) 71–139; "Introducción crítica a la antropología filosófica de Zubiri," *Cuadernos Salmantinos de Filosofía* (No. 2, 1975) 157–184.

55. "Filosofía y política," *ECA* (No. 284, 1972) 373–385; see also "Seguridad social y solidaridad humana: Aproximación filosófica al fenómeno de la seguridad social," *ECA* (No. 253, 1969) 357–366; "Los derechos humanos fundamentales y su limitación legal y política," *ECA* (No. 254–255, 1969) 435–449, cited in *VA*, Vol. 1, 501–520, trans. by Phillip Berryman as "Fundamental Human Rights and the Legal and Political Restrictions Placed on Them" (*TSSP*, 1991) 91–104; "Un marco teórico-valorativo de la reforma agraria," *ECA* (No. 297–298, 1973) 443–457; "Aspectos éticos del problema poblacional," *ECA* (No. 310–311, 1974) 565–592.

56. Ignacio Ellacuría, *Teología política* (San Salvador: Ediciones del Secretariado Social Interdiocesano, 1973), hereafter cited as *TP*. The publication of *Teología política* touched off a minor furor within local ecclesiastical circles, largely because of the third section which deals with revolutionary violence. The book came out in English in 1976 with the rather colorful title, *Freedom Made Flesh: The Mission of Christ and*

*His Church*, trans. by John Drury (Maryknoll: Orbis, 1976), hereafter cited as *FMF*. Because Ellacuría actually wrote these pieces as individual essays, I cite the original essay titles and publication dates in all notes and bibliographical references to *Teología política [TP]*. I also include the page references to *Freedom Made Flesh [FMF]* in all my citations of this work. Although most of my citations are to Drury's English translation, I occasionally use my own translation; therefore, I note the translator in all citations to the essays that comprise *Teología política*.

57. "Hacia una fundamentacíon filosófica del método teológico latinoamericano," in E. Ruiz Maldonado, ed., *Liberación y cautiverio: Debates en torno al método de la teología en América Latina* (Mexico City, August 11–15, 1975) 609–635, hereafter cited as "Hacia."

58. "Tesis sobre la posibilidad, necesidad y sentido de una teología latinoamericana," in *Teología y mundo contemporaneo: Homenaje a Karl Rahner en su 70 cumpleaños* (Madrid: Ediciones Cristiandad, 1975) 325–350; hereafter cited as "Tesis sobre teología."

59. Ignacio Ellacuría, *Filosofía de la realidad histórica* (San Salvador: UCA Editores, 1990) 442–460, cited throughout as *FRH*; also published in Spain (Madrid: Trotta, 1991) but with different pagination. It should be recalled that Ellacuría never finished this book. Mimeographed versions of it were produced for his philosophy classes, but it was not formally published during his lifetime. Antonio González edited Ellacuría's original manuscript for publication in 1990.

60. The longer review of Zubiri's work is "Aproximación" (1983); the shorter pieces appear in the bibliography. Articles on Zubirian themes include "La antropología filosófica de Xavier Zubiri," in P. Lain Entralgo, ed., *Historia universal de la medicina*, Vol. 7 (Barcelona: Editorial Salvat, 1975), hereafter cited as "Antropología"; "Fundamentación biológica de la ética," *ECA* (No. 368, 1979) 419–428, hereafter cited as "Fundamentación biológica"; "Biología e inteligencia," *Realitas III-IV: Seminario Xavier Zubiri* (Madrid: Sociedad de Estudios y Publicaciones and Editores Labor, 1979) 281–335; "El objeto de la filosofía," *ECA* (No. 396–397, 1981) 963–980; "La nueva obra de Zubiri: 'Inteligencia Sentiente,' " *Razón y Fe* (No. 995, 1981) 126–139, hereafter cited as "Nueva obra."

61. Other philosophical articles from his mature period include "Filosofía ¿para qué?" (San Salvador: UCA, 1976, 1987), trans. by T. Michael McNulty as "What Is the Point of Philosophy?" *Philosophy & Theology* (Vol. 10, No. 1, 1998) 3–18; "Propiedad" (1976); "Historización del bien común y de los derechos humanos en una sociedad dividida," in E. Tamez and S. Trinidad, eds., *Capitalismo: Violencia y anti-vida*, Vol. 2 (San José, EDUCA, 1978) 81–94, hereafter cited as "Bien común"; "El concepto filosófico de tecnología apropiada," *ECA* (No. 366, 1979) 213–223; "Función liberadora de la filosofía," *ECA* (No. 435–436, 1985) 45–64, hereafter cited as "Función liberadora"; "Voluntad de fundamentalidad y voluntad de verdad: Conocimiento-fe y su configuración histórica," *RLT* (No. 8, 1986) 113–132; "Beitrag Zum Dialog mit dem Marxismus," in P. Rottländer, ed., *Theologie der Befreiung und Marxismus* (Münster: West, 1986) 77–108; "La superación del reduccionismo idealista en Zubiri," *ECA* (No. 477, 1988) 633–650, hereafter cited as "Reduccionismo"; "Historización de los derechos humanos desde los pueblos oprimidos y las mayorías populares," *ECA* (No. 502, 1990) 589–596, hereafter cited as "Derechos humanos."

62. See Ignacio Ellacuría, *Veinte años de historia en El Salvador (1969–1989): Escritos políticos* (San Salvador: UCA Editores, 1991) 3 Volumes, cited throughout as *VA*. Ellacuría wrote some ninety-eight essays devoted specifically to social-political analysis and commentary. Most of these are included in *Veinte años*, along with several

articles on political philosophy. Of those ninety-eight, all but fourteen were written between 1979 and 1989.

63. Ignacio Ellacuría, *Conversión de la Iglesia al Reino de Dios: Para anunciarlo y realizarlo en la historia* (Santander, Spain: Editorial Sal Terrae, 1984), cited throughout as *CIRD*.

64. O. Romero, A. Rivera y Damas, I. Ellacuría, J. Sobrino, and T. Campos, *Iglesia de los pobres y organizaciones populares* (San Salvador: UCA Editores, 1979), cited throughout as *IPOP*. In addition to those already cited, important theological essays from this period include Ignacio Ellacuría, "Iglesia y realidad histórica," *ECA* (No. 331, 1976) 213–220; "La Iglesia de los pobres, sacramento histórico de la liberación," *ML*, Vol. 2, 1991, 127–154, first published in *ECA* (No. 348–349, 1977) 707–722, hereafter cited as "Sacramento histórico"; trans. by Margaret Wilde as "The Church of the Poor, Historical Sacrament of Liberation," *MLT*, 543–564; "El pueblo crucificado" (1978); "La teología como momento ideológico de la praxis eclesial," *Estudios Eclesiásticos* (No. 207, 1978) 457–476, hereafter cited as "Teología como praxis"; "Historicidad de la salvación cristiana," *ML*, Vol. 1, 1991, 323–372, first published in *RLT* (No. 1, 1984) 5–45; trans. by Margaret Wilde as "The Historicity of Christian Salvation," *MLT*, 251–289; "Aporte de la teología de la liberación a las religiones abrahámicas en la superación del individualismo y del positivismo," *RLT* (No. 10, 1987) 3–28, hereafter cited as "Religiones abrahámicas"; "La teología de la liberación frente al cambio sociohistórico de América Latina," *RLT* (No. 12, 1987) 241–263; trans. by James Brockman as "Liberation Theology and Socio-historical Change in Latin America," *TSSP*, 19–43, hereafter cited as "Teología frente al cambio"; "Utopía y profetismo desde América Latina: un ensayo concreto de soteriología histórica," *ML*, Vol. 1, 1991, 393–442, first published in *RLT* (No. 17, 1989) 141–184, hereafter cited as "Utopía y profetismo"; trans. by James Brockman as "Utopia and Prophecy in Latin America," *MLT*, 289–328; "Salvación en la historia," in C. Floristán and J. J. Tamayo, eds., *Conceptos fundamentales del cristianismo* (Madrid: Editorial Trotta, 1993) 1252, also published, with minor variations, as "Historia de la salvación," *RLT* (No. 28, 1993) 3–25, hereafter cited as "Salvación en la historia."

65. "Luces y sombras de la Iglesia en Centroamérica," *VA*, Vol. 1, 293–302, first published in *Razón y Fe* (No. 1020, 1983) 16–26; see also the articles cited above in nn. 25 and 26.

66. I. Ellacuría and J. Sobrino, eds., *Mysterium Liberationis: Conceptos Fundamentales de la Teología de la Liberación*, 2 Vols. (San Salvador: UCA Editores, 1991), trans. as *Mysterium Liberationis: Fundamental Concepts of Liberation Theology* (Maryknoll, Orbis, 1994), cited throughout as *ML* and *MLT* respectively. The four articles by Ellacuría included in *Mysterium Liberationis* are "Sacramento histórico" (1977), "El pueblo crucificado" (1978), "Historicidad de la salvación cristiana" (1984), and "Utopía y profetismo" (1989).

*Chapter Two*

# Philosophy of Historical Reality

*The formal structure and differentiating function
of intelligence, within the structural context of
human notes and of the permanently biological
character of the human unity, is not the
comprehending of being or the capturing of
meaning, but rather the apprehending and facing
of reality.*

Ignacio Ellacuría[1]

Agreat paradox dawned with the Enlightenment. The empirical sciences came into being and appeared capable of explaining in detail the inner workings of the physical universe. But even as they grew and threw their light on the world, the font from which they sprang, human reason, covered itself in a dark shroud of doubt. With the reflections of Rene Descartes on the nature of the mind, philosophy began to focus on questions of method. Following his new method, he arrived at his famous maxim, *cogito, ergo sum.* More importantly, his meditations focused attention as never before on the human person. The human subject became the starting-point and goal of philosophical research. A century after Descartes, the great German idealist, Immanuel Kant, summed up that intellectual revolution with his formulation of the threefold philosophical quest: What can I know? What should I do? What may I hope for? The anthropological focus that underlies and unifies these questions is unmistakable. It can be further compressed into a single, austere query: Who is the human subject? With the turn to the subject, philosophy entered its own version of the profound paradigm shift initiated in cosmology by Galileo, Copernicus, Newton, and others. In this historic shift a new world emerged, one that constructed many of the institutions with which we remain familiar today. But the shift was never fully accomplished. Modernity never made peace with itself, never completed its search for new foundations, never answered Kant's questions with complete satisfaction.

## The Character of Human Intellection

The paradox of modernity generated numerous efforts to complete the Kantian quest, to take up the project anew or bury it for good. In this context Zubiri produced his own philosophical inquiry, beginning with a thorough critique of the idealism he saw running through every branch of Western philosophy. When the first volume of his work on human intelligence was published, Ellacuría appraised it in the light of the modern turn to the subject. Alluding to Kant, he encapsulates Zubiri's quest in three guiding questions: "What is reality? In what does knowing consist? What access to God might there be?"[2] Ellacuría's rhetorical device subtly combines contrast and comparison. In his view, Zubiri was attempting to get beneath the turn to the subject in order to probe certain crucial issues that modernity had been unable to address adequately. While he frames Zubiri's project in a way that broadly corresponds to Kant's three questions, behind that correspondence sharp differences also appear. Ellacuría does not see Zubiri as dismissing Kant's anthropological perspective, but as reformulating the question about the human within the larger compass of reality. In an essay which he wrote as an introduction to the study of philosophy, Ellacuría observes:

> The classical Kantian questions—what can I know, what should I do, what may I hope for—are summarized in this one question: what is the human? But, I must add, what is the human in reality, because only in this way can we capture what the human really is. Here history appears as the place of the fulfillment and revelation of reality. The human, considered socially and as the one who makes history, is the place of the manifestation of reality.[3]

Following Zubiri, Ellacuría claims that modern philosophy "does nothing but draw out the ultimate implications of the idealistic roots hidden in classical theories of intelligence since Parmenides, Plato and Aristotle."[4] However, he makes this point to rescue modernity's anthropological concern, not to reject it. He criticizes modern philosophy for failing to find an adequate way to deal with reality and to grasp the human as the place where reality makes its appearance, but argues this does not invalidate its entire project. It points instead to the deep source of the problem. The Zubirian critique focuses not only on modern philosophy, but on the entire history of Western philosophy insofar as that history manifests a proclivity for an idealism that is reductionistic. Stated simply, idealism becomes reductionistic when knowing is separated from sensing. In Parmenides, for example, the metaphysical identification of being and thinking requires the prior separation of sensation (perception) from intellection (the integrated process of understanding). "This approach to the problem of intelligence contains in its depths an affirmation: intellection is posterior to sensation, and this posteriority results in opposition."[5] To complicate matters, knowing a thing becomes primarily identified with capturing the essence of a thing. It is important to note that, in Zubiri's judgment, this identification proves characteristic not only of idealist traditions (Platonism and Neoplatonism, for example) but also of such realist approaches as Aristotelianism and medieval scholasticism.

> This same detour was taken by scholastic philosophy which, in its great appreciation for what differentiates Aristotle from Plato, failed to take account of the very grave consequences which the Aristotelian theory of intelligence contains for true realism. Outwardly the idea of Aristotelian and medieval philosophy, that the real things in the world are made present to the intelligence in its own worldly reality, could be taken as the supreme affirmation of realism. However, for Zubiri "it is strictly untenable and formally absurd."[6]

With the turn to the subject, Descartes hoped to arrive at an indubitable starting point for philosophy. However, he did not escape the idealistic reductionism afflicting the preceding philosophical tradition. Like Parmenides, he failed to clearly distinguish reality and concept. Instead he virtually identified them. Even more importantly, he brought this identification to bear on the analysis of human consciousness itself. In this way he implicitly equated mental acts and the conceptualizations of those acts. Kant, under the impact of Hume, recognized that this identification was uncritical and problematic. He attempted to resolve the ensuing dilemma via his masterful series of critiques. For this reason, he serves as Zubiri's most important interlocutor in *Inteligencia sentiente*. However, even Kant failed to address the problem in all its radicality. Ellacuría observes:

Zubiri did not initially reproach Kant for having undertaken a critique of reason but for starting with the supposition that there already existed an indisputable science which could serve as a model of knowing. Before constructing a theory of reason or an epistemology, that is, a critical study of the conditions of objective knowing (regardless of how critical it might be) one must analyze the very fact of intellection as it is given in its unity and not separated into its sensible and intellective components.[7]

Zubiri seeks to surmount the limitations of the Kantian critique by developing his own constructive position. He questions and ultimately rejects the presumption that knowing has intrinsic priority over reality, i.e., that "forms of knowing" constitute "empirical reality." He also calls into question the supposition that reality has priority over knowing, i.e., that "knowing" simply mirrors "reality." He aims instead for a starting point more radical than either of these. "It is impossible to assert an intrinsic priority of knowing over reality or of reality over knowing. Knowing and reality are, in their very roots, strictly and rigorously co-determining. There exists no priority of one above the other."[8] Zubiri thus argues that the human, embedded in reality, apprehends reality through the exercise of sentient intelligence. Moreover, "reality is the formal character, the formality, according to which that which is appre-hended is something 'in itself,' something 'of its own.' To know is to apprehend something according to that formality."[9] He encapsulates his account of human knowing in a thesis statement. *"Human intellection is formally the simple actualization of the real in the sentient intelligence."*[10]

Zubiri argues that human knowing is the sensible-intelligible appre-hension of the real as real, not the grasp of a conceptualized essence or idea. He refers to human intelligence as "sentient intelligence" to suggests that human sensation and intellection, although formally dis-tinct, remain intrinsically linked in the intelligent apprehension of reality. This differentiation in unity is reflected in his definition of each activity. "I think that intellection consists formally in the apprehension of the real as real, and sensation is the apprehension of the real in impression."[11] Thus, he not only resists the conceptual separation of knowing and sensing, intelligence and sentience, but he emphasizes that the human is open to real things as realities by virtue of sensibility, that is, by sensing them.

The human . . . senses things not only as stimuli, but also as realities; the stimulus itself is ordinarily sensed as a stimulating reality, that is, as a "real" stimulus. The opening to things, as realities, is what formally constitutes intelligence. The particular formality of intelligence is "reality."

> Now this formality is not something primarily "conceived" but rather something "sensed;" the human not only conceives that what he has sensed is real; he senses the very reality of the thing. Hence it is that this mode of sensing things is an intrinsically intellective mode.[12]

Clearly, then, sensation does not disappear with the appearance of human intelligence. Rather, it is assumed and ordered on a higher level. This means that human sentience is intelligent sentience just as human intelligence is sentient intelligence. It also implies that the sentient intelligence of the human represents an evolutionary leap without implying a radical discontinuity between nonhuman animals and humans.[13]

If we were to characterize Zubiri's thought under the overwrought rubric of a historic "turn," it could be said to represent a turn to reality, to reality as unified and differentiated, material and historical. But such a turn should not be misconstrued. Zubiri's investigation involves neither an abstract concept of being nor the apprehension of some immediate reality-in-itself. These formulations recapitulate respectively the basic errors of reductionistic idealism and naïve realism. Rather, he analyzes the formal structure of reality as it is apprehended in sentient intelligence. "Zubiri, therefore, takes sensibility as the access to true reality with utmost seriousness. Reality is sensed, is apprehended, as reality by the senses, and only if reality is in some way sensed can it really be conceived or thought, that is, as reality. The senses not only provide us with contents, but make reality formally present to us. They make the very formality of reality formally present to us."[14] To repeat, through their sentient intelligence, humans have real access to reality. Ellacuría restates this basic insight in terms of the fundamental purpose and logic of human knowing. "The formal structure and differentiating function of intelligence, within the structural context of human notes and of the permanently biological character of the human unity, is not the comprehending of being or the capturing of meaning, but rather the apprehending and facing of reality."[15]

Following Zubiri, Ellacuría stresses the primordial unity of sensation and intellection in the sentient intelligence. This forestalls idealistic interpretations of the access of the sentient intelligence to reality. Theories of knowledge that sunder this primordial unity tend either towards idealism or positivism. The consequences of such a split, especially in the area of ethical responsibility, are often devastating. Thus, for example, while the scientific impulses of modernity have proven spectacularly fruitful, they have contributed to a real moral confusion which, in the twentieth century, has assumed tragic and even lethal proportions. Zubiri seeks the rehabilitation of these empirical urges and their ethical orientation by reuniting both with reality. As such, his turn to reality aims not in the first place to attack modernity but to correct it. Ellacuría sees this point as crucial. The turn to reality grounds the internal coherence of numerous other disciplines. It enables them to overcome the dichotomies of perception and truth, the world we sense and the world we understand. Most importantly, it employs them in the crucial task of mending the divisions among thinking, opting, and acting.

> Concretely, with regard to sensibility it remains clear that true reality, reality as true, is not reached by fleeing the senses or nullifying the sensorial life, but on the contrary by putting it to full and fecund use. The consequences of this approach for pedagogical theory, communication theory, aesthetics, etc., are evident, *as are those for doing theology correctly*, for the transcendent would not have to appear as something beyond the senses, as a world apart from the reality which is given to us immediately. We should not forget that the duality of sensible/suprasensible, material/spiritual began ultimately in the dissociation and opposition between sensibility and intelligence.[16]

Zubiri's understanding of the real link between human intellection and reality contains numerous implications for theology as well as for spirituality. I call attention to two that have a direct bearing on the theological method that Ellacuría develops.

**The Theologal Dimension of Reality.** Zubiri's theory of human intellection highlights what could be called the theologal implication of the fact that one is grounded in reality. Zubiri explains how, through our sentient intellection, we apprehend real things that exist on their own apart from us. We also discover ourselves to be realities that exist in the midst of other realities. Moreover, we apprehend that we depend on these external realities in a constitutive way in order to be human. Hence, "humans are found constitutively inclined 'from themselves' *towards* things. In other words, the human is 'something in itself,' but as a radical and formal principle of openness. Human being entails being open to things. This is the formal ontological structure of the human: exteriority. In himself/herself, the human without things would be nothing."[17]

In his examination of this human inclination toward things, Zubiri begins with reality as a formal principle grasped by the sentient intelligence, then moves to reality as fundament, that is, as something more than the thing which I apprehend as real. It should be noted that Zubiri does not locate a conceptual foundation for philosophy in the apprehension of reality as fundament. Hence, Zubirian fundamentality should not be confused with philosophical foundationalism. "A fundament is, primarily, that which is root and support at the same time. Hence, 'fundamentality' does not here have a meaning exclusively or primarily conceptual, but rather something much more radical. Nor is it simply the mere cause of our being in one way or another, but rather of our being in being, if I may be pardoned the expression."[18] In his view, the fundament predominates in reality. "To predominate is to be *more*. . . . And to be *more* is to have power. Reality exercises this power upon the thing as *this* thing. But it also exercises it upon the subject who apprehends it. This means that reality as fundament exercises its power upon me. 'Reality is the *power of the real*.' "[19]

As the power of the real, reality imposes itself upon me; in the apprehension of reality, I encounter the *more* of reality. Zubiri highlights three dimensions of this *more* that emerge in my encounter with reality. First, I encounter reality as something ultimate. Second, reality functions as the ground of possibility. It is "precisely that which makes possible my reality as human."[20] Finally, reality has an urgent quality: it urges or impels the human to "sketch out a system of possibilities among which he/she must choose and which constitute the final demand of his/her own reality."[21] Humans thus live in reality as something ultimate, from reality as the ground of possibility and for reality as the terminus of their most urgent longings. As will be seen in chapter 4, Ellacuría derives the essential logic of his theological method from the threefold structure of this encounter with the power of the real.

**The Historicity of Sentient Intelligence.** There emerges a second, historical implication of this account of sentient intelligence and the overcoming of idealistic reductionism. It makes its appearance in the recovery of the social and historical constitution of intelligence initiated by Zubiri and amplified by Ellacuría. Zubiri himself relied on two crucial intuitions that he inherited from post-Hegelian philosophy. (1) The first, to which I have already alluded, received forceful articulation in Nietzsche. The Parmenidean divorce between sensibility and intelligence, embedded in all manner of idealistic reductionism, results in a metaphysical split between the sensible and intelligible worlds. Ellacuría takes this a step further. The epistemological-metaphysical division is not merely intellectual or academic. Rather, its concrete effects appear sociologically in such examples as the division of society into educated ruling elites and an illiterate peasantry. Because the more destructive moments of this latter division represent not only an epistemological error but a historical injustice, Ellacuría's task entails not only elaborating a liberative social theory but promoting concrete historical liberation. Moreover, while new and improved theories of human knowing cannot overcome idealistic reductionism, either conceptually or in reality, the turn to historical reality, because it is not merely conceptual, can. This suggests that reality itself contains a deideologizing potential. At the same time it demands a response from the human who apprehends it: the response of an embodied praxis.

(2) The historical implication of this account of sentient intelligence builds upon a second intuition that Zubiri bequeathed to Ellacuría. Closely related to the first, it appears in the young Marx's critiques of idealism and inadequate versions of materialism. Sensibility cannot be regarded as primarily passive and receptive. Rather, it exhibits a radical dynamism in relation to the world in which it is inserted. It not only apprehends that world but responds to it, affects it and so changes it. Therefore, "the relation of the human person with the natural and social world does not primarily consist in contemplation but in a transformative activity."[22] Here, too, Ellacuría manifests a brilliant capacity to utilize the transformative power of the Zubirian vision of reality in his philosophy, theology, and praxis of liberation. The primary move in Ellacuría's appropriation of the Zubirian vision of reality involves his examination of reality as historical reality. While Ellacuría remains firmly rooted in Zubiri's philosophical vision, the accent is shifting. Certainly Zubiri employs the concept of historical reality, but in Ellacuría, it becomes the central category. This can be seen in the way he approaches the object or ultimate concern of philosophy and in his summary of the Zubirian understanding of intramundane reality.

## THE OBJECT OF PHILOSOPHY

If, as Ellacuría argues, historical reality is the object of philosophy, then clarifying the status of this object will shed light on the meaning, role, and possibility of developing an adequate concept and praxis of historical reality. Obviously, from Ellacuría's perspective, the notion of historical reality will be adequate only if, among other things, it does not lose itself in abstractions, only if it resists subtly reintroducing some form of idealistic reductionism into its arguments or actions. So he starts with the philosophical task itself. Philosophy, he points out, experiences an initial lack of definition with regards to what it is looking for. "Zubiri thus interpreted the famous Aristotelian expression (the science which looks for itself) to mean that it is the knowledge [saber] which before anything looks for what is its object."[23] In the effort to identify its object and central theme, philosophy immediately encounters the temptation to compartmentalize its tasks and, indirectly, its object, into what scholastic philosophy calls general and special metaphysics, or first and second philosophy. But in Ellacuría's view, "nature cannot be treated without reference to history, nor the human without reference to society, and, reciprocally, history cannot be addressed without reference to nature, nor society without reference to the human."[24] Thus, Ellacuría's interpretation of Zubiri is framed as a search for the object of philosophy. At the same time, it is grounded on the assumption that that prethematic object is radically and constitutively unified.

Ellacuría contemplates Zubiri's project against the backdrop of Marx's critique of Hegel. He does so both to highlight what these three formidable thinkers share in common and to register the differences that arise in their approaches to and understanding of *lo último de realidad*. All three begin from the presumption that the whole of reality is unified. Likewise, although in different ways, they understand philosophy as the effort to mediate between the real unity of reality and the concepts we use to grasp this unity. Hegel is a philosophical idealist. He conceptualizes the really real as ideal and articulates the unity of reality in terms of Absolute Spirit. This does not imply that for Hegel the unity of reality is merely conceptual. However, it does suggest that "all that exists and that occurs is nothing but the historical process of the Absolute, or the Absolute historicized in search of its full self-realization and self-identification."[25] Like Hegel, Marx insists that reality remains unintelligible if not taken unitarily and dynamically as a single totality. He also agrees that reality must be captured and conceptualized as a dialectical, evolutionary process which, by its very nature, manifests a unity of contraries. But ever the social scientist, Marx resists Hegel's idealism and challenges the abstractness of his philosophy of history. He inverts the Hegelian dialectic and locates the single, real unity of all that exists in the whole of socioeconomic relations. In his view, the totality of socioeconomic relations represents "the final instance of all of social and historical reality, making a single reality, therefore, of all natural and historical reality."[26]

"The 'object' of philosophy for Zubiri is the totality of reality considered dynamically."[27] Like Hegel and Marx, Zubiri views reality as a single, unified whole. Furthermore, the structuring and structural dynamism implicit in reality serves as the principle of this unity. But Zubiri sets himself apart from both Hegel and Marx by the way he inserts a strict commitment to the physicality of intramundane reality within a radical openness to extramundane reality. His philosophy stands in stark contrast to Marx's atheistic materialism as well as Hegel's pantheistic idealism. Up to a certain point, Zubiri manifests a philosophical reserve bordering on agnosticism: one can formulate an intramundane ontology without explicitly posing the question of God because "the real and observable physical unity of the world does not recognize something as 'part' of this physical unity which cannot enter into it."[28] This does not mean, of course, that Zubiri is agnostic before the mystery of God. Nor does he bracket the question of God in the fashion of Husserl's *epoche*. Instead, he addresses the relationship between God and intramundane reality in a distinctive and profound way.

> God and intramundane reality do not, strictly speaking, form a whole. This does not necessarily mean that there is not or cannot be a certain unity of that whole with God, and of God with that whole; but it will be a unity of another, completely distinct, type. Neither does this mean that God cannot make Godself present in some fashion within intramundane reality. But that presence will be different from the type of presence—what Zubiri calls actuality—of some intramundane things with respect to others.[29]

What is Zubiri up to here? First of all, he stands solidly within that philosophical tradition that commits itself to the radical unity of reality. Second, with an excellent grasp of the physical sciences and their impact on philosophical knowing, he likewise stands committed to locating the principle of this real unity of intramundane reality in material reality. However, "the unity of the object of philosophy is not the formal unity of an object."[30] The implication of this claim appears in the contrast between the way realities are studied and the way reality is approached. Physical things can be studied as physical things. The task of doing so belongs to science. Philosophy, for its part, studies physical things *as real*, from the perspective of the real. "That which physically is the principle of unity is what metaphysically is converted into the object of philosophy."[31] Third, however, this move towards a "materialistic realism" cannot be made at the expense of collapsing reality into a closed system wherein contact, relationship or unity with extramundane reality, God and the Reign of God, is excluded. Thus, Zubiri distinguishes between the unity binding intramundane realities to one another and that form of unity that he calls "religation," which binds intramundane reality as a whole to its fundament.

Like Zubiri, Ellacuría wants to articulate the possible relation between the world of God and the human world, between extramundane and intramundane reality. But Christian theology has been a major producer and consumer of the idealistic reductionism afflicting Western philosophy throughout its history. In recent times this has undermined its credibility, its critical capacity, and its relevance to everyday life. Moreover, Christianity perennially faces the temptation of degenerating into deadly forms of ideology. This gives rise to legitimate suspicions of its theological attempts to conceptualize the link between the world of God and the human world. Seen in this light, Ellacuría's exploration of intramundane reality on its own terms represents a continuation of Zubiri's effort to construct and maintain good philosophical boundaries. But Ellacuría also recognizes that such boundaries are not enough. Ever the disciple of Zubiri's philosophy, he goes beyond both Zubiri and philosophy.

The object of philosophy for Zubiri is the dynamic totality of all intramundane reality *qua* real. Ellacuría refers to this distinctive philosophical position as an "open materialistic realism." He clearly aligns himself with it. Just as clearly he develops it. He identifies the object of philosophy as historical reality, which implies no repudiation of Zubiri, but does result in a subtle shift to an "open historical realism." As will be seen below, historical reality is material reality taken up and realized as history. Yet this refinement is not merely linguistic. The problems that have plagued the history of Western thought have also plagued the history of Western praxis. They have contributed to a succession of rationalizations which aim to obliterate the memory of that history's acquisitive, oppressive, and murderous side. These matters stand out in Ellacuría's writings with a passion and clarity not found in Zubiri. Ellacuría's understanding of reality as historical reality grounds the operation of his critical method of historicization, his sense of historical place, and his commitment to liberative praxis. That is, first, his philosophy of historical reality not only connects concept and reality, philosophy and life in new ways, but transfers the impact of these connections to questions of method, thus augmenting the philosophical density of liberation theology. Second, his convictions about the idea of historical place appear in his choice to live in a particular historical place. Third, his commitment to a theory rooted in praxis gets embodied in his actual historical praxis.

## THE STRUCTURE OF REALITY

Zubiri took up the study of philosophy under the lengthening shadows of late modernity, but as we have seen, the whole course of Western thought, from the pre-Socratics through Heidegger, forms the ultimate horizon of his philosophical quest. He labored to identify and overcome the idealistic bias that afflicts that entire tradition in order to recover a sense of reality that is not divorced from history. Ellacuría appreciated the importance of his mentor's labor. As was indicated above, his major work, *Filosofía de la realidad histórica*, depends heavily on Zubiri. Although a detailed exegesis of this text is unnecessary for our purposes, an introduction to the Zubirian-Ellacurian understanding of the dynamic structure of reality will facilitate our interpretation of Ellacuría's theological method. For that reason I trace his sketch of that structure with a series of the five theses.

**The Unity of Intramundane Reality.** The radical unity of reality seems to exclude the multiplicity of real things and visa versa. Ellacuría initiates his discussion of the structure of reality by addressing this tensive relationship. *"The totality of intramundane reality constitutes a single physical unity that is complex and differentiated in such a way that the unity does not nullify the differences and the differences do not nullify the unity."*[32] In this thesis he engages a philosophical problem of great richness and antiquity. "Like all reflective civilizations, the Greek one experienced the need to justify the simultaneous presence of unity and multiplicity, of order and chaos, of harmony and strife. . . . But what distinguishes the Greek solution is its particular mode of holding these opposite principles in balance."[33] As we have seen already, Ellacuría, following Zubiri, both stands in that tradition and criticizes its disfiguring predilection for idealistic reductionism. Because of the problems associated with traditional views of metaphysics, it is important to recall that he dissociates himself from all abstract or conceptualistic metaphysics. His approach to reality *(realidad)* proceeds by way of the real exigencies of specific historical situations *(realidades)* in order to develop the tools needed for analyzing and unmasking them. Even though this thesis emits metaphysical overtones, it emerges from an investigation that shares much in common with theories of knowledge, ethics, and politics best described as postmetaphysical. At the very least Ellacuría's philosophy of historical reality must be viewed as resolutely postidealist. This assertion provides a context for interpreting his first thesis.

His first thesis specifically focuses on the totality of reality. It is possible to verify that things exist in relationship to other things, that things can be said to exist in virtue of other things. But Ellacuría points out that there exists a prior and primary unity of reality that grounds all relations and functions. It constitutes all real things both as things and as real, and because of it we can and must speak of all reality as forming a totality, a unified whole. "The transcendental principle of unity is the very reality of every real thing which, by being real, is intrinsically and constitutively respective to any other real, intramundane and material thing. Every other subsequent form of unity, whether of a relational or functional type, is grounded on this respective character of reality *qua* reality."[34] The Zubirian neologism for the prior and primary unity of reality, respectivity, thus refers to the foundational intraconnectedness of reality *qua* reality. As religation names the power of the real that binds reality to its fundament, respectivity denotes the power that links any real thing to every other real thing in the cosmos. However, this unified "totality is not an abstract but a concrete totality."[35] For philosophy to grasp this concrete unity it must recapitulate the painstaking journeys of the sciences. It must gradually uncover the unity of the real in real things, just as biology arrives at an understanding of evolution through the study of various concrete species, or unified field theory in physics proceeds in tandem with particle theory, or any macroeconomic theory must engage multiple microeconomic realities. Not only must philosophy follow a similar path, it must help the sciences subvert the imperial tendency of the senses to view reality as atomized. Yet while defending against this atomization on one side, Ellacuría sees the need to forcefully repudiate monism on the other. The totality is not unified at the expense of multiplicity and difference, including even contradictions, oppositions, and negations. Rather, it formally maintains a careful balance between identity and multiplicity.

**The Dynamic Character of Intramundane Reality.** The second thesis brings out a key element already present but not yet fully explicit in the first statement. *"Intramundane reality is intrinsically dynamic. Thus, the question about the origin of movement is either false or, at the very least, secondary."*[36] Ellacuría insists that "reality is always dynamic and its type of dynamism corresponds to its type of reality."[37] This raises the problem of continuity through change. The key element shows up in the phrase, "intrinsically dynamic."

> We might say that dynamism is inscribed in the very reality of each thing and each thing is thus transcendentally dynamic. Reality is neither the subject-of a dynamism nor subject-to a dynamism, but rather is something constitutively dynamic. Reality is dynamic from itself [de por sí], it is dynamic of itself [de suyo], and its moment of dynamism consists initially in a giving-of-its-own [dar de sí]. The world, as the respectivity of reality *qua* reality, does not have dynamism, nor is it in dynamism, but rather, it is itself dynamic: worldly respectivity is essentially dynamic.[38]

Ellacuría suggests further that "a certain circularity must be recognized in the very reality of things: dynamism interrupts identity and non-identity actualizes dynamism."[39] So the intrinsic dynamism of reality cannot in the first place be identified with either movement or process. It is prior to both. The intrinsic dynamism of reality belongs to reality in a most basic and fundamental way. "Zubiri characterized the formal character of dynamism as a giving-of-its-own, an expression which, among other things, implies an original unfolding between what is that 'of-its-own' and what it can 'give,' but always as a 'giving-of-its-own' in such a way that the giving does not sunder the of-its-own."[40] This will prove especially significant when Ellacuría turns to the unique instance of human reality which, as intrinsically dynamic in a distinctly transcendental way, gives not only "of-its-own" but "of-him/herself."[41]

**Rethinking Dialectical Method.** Ellacuría introduces the dialectical character of reality at this point, but sounds a cautionary note. *"Reality, which is systematic, structural and unitary in itself, is not necessarily dialectical or, at least, is not univocally dialectical."*[42] The dialectic displays its greatest usefulness in the analysis of society and history, precisely where the tensions produced by class struggle render such analysis especially difficult. Moreover, this type of analysis appears crucial in a philosophy which takes historical reality as its object. Therefore, Ellacuría does not draw battle lines against Hegel and Marx and reject the notion of the dialectic, although he does sharply criticize mechanical and formalistic uses of it (which, he adds, they too would find abhorrent). At the same time, Ellacuría appreciates Zubiri's reluctance to embrace the term "dialectic." It carries idealistic connotations. Hence, Ellacuría carefully nuances his understanding of dialectic in order to make room for an analysis of social reality that takes into account the crucial insights of Marx, while retaining the postidealist realism and theologal openness provided by Zubirian metaphysics. This allows Ellacuría to affirm a sense in which the structural dynamism of individual realities can be understood as dialectical.

"Each real thing is primarily a reality in which the parts receive their reality from the whole, although they themselves constitute that reality as a whole. Already this could be considered in a certain sense dialectical, inasmuch as the parts and the whole give and receive reality among themselves in a sense that is not univocal."[43] This reasoning applies not only to individual real things in their structural dynamism, but to the structural dynamism of the totality of intramundane reality. However, the key issue at stake here concerns the Hegelian thesis that negation serves as a principle of creation. In its favor, Ellacuría notes that this thesis posits as a universal principle a theme which runs through a number of images derived from and essential to the Christian perception of reality: only the seed that dies will multiply, the resurrection comes only after a certain death, the Reign of God can be reached only if one sells or denies everything else, one is a disciple of Jesus only by negating oneself, etc. Seen from the perspective of the dialectic, these crucial Christian images can (and must) be rescued from becoming overly spiritualized or privatized. Still the question remains whether negation can serve as a positive principle of reality. Ellacuría's qualified affirmative includes two points.

First, the negation that overcomes negation, what Christians call conversion, exercises a positive and creative function. "The Christian 'dialectic' achieves its full meaning when it comes face to face with sin and/or with a self-enclosed end that makes an absolute of each thing or each human. That is, it recovers its full meaning before a reality that is itself negation."[44] Hence, it should be asked whether this resistance emerges from negation or from an affirmation. Second, the negation runs the risk of not going beyond the sphere of the negated. This in turn seems to imply that "that which is qualitatively new cannot appear by the road of mere negation. Rather, negation is the form necessary for the positive to make itself present here where the negative gives itself. In other words, something positive, 'always greater' than the negative, renders the negation positive so that the negation does not annihilate its contrary, but only annuls and overcomes it."[45] Insofar as reality manifests itself in a dialectical fashion, as in social-historical reality, for example, some form of the dialectic can and must inform philosophy and praxis. Thus, this thesis sets limits. While it keeps the door open to a qualified use of a dialectical method in social analysis, it guards against its deployment in a totalizing manner.

**The Ascending Process That Characterizes Reality.** Ellacuría calls the next step a deduction whose contents proceed from the self-disclosure of reality itself. *"Reality not only forms a dynamic, structural and, in some sense, dialectical totality, but is a process of realization in which ever higher forms of reality emerge from, retain and elevate those forms which preceded them."*[46] This thesis brings us into the very heart, the dynamic core, of Zubiri's thought. Its truth does not rest upon the theory of evolution, although in the empirical verification which that theory provides, the philosophical truth of reality can be sensed. But as Ellacuría points out, even were there no evolution, this thesis would stand, for it describes the very structure of reality itself.

> Thus, the dynamisms of the purely material make themselves present and operative in the dynamisms of life, and the dynamisms of life in those of animal life, and those of sensing animals in those of human reality, and those of human reality in those of social and historical reality. This is a more or less complex verification, but a verification all the same. What the theory or fact of evolution adds is the process-grounded explanation of why the lower levels make themselves present in the higher, how the higher come from and maintain the lower, and how the higher really transcend the lower without nullifying them.[47]

The dynamic thrust intrinsic to reality emerges in the process of *realization* by which higher forms of reality emerge out of lower forms. It is reality that realizes itself. When Ellacuría speaks of higher and lower forms or modes of reality, he means literally that the degree of reality can be compared and evaluated.

> Consequently, some of the real processes not only give way to new realities, but they give way to new forms of reality. Life is not only a reality distinct from pure matter, but is another form of reality, a subsequent and higher form of reality. This means that there is a strict process of realization, meaning a process in which reality continues giving of itself, such that forms of superior reality continue appearing through the inferior. The world of real things is not only open to new real things, but to new forms of reality as such.[48]

In Ellacuría's example, the self-realization of reality is at work in the evolution of animal life from inanimate matter. This does not mean that the lower form of reality disappears, allowing us to talk about life apart from its material foundations, as if its reality resided beyond the physical. At the same time, this thesis does not suggest that the lower reality (i.e., inanimate matter) already contained the higher (i.e., animal life), at least formally, the way a seed contains the germ of a tree. The movement from lower to higher forms of reality springs from the intrinsic dynamism of reality itself. It involves a more radical interlacing of connectedness and newness. This flies in the face of a static view of reality that maintains that there is nothing new under the sun. Something new is being given, but within the same unified totality of the real.[49]

**Historical Reality as the Object of Philosophy.** We come, then, to Ellacuría's thesis on the object of philosophy. " *'Historical reality' is the* *'ultimate object' of philosophy understood as intramundane metaphysics, not only because of its encompassing and totalizing character, but inasmuch as it is the supreme manifestation of reality."*[50] Ellacuría's conclusion flows directly from the preceding line of argument. At its highest level of realization, intramundane reality appears as historical reality.

> Thus, by "historical reality" is understood the totality of reality such as it gives itself unitarily in its qualitatively highest form. That specific form of reality is history, where we are given not only the highest form of reality, but the disclosure of the maximum possibilities of the real. It is not simply history, but historical reality. This means that the historical is taken as the *realm* of the historical more than historical *contents*. In that realm, the question concerns its reality, what reality gives of itself and what it reveals in itself.[51]

Several points deserve to be highlighted here. Ellacuría unifies the categories of history and reality into the ultimate object of philosophy, historical reality. In the phrase, "historical reality," "historical" refers not so much to the succession of discrete historical happenings, the various events that happened in history, nor even to the weaving of these various events into an orderly, systematized account of the whole. Historical events are realized in the realm of the historical. Therefore, "the historical" refers both to the field, sphere, or area of reality that serves as reality's realm of ultimate realization, and to the unity underlying the various historical happenings, the contents of that realization. This unity is given in reality by reality. It emerges through the totality of history's actors, authors, editors and auditors, all the players, all the parts, the audience, the stage, and every other aspect of the cosmic theater, but the unity as such is not imposed by any of these.

Historical reality represents the qualitatively highest form of reality in that something "new," something "more," appears on this level of realization. This "something new, something more" does not eliminate or annul the dynamisms of the previous levels of realization, but integrates and orders them in a new way. "What does human history add to reality? For Ellacuría, it adds praxis, understood as a new level of reality (historical reality). History evolves from, incorporates, and transforms (within limits) all of reality's other aspects (including the systemic and material properties of matter, biological life, sentient life, and human life). It also adds the content of history itself."[52] The previous thesis looked at reality as a dynamic, structured, and dialectical process. In the course of this process, ever higher forms of reality emerge incrementally out of the lower forms. But the higher forms do not annihilate the lower, nor can they exist in isolation from them, "rather, on the contrary, a dynamic 'more' of reality gives itself from, in and through the lower reality, in such a way that the latter is made present in many forms and always necessarily in the higher reality."[53] Ellacuría concludes that the final stage in this process occurs when reality becomes historical. "In it, reality is more reality, because all of the prior reality is found, but in that modality which we call historical. It is reality as a whole, assumed under the social reign of freedom. It is reality disclosing its richest potentialities and possibilities."[54]

As the object of philosophy, historical reality not only serves as *a* metaphysical category, buts as *the* category which lends weight to so-called "thick descriptions" of social, political, economic, and cultural phenomena. The logic behind this claim draws together the realization of reality and its manifestation to sentient intelligence. First, historical reality encompasses every other kind of reality, including the material, the biological, the personal, and the social. Second, in the realm of the historical, reality reveals itself and discovers at the same time its reason for being. Third, historical reality is where reality is more, more itself, and more open to what is beyond it. Historical reality, Ellacuría's primary metaphysical category, what he calls "the object of philosophy," thus appears as a theologal category. For this reason it can function simultaneously as the dynamic structure of theological method and the ground beneath the cross.

## THE GROUNDS OF HISTORY

The problems inherent in many post-Hegelian philosophies of history spring from the tendency to view the comprehensiveness of the whole in an idealistic fashion. By taking historical reality as the object of philosophy, Ellacuría firmly commits himself to a realistic understanding of a unified history. But such a comprehensive view cannot simply be asserted. If, as Ellacuría maintains, the dynamism of history emerges from prior material and biological dynamisms, both assuming and transcending them, then an adequate interpretation of the human situation in both its individual and collective dimensions must pay attention to the material foundations and biological roots of the human species in its history. To put this another way, a postidealist comprehension of history must both analyze the grounds of history and address their manner of being historical.

To seek the grounds, the material and biological foundations, of history might appear strange, for we are used to contrasting and even opposing history and material-biological nature. The word, "natural," is often used to refer to that which has not been sullied by history. But these simplistic dualisms obscure the basic and verifiable truth that "history emerges from material nature and remains indissolubly linked to it."[55] Ellacuría lends special attention to the material foundations of the human person in society and history and examines four such grounds of the real unity of history: matter, space, time, and biological life. I briefly describe these four, noting how they function as grounds of history.

**Matter Itself.** "The materiality of history, it goes without saying, arises from the presence of matter in history. But it is necessary to speak about what matter really is and about the way that matter is made present in history."[56] The relationship of matter to material things and the problematic but necessary question—what is matter?—lead into a metaphysical and scientific labyrinth older than Aristotle and denser than Einstein. But Ellacuría takes up this perplexing issue for a specific purpose: he wants to establish the materiality of history and, in this materiality, to ground the formal unity of historical reality. His theory of reality turns away from idealism and turns toward historical materialism. His is not the dialectical materialism of Engels, however, but an open historical materialism patterned on Zubiri.

It is necessary to say what matter really is, but it proves far easier to establish what it is not. Modern science, especially particle physics, has been able to push the boundaries of our knowledge of matter, but in the final analysis, matter can be neither seen nor represented in the fashion of material things. This is partly because "what exists primarily are not material things which are each, by themselves, individual unities, something independent; rather, all of them form an original and single unity among themselves: that is matter itself."[57] So rather than talk about matter as if it were a thing, Ellacuría refers to it as a determinative, structuring principle, a positive activity constitutive of all intramundane reality. "Hence, matter is the very essence of material things, understanding these as structures of notes. What formally and immediately determines matter is the unity of the system itself, its structural character, together with the content of all the notes which pertain to a material thing. Those ultimate notes, foundational of all the rest and determinative of what they are in their primary unity, equal matter itself."[58] As a structural principle, matter grounds both the unity and multiplicity of historical reality. More precisely, then, matter refers to a "positionally constitutive structure: by reason of its structural character it is a multiple *unity*, and by reason of its positional character it is a unified *multiplicity*."[59]

Matter includes both mass and energy and, for this reason, exhibits both static and dynamic characteristics. It serves, therefore, as the foundation of the unity and the intrinsic dynamism of reality, including historical reality.

This is the main point Ellacuría wants to establish. However, he does broach one final issue. Is matter in itself eternal and infinite? The answer, in the final analysis, is that we do not know. However, and this is crucial from Ellacuría's point of view, the key theological issues regarding the presence of God to history lie completely outside of this discussion. "It cannot be said that God is not made present in history because matter is eternal and infinite, just as it cannot be said that God is made present because it is neither eternal nor infinite. The theological meaning of history should be approached from other points of view. Matter is not in some mode the negation of God."[60] Ellacuría observes that when Engels rejected idealism in favor of dialectical materialism, he also rejected the possibility of a doctrine of creation. For Engels, such a doctrine is contradicted by the turn to matter. In his view, the idea of creation implicitly betrays a form of idealism. But Ellacuría finds in Zubiri's analysis an even more radical assessment. Not only does the question about the eternity and infinity of matter lie beyond science, the question about the creation or eternity of matter lies beyond philosophy. One can argue theologically for the possibility of God's self-disclosure regardless of whether or not matter is conceived as eternal and infinite. In part four it will be seen how Ellacuría takes up this question "from below," that is, from within historical reality. Correlatively, the primary idiom of God's self-disclosure, at least in the Jewish and Christian Scriptures, proves to be a salvific historical liberation. For this and for other reasons, soteriology occupies center stage in his theological writings. In order to prepare the ground for an adequate interpretation of his approach to historical salvation, it is helpful to note first how he affirms and conceptualizes the materiality, and hence the unity, of intramundane historical reality.

**The Spatiality of the Real.** Every real thing is spatial. Ellacuría regards spatiality, the quality of being extended in space, as the second basic moment of the materiality of history. For one thing, it operates as a necessary condition of matter. Thus, in the same way that things emerge from and remain intrinsically united to all other things because of their materiality, they have their own proper "position" relative to all other things and within the whole of reality because of their spatiality. This having-a-position operates as a structural principle of real things. Each real thing extends outward from itself toward all other things. But this *extension* must not be viewed statically. The whole remains dynamic, although as a structured dynamism, not a vibrant chaos. Likewise, individual things within the whole possess a dynamic respectivity or positionality in relation to all other things. In other words, within this dynamically structured physical cosmos, it is possible for things to move about freely with respect to one another. At the same time, spatiality ensures a certain stability within the structured dynamism of the whole. Both stability and movement belong to the real.

The ascending process of realization in which higher forms of reality emerge from and leap beyond earlier, lower forms, both retaining and transforming them, also manifests spatiality. The dynamic stability of reality emerges at each level on which reality realizes itself. Thus, as the physicist can study the dynamic stability of matter and the material cosmos, the biologist can study the dynamic stability of the ecological habitat. And neither of these disappears when we arrive at the level of history. "More generally, the dynamism of history cannot be what it is without all the antecedent spatial dynamisms: the dynamism of history is not only a strict spatial dynamism but its distinctive spatiality exhibits the underlying tensions of all the other spatial dynamisms. In both general, theoretical formulations of history and interpretations of historical facts, this should not be forgotten."[61]

All this becomes important when we consider our own human reality, with our peculiar capacity for interiority and nonspatial extension and presence. "The mode of reality proper to the human continues being spatial. It breaks the limits of the basic spatial definition and even those of the basic definition of the cosmos, but from within these limits. The openness of the human is a sentient openness, sustained and conditioned by the organic limits themselves, which the person can never abandon."[62] Therefore, the spatial dimension of human reality must not be minimized or absolutized. In his description of the human's openness to reality, Ellacuría guards against any tendency to idealize or spiritualize that openness, on the one hand, while rejecting any materialistic interpretations which deny that openness, on the other.

> The human occupies space, is defined by space and is really present in space. She can have this real presence . . . because she is defined by an organic space and occupies a local space. The local and organic qualities of her space never disappear in her form of being really present. Many idealistic abstractions of the comprehension of the human and of history forget this modest dimension of the local and organic qualities of human spaces. On the other hand, many materialistic abstractions forget that

human reality assumes in a distinct manner those distinct modes of being in space.[63]

Moreover, because reality is not grasped abstractly, but sentiently and locally, in the concrete space where one is located, all constructive accounts of reality and all historical narratives betray the openness and limits of spatiality. Finally, as will be seen further, Ellacuría's theological method gives special prominence to the notion of *place* in any encounter with historical reality. In his attention to the importance of *theological place,* he capitalizes on this rigorous philosophical account of the spatial dimension of historical reality.

**Material Temporality.** Every intramundane reality presents itself as extended in space and, in this way, as spatially intraconnected to every other reality. In a similar manner intramundane realities are distended in time. "The temporal phenomenon is, for one thing, a phenomenon that appears in those realities where some notes come 'after others,' possessing an exteriority that is not spatial, but successive."[64] To ordinary perception time appears as a complex unity of "nows" which follow one another in a unified pattern of "before-now-after." But with the modern turn to the subject and the subsequent rise of historical consciousness, ancient questions about the status of time were unleashed anew. What grounds the unity of time? Do humans project temporal structure on the otherwise chaotic flow of their experiences so as to order and measure them? Does time exist ultimately in or apart from the human mind? Naturally, such questions about time bear directly on a formal interpretation of history. Therefore, it is with an eye to history that Ellacuría, again following Zubiri, dives into a technical, scientific-philosophical discussion of the temporality of intramundane reality.

Ellacuría approaches the theme of material temporality by introducing the three features of time, connection, direction, and measurement, which constitute its unifying thread. First, he notes that the internal connection of time shows up in several ways: time as continuous, open, aperiodic, and ordered. Second, he notes that time flows in only one direction. This feature of time is strictly determined and cannot be modified or reversed. Third, while time can be objectified and measured quantitatively using clocks and calendars, this fact proves secondary to and dependent on the qualitative spatial-temporal unity of material reality. "Time cannot be measured independently from what happens in time."[65] Behind this entire discussion lurks a crucial issue regarding the unity of time and the reality of that unity. "That the unifying thread of time does not have substantiality does not mean that time has no reality, that is to say, that it is a concept or a pure intuition. It just means that its reality is not independent of its linkage to the now-present, a linkage so intrinsic that without it the now-present not only cannot be conceived or intuited, but simply does not exist."[66] Moments in time do not exist. Rather, they pass. Using the technical Zubirian term to describe this passing, Ellacuría concludes, "each moment, therefore, is in real continuity with all other moments in a real and really transcurrent way. There is a real continuity, but this continuity stems from transcurrence."[67]

Within the horizon of temporal transcurrence, Ellacuría can pursue the issue of the universality and relativity of time that will prove critical to his conception of history. Time is universal. However, this claim does not mean to imply that all real things exist in some absolute, universal time. For, in fact, things do not exist *in* time at all. They exist, or rather, they transcur, temporally. The universality of time stems from this fact. Therefore, as with spatial universality, temporal universality does not demand uniformity. Time is universal but things have their own time. "The unique internal necessity of things is what is determined by the intrinsic feature of their being constituted by the structure of process. And this feature is what takes the form of each one of the phases, that is, of time. Therefore, things devour time; time does not devour things. Time is always and only 'time-of' something, of something in process."[68] The universality of time, therefore, does not contradict either unique, culturally bounded experiences of time nor a theoretical account of temporal relativity. The respective relationship among all real times constitutes a real unity, but not an inflexible law of universal time.

From the analysis of the material temporality of history, the further issue remains of adequately conceptualizing time's manner of being historical. Zubiri identifies four types of processes, each of which uniquely manifests the unifying thread of time. In physical processes, time has the character of *succession*, while biological processes reveal time as *age*; psychical processes suffer *duration*, but biographical/historical life processes are distinguished by *precession*, a capacity unique to sentient intelligence by which it can projectively anticipate within time. Historical time includes all of these in one way or another, for natural, biological, and psychological processes continue to accompany humans as underlying, integral aspects of their properly biographical and historical processes. This descriptive overview of the temporal processes at work in historical reality retains its primary purpose of explicating the material conditions of a unified and differentiated historical reality.[69]

**The Biological Foundation of History.** "History has profound biological roots."[70] This assertion seems innocent enough, but it admits of very
different interpretations. Ellacuría wants to avoid two extremes from the
start. One confuses history with evolution. The other, in viewing history
as the ideal manifestation of the spirit, denies the importance of the
biological to history, at least in theory. "To believe that history has
nothing to do with biological evolution is a form of idealism and a
falsification of history. But, at the same time, to believe that history is
substantially the same thing as evolution is also a falsification of history,
an unjustified materialism of history or an unjustified naturalization of
the historical."[71] These two mistaken postures can be avoided by taking
seriously an analysis of "the biological in the constitution of the individual, or in the constitution of humanity."[72] Ellacuría conceptualizes the
material grounds of the unity and reality of history starting from the
biological unity of the species.

Anthropological research indicates that, in the process of evolution
and before arriving at the human of today, different types of humanity
have appeared, distinguishable by virtue of different social structures
and habits but, above all, by crucial somatic differences (such as cranial
capacity). Thus, biological and historical factors flow together and overlap
in the appearance, configuration, and evolution of different types of
hominids: "[T]he recognition of distinct types of humanity—and that
these distinct types emerge through a strictly evolutionary process—
highlights the importance of the biological in history. . . . Nature and
history intervened positively and immediately in the appearance of *homo
sapiens*."[73] I have already noted, in my précis of Ellacuría's "realization"
thesis, the way the natural makes itself present in the historical: reality
is a process of realization in which ever higher forms of reality emerge
from and elevate those forms which preceded them. Now the argument
becomes even more concrete, as Ellacuría argues that the dynamism of
*species*, in this instance, the human species, undergirds the dynamism
of history. What, then, constitutes a species?

"In the first place, 'species' refers to a physical feature that is really
present in each individual, according to which this individual, through
the very structure of his own reality, formally and actually constitutes a
schema of viable genetic replication through which other individuals
can and do emerge from him."[74] By virtue of this common, constitutive
schema, all the individual members of a species are linked to all the
rest. Like a hologram, each individual carries the pattern of the whole
species, and the whole species is manifested in each individual member
of it. Three implications stem from this. First, the species represents not

the mere adding up of equal individuals but "a previous primary unity that is *pluralized* in individuals."[75] Second, the evolutionary development of the species exhibits *continuity*; it is because of this that the individuals share the same life. Third, the species is *prospective*; it represents a genetic prospection or exploration. "It is not only that each individual has had genetic predecessors and could have genetic successors with whom they share their lives. The phylum itself is formally prospective."[76] Therefore, without this biological genesis, without each individual belonging formally to the species as such, there would be no history. "The three characteristics, precisely because they are structural, prove essential to history and to the historical dynamisms. In the first the individual stands out; in the second, the social; in the third, above all, the historical."[77] The prospective element of this vital condition of history means that history not only has to do with temporal succession but with genetic succession. "The time of history . . . is thus a biological time and will have all the modulations which a biological process carries with it. The process-structured unity of the species, in the plurality of the successive individuals, specifies metaphysically the biological character of history."[78] Thus, rather than history conceptualized in terms of the transcendental structures of Spirit, history starts from, exists through, and leads back to biogenetic structures. The beauty of this interpretation: it embraces the individual while at least formally overcoming individualism; it makes room for a serious description of human sociality and locates the ground of human solidarity in reality; it escapes the traps of idealism, for the elements essential to history, prospection and succession, are rooted in (without being reduced to) biology.

Ellacuría's account of the grounds of history—materiality, spatiality, temporality, and vitality—emphasizes the integral relationship of nature and history. Both categories are taken up into the overarching term, "historical reality." He underlines the continuity and presence of organic nature in history, without separating nature from history or reducing history to nature. At the same time, he rigorously describes the physical-biogenetic unity of the human species that in turn conditions the differentiated unity and genuine openness of historical reality itself. His turn to physical reality accompanies the effort to surpass philosophical idealism while integrating historical consciousness and ontology. But taken alone, this articulation of the material-biological grounds of history does not represent a complete philosophy of history, much less an integrated account of historical reality. Beyond naming the material conditions of history, a further step appears: identifying the impact on history of human creativity in both its personal and social dimensions. A philosophy seriously rooted in biology which fails to investigate the human ability to apprehend, generate, and actualize new real possibilities in history runs the risk of identifying history with its material-biological conditions and degenerating into some form of biological determinism. In contrast to this, Ellacuría's investigation of the human focuses on the integral totality of historical reality. He seeks not only to understand the human in historical reality, but to generate new possibilities for liberative historical praxis.

## Notes to Chapter 2

1. "Hacia" (1975) 625.
2. These questions appear in Spanish as follows. ¿Qué es la realidad? ¿En qué consiste el inteligir? ¿Qué hay acerca de Dios? See "Nueva obra" (1981) 133, trans. mine.
3. Ignacio Ellacuría, "Filosofía ¿para qué?" (1976) 8, trans. mine; see also Philosophy & Theology (vol. 10, no. 1, 1998) 11.
4. "Nueva obra" (1981) 133. In his final article on Zubiri's thought, "Reduccionismo" (1988), Ellacuría develops most fully what he means by "the overcoming of idealistic reductionism" (la superación del reduccionismo idealista). This notion serves as the hermeneutical lens through which he interprets Zubiri's criticisms of and contribution to the tradition to which he belonged. My aim here is not to assess the accuracy of this interpretation but to indicate the critical context within which Ellacuría develops his epistemology.
5. Zubiri, IS, 11, trans. mine.
6. "Reduccionismo" (1988) 634, trans. mine, which quotes Zubiri, IS, 147. The influence of Heidegger on Zubiri can be detected here. A close examination of this influence, while relevant to a complete assessment of Zubiri's philosophy, exceeds the limits of the present investigation.
7. "Reduccionismo" (1988) 635. The recognition of Kant's importance combined with the judgment that Kant ultimately failed to effect the Copernican revolution that modern philosophy sought also permeates the work of Bernard Lonergan; see Insight: A Study of Human Understanding (New York: Harper & Row, 1957, 1978); Method in Theology (New York: Seabury, 1972). A Catholic philosopher-theologian schooled in the thought of Thomas Aquinas, Lonergan, like Zubiri and Ellacuría, was convinced that a productive engagement between the Catholic tradition and modernity was both necessary and possible. For this reason he, too, engages Kant as a key interlocutor. The fascinating parallels and important differences that exist between Lonergan and Ellacuría (not to mention Lonergan and Zubiri) go beyond the limits of this book, but represent worthy topics for future study.
8. Zubiri, IS, 10. "The indefinite idea 'knowing' [saber] does not become definite first of all in understanding [conocer] but in intellection [intelección]," ibid., 11. Zubiri uses the verb saber (to know) in a neutral sense here. He wants to engage the modern question, in what does knowing consist? However, he does not want to uncritically take on certain modern assumptions or terms, i.e. knowledge (epistéme), understanding (conocimiento) and the science of knowledge (epistemología). Throughout his writings Zubiri uses a range of Spanish words to designate human knowing. Some

of these have English cognates and/or commonly accepted translations. Unfortunately, the key verb that he employs in Spanish, *inteligir*, contains no suitable parallels in English. The noun form of this verb, *intelección*, translates as a workable English neologism, "intellection." At times he also uses *inteligir* as a noun (*el inteligir*); this, too, I translate with "intellection," including *el inteligir* in brackets. Finding a verb form parallel to the verbal use of *inteligir* creates problems, however. The cognate, "to intellectualize," is simply inaccurate; other possibilities (i.e., "to intelligize") are excessively awkward. Therefore, I usually translate *inteligir* as "to apprehend" (or "to intelligibly apprehend," when it is necessary to distinguish it from *aprehensión*.) Occasionally, the context will demand some form of "to understand" or "to know." In these cases, I again include *inteligir* in brackets.

9. Ibid., 10.

10. Ibid., 13, emphasis mine.

11. Ibid., 12. It is worth noting what Zubiri means by "real" in these definitions. He continues: " 'real' signifies that the features which the apprehended thing possess in the apprehension itself, are possessed 'in themselves,' 'of their own,' and not only by virtue, for example, of an instinctive response," ibid., 12.

12. Zubiri, *OE*, 375.

13. Zubiri supports this claim with a formal anthropological analysis. "The first form of reality which the human apprehends is that of his/her own stimuli. He/she perceives them not as mere stimuli but as real stimuli, as stimulating realities, so much so that the first function of intelligence is purely biological. It consists in finding an adequate response to real stimuli. This fact alone proves that the further we descend toward the beginnings of life in both individual and species, the more subtle the distinction between mere stimulus and real stimulus becomes until it seems to disappear—and that is exactly what proves there is no break between animal life and life which is properly human," Xavier Zubiri, "The Origin of Man," in Robert Caponigri, ed. and trans., *Spanish Philosophy: An Anthology* (South Bend, Ind.: Notre Dame Press, 1967) 46, trans. emended.

14. "Nueva obra" (1981) 135.

15. "Hacia" (1975) 625. Zubiri's concept of "notes" (*notas*) helps him account for the differentiation among realities within the unity of reality. This concept refers to the differentiated parts and properties of a real thing. Without going into all the differences between formal and causal, constitutional and adventitious, additive and systematic notes, it should be observed that *essential* notes establish the thing as *this* thing, i.e., a real thing which exhibits both real unity through differentiation and real differentiation in unity; see below, n. 58.

16. "Nueva obra" (1981) 136, emphasis mine.

17. Fernando Llenín Iglesias, *La realidad divina: El problema de Dios en Xavier Zubiri* (Oviedo: Seminario Metropolitano, 1990) 25, trans. mine, author's emphasis.

18. Zubiri, *NHG*, 327.

19. Diego Gracia, *Voluntad de verdad: Para leer a Zubiri* (Barcelona: Editorial Labor, 1986) 213, trans. mine. The emphasis of the word "this" is mine: in attempting to render the neologism, *talidad*, I chose the circumlocution "the thing as *this* thing" rather than a more literal but obscure rendering such as "this-ness" or "such-ness." All other emphasis is Gracia's. The final sentence is a quotation from Zubiri, *HD*, 88, trans. mine. Zubiri's originality in attempting to articulate this theologal power of the real finds expression in yet another neologism, *religación*. Rather than attempt to translate the word, I use the English cognate, "religation," drawing on the same

Latin root *(religatum esse, religio)* from which we also derive the term, "religion." To be religated to reality, means, above all, to be rooted or anchored in reality.

20. Zubiri, *HD*, 82.

21. Ibid., 82–83.

22. Ibid., 986.

23. "El objeto de la filosofía" (1981) 15, trans. mine. When he edited *Filosofía de la realidad histórica* for publication, Antonio González used Ellacuría's earlier article, "El objeto de la filosofía," as the introduction and postscript to the book. When citing this article, I refer to it by name and date of original publication, but because the article can be most easily located in *FRH*, page references will be to the article as it appears there (*FRH*, 15–47, 599–602).

24. Ibid., 16.

25. Ibid., 30; see also ibid., 18.

26. Ibid., 19.

27. Ibid., 25.

28. Ibid., 26.

29. Ibid., 27. This discussion bears on the earlier comments regarding the "theologal" character of Zubirian realism. Zubiri approaches the whole question of God through his analysis of *religación*. Moreover, the relationship between intramundane reality and God penetrates the relationship of philosophy to theology. Hence, this aspect of Zubirian thought forms the larger framework within which Ellacuría formulates his theological method.

30. Ibid., 27.

31. Ibid., 28. Again we note Zubiri's insistence that the turn to physical reality does not mean we turn to things in themselves nor to some reality beyond apprehension. Rather, we turn to reality as it is revealed in real things, and we turn to the place where reality manifests its highest degree of realization, i.e., history. I address this second point more fully in chapter 3.

32. "El objeto de la filosofía" (1981) 31.

33. Louis Dupré, *Passage to Modernity: An Essay in the Hermeneutics of Nature and Culture* (New Haven, Conn., and London: University of Yale Press, 1993) 18.

34. "El objeto de la filosofía" (1981) 31.

35. Ibid., 32.

36. Ibid., 33.

37. Ibid., 33. The second part of thesis two intensifies the main point: looking for the "origin" of the dynamism assumes the existence of a prior, static, self-contained "reality." But there is no "hyperreality" prior to or above "reality." Moreover, reality as such is dynamic. Therefore, it is misleading to ask, why is there dynamism and change? Or again, where does dynamism come from? Instead, Ellacuría asks, "Does dynamism spring from the non-identity of everything with itself, or does the non-identity spring from the essentially dynamic character of every reality?" Ibid., 33.

38. *FRH*, 591.

39. "El objeto de la filosofía" (1981) 33.

40. Ibid., 34.

41. *FRH*, 592; see chapter 3, n. 14.

42. "El objeto de la filosofía" (1981) 35. With this thesis Ellacuría aims, among other things, to distinguish his view of dialectic from that of Friedrich Engels.

43. "El objeto de la filosofía" (1981) 35.

44. Ibid., 37.

45. Ibid., 38.
46. Ibid., 38. Compare this important theme in Zubiri and Ellacuría to Lonergan's understanding of "emergent probability"; see *Insight*, op. cit., 121–128.
47. "El objeto de la filosofía" (1981) 39.
48. Ibid., 40.
49. Further implications of this thesis will emerge when we look at the notion of *species* below, in the context of the discussion of the biological roots of history. Moreover, this process of realization, which is achieved in the emergence of each new and higher species, also shows up in each individual member of any given species.
50. Ibid., 42.
51. Ibid., 43–44, emphasis mine.
52. Lassalle-Klein, "The Body of Christ," 65. I examine Ellacuría's understanding of *praxis* in the context of his theological method; see chapter 4.
53. "El objeto de la filosofía" (1981) 42.
54. Ibid., 43.
55. *FRH*, 49.
56. Ibid., 51.
57. María Luz Pintos, "La realidad histórica en Ignacio Ellacuría: Fundamentación material para una filosofia de la historia comprometida," *Estudios Eclesiásticas* (No. 262–63, 1992) 337, trans. mine, hereafter cited as "Pintos."
58. *FRH*, 53. Regarding the relationship between the unity of matter and the differentiation among material things, Zubiri writes: "Essentiality belongs to both terms, to unity and to the notes, but to each in a different way. Unity is the absolute term. Based on itself, it is actual in the notes as something prior to them. Its essentiality consists in conferring essential reality on, in 'essentiating,' the notes. These notes are, in their turn, actualized in unity, and for this reason their essentiality consists in being 'notes-of,' in being 'essentiated.' The way in which unity is actual in the essence is, then, different from the way in which its notes are actual: the unity is actual by being 'in' each note, and each note is actual as being 'note-of,' " Zubiri, *OE*, 313.
59. Ibid., 52, author's emphasis.
60. *FRH*, 68.
61. Ibid., 71.
62. Ibid., 72.
63. Ibid., 72.
64. Ibid., 76.
65. *FRH*, 81. Zubiri observes that "time is not so much a straight line as a qualitatively structured curve. This means that, at least locally, the *nows [las ahoras]* remain fixed with respect to one another according to this modulation. Measuring instruments (the watch and the calendar) are always founded on this qualitative structure," ibid., 81, emphasis mine; quoted from Xavier Zubiri, "El concepto descriptivo del tiempo," Realitas II (Madrid: Editorial Labor, 1976) 21, trans. mine; hereafter cited as "Zubiri, Tiempo."
66. *FRH*, 82.
67. Ibid., 83. "Transcurrence consists in the now-present itself being constitutively and formally a now-from-to, something that is open in itself and from itself to its own past and future," ibid., 82. Ellacuría draws a parallel to the unity of spatiality: "[T]ime thus appears as the respective unity of things which transcur temporally," ibid., 83. Zubiri observes that to "the 'now-present' there is not *added* a before-moment and an after-moment. Rather, the 'now-present,' in itself, *is* currently and formally a

'now-after-before,' that is, a 'now-from-to.' The past and future constitute the formal structure of the 'now-present.' Therefore, the 'now-present' has in and of itself *real* temporal continuity with its own past and future," ibid., 83; quoted from Zubiri, "Tiempo," 26, author's emphasis.

68. Ibid., 86; quoted from Zubiri, "Tiempo," 36–37.
69. For a further discussion of the temporal structures of human reality, see *FRH*, 420–439.
70. Ibid., 91.
71. Ibid., 102.
72. Ibid., 93.
73. Ibid., 101.
74. Ibid., 116. Therefore, to belong to a species means to belong to a biologically specific *phylum*. But this can be approached from two sides: *species*, here, refers to the specific physical essence (i.e., the unity of constitutive characteristics) by means of which each member of the species belongs to the *phylum*; it also references the *phylum* itself, which is made up of all the individuals in it; see *FRH*, 116–117. "It is very important to keep this fact in view . . . for the schema of the species is so intrinsic to the very essence of the individual human that, without it, she would have no reality," Pintos, 341.
75. *FRH*, 117, emphasis mine.
76. Ibid., 117–118. Ellacuría quotes Zubiri on the connection between this genetic exploration and the possibility of history. "Each human is prospective because he belongs to a *phylum* that, as *phylum*, is constitutively prospective. . . . If the human had no biological genesis we could not speak of history. Through the biological genesis in its prospective aspect, humans not only maintain diversity while living together, but their individuality and sociality have an historical character," *FRH*, 119; Zubiri, "La dimensión histórica del ser humano," *Siete ensayos de antropología filosófica* (Bogotá: Universidad Santo Tomás, 1982) 123–124, trans. mine; this article hereafter cited as "dimensión histórica."
77. *FRH*, 118.
78. Ibid., 121–122.

*Chapter Three*

# The Human in Historical Reality

*It could be said that very recently history entered
a new and distinct epoch characterized as much
by its universal and real, historically real, unity
as by the possibility, also historically real, of
having to consider its own ending, an ending
that in good measure depends on history itself
and on what it is going to do.*

Ignacio Ellacuría[1]

Zubiri's philosophical project began taking shape in the twilight
of late modernity. Ellacuría valued it because it responds to the
legitimate, classical impulses of philosophical realism without ca-
pitulating to a decadent version of neoscholasticism. Likewise, he appreciated its positive assessment of the significant achievements of the
last three centuries, including the development of scientific method, the
growth of the social sciences, and the emergence of historical consciousness. Specifically, Ellacuría felt that Zubiri had forged a distinctive and
useful way to approach a variety of burning issues in the areas of philosophical anthropology, social ethics, and theological method. Having
introduced Ellacuría's appropriation of Zubiri's postidealist metaphysics,
I now turn to examine implications of his metaphysics on his understanding of the human in historical reality.

# THE HUMAN AS REALITY ANIMAL

**The Personal Dimension of the Human.** Zubiri's philosophical anthropology capitalizes on the correlation between sentient intelligence and reality. This correlation underlies Ellacuría's theological method. It also provides the central metaphor in my interpretation of his thought, the metaphor of ground. The human is intrinsically grounded in and related to historical reality. Therefore, to interpret history one must stand on its material ground, in particular, its biological ground. Stated differently, Ellacuría grounds his critical, postidealist anthropology in the Zubirian axiom that the biological represents a constitutive aspect of the human.[2] This does not mean that the human *has* a body or a psyche. Instead, Zubiri speaks of humans *as* psycho-organic. The human is a whole personal reality in whom the biological and the psychological are structurally integrated. Moreover, this thesis underscores the fact that the biological represents a constitutive aspect of sentient intelligence. The exercise of human intelligence itself "not only remains essentially and permanently sensitive, but initially and fundamentally a biological activity."[3] This has important ramifications. First, human intelligence can only act from the senses and in reference to them. Second, the senses and the intelligence, which in the human species emerge in complete unity with one another, serve above all to protect the biological viability of the human. Third, sentient intelligence thus emerges with an initial biological imperative to sustain life, both the life of the individual human organism and the viability of the species.

> Zubiri used to say that, even though a species of superior animals without intelligence is perfectly biologically-viable, a species of idiots is not. . . . The first human utilized intelligence in order to continue living, and this essential reference to life, given the primary unity which is the human as a living being, is the primary "whence" of intelligence and, correctly understood, also the primary purpose of all knowing [*inteligir*]: in order that they might have life and have it more abundantly, we might say, if allowed to use a secularized version of the formula so essential to the Christian faith.[4]

Zubiri appraises this biologically grounded, sentiently intelligent human reality from two distinct but related perspectives. One studies the emergence of the human species as species. The other analyzes the stages of development of individual living members of this species. The former amplifies Ellacuría's thesis that reality involves a process of realization in which ever higher forms of reality emerge from, retain, and elevate lower forms preceding them. He moves from the understanding of matter as "an internal dynamism that is both structural and structuring," to an enriched notion of body, which viewed successively includes all the prior structural moments of a living thing, including the stabilization of matter, the vitalization of the stabilized matter, etc.[5] This dynamism "achieves its fulfillment in its final giving-of-its-own in the human person."[6] The formality of animal, that is, the way the animal exists, is assumed into the "hyperformality" of human animal. The key, of course, is that the human animal does not appraise its situation according to mere sentient stimulation, but according to the formality of the real. As was noted above, this point grounds Zubiri's anthropology.

Zubiri also examines the human in historical reality in terms of the integral steps involved in the development of individual humans. He observes that the human, although an animal, demonstrates a manner of being embedded in reality that proves essentially different from that of all other animals. This unique fact of being embedded in reality can be further qualified in terms of three specific movements: apprehension, affection, and response. These activities also occur in other animal species, but the way the human apprehends, feels affected by, and responds to real things as real involves a singular quality of openness. Summarizing Zubiri, Ellacuría notes that in humans "the stimulus is not just 'merely' stimulating, it does not exhaust itself in awakening a response and nothing more, but it is apprehended as a stimulating 'reality.' Affection (the modification of one's vital tone) is not just 'mere' affection, for the human feels herself affected in her reality and in her mode of being in reality. The response is likewise in function of reality, a determination of what I want in reality."[7] Thus, it is not intelligence *per se* that distinguishes the human animal from all other animals, but rather the human's embeddedness in and among realities, an embeddedness mediated by the sentient intelligence.

Zubiri finds a colorful nickname for the human to correspond with this analysis: the reality animal. "Because the biological unity of sensing, feeling and tending is the essence of animality, the human encounters things as real things, the human animal is, from this point of view, the reality animal."[8] Although she never ceases to be animal, the human is placed not only among realities but in reality. She is, therefore, a transcendental animal.[9] However, this transcendental character of human reality does not annul human animality. "Although the human animal is embedded not only *among* realities, but *in* reality and is, in this sense, a transcendental animal, her openness to the transcendental does not cause her to stop being an animal. Without animality, that openness is impossible in the human. This is not because animality is a type of substrate without which the transcendental cannot be achieved. Rather, it is because that openness is formally sentient."[10]

A revealing contrast can be drawn between "reality animal" and the well-known construct, "rational animal." This shift in terminology reflects Zubiri's effort to project his epistemological corrective into the heart of the quintessentially modern science of anthropology. As such, it summarizes his entire project. He does not want to indiscriminately jettison modernity's turn to the subject. Rather, he aims to situate that turn within a robust, postidealist recovery of the real. Ellacuría grasped fully the import of this strategy.

> The human is animal, because reality is only accessible to her in a sensible, stimulatory manner. However, she is not a pure animal, for she does not remain enclosed in a stimulatory medium, but open to a real world. For this reason she is the reality animal, since she unitarily apprehends reality in a stimulatory manner. This goes far beyond saying that all knowing starts with the senses (Aristotle, St. Thomas) or begins with experience (Kant), for what is at stake are not contents but, much more radically, the mode or formality by which any content, and not only the primary contents, is apprehended by the human.[11]

The fact that the human stands open to a real world points to something else. The person is what she is both materially and formally. As an open essence she "is open to her own character of reality and conducts herself with respect to it."[12] That is, the person is not only a real thing but a self, a reality among realities. Her reality exhibits the formality of selfhood. The human *what* is a *who*. Because she is herself, her acts are her own acts, and the entire action of her life as a whole belongs to her. By virtue of her openness to reality, her life takes on the character of self-possession. "This is what should be understood by life. To live is to possess oneself, and to possess oneself is to belong to oneself as reality."[13] Zubiri captures this with the common Spanish phrase, *de suyo*, which can be translated "in itself," "on its own," "intrinsically," etc. The human is herself *de suyo*. This is not meant as a definition but rather an explication. "All explication places the thing explicated in a certain line or order. In the case of reality, it has been customary to place it in the order of concepts. Here, by contrast, we place reality in the order of immediate confrontation with things. And in this order, the reality is the 'of its own' [*de suyo*]."[14] This openness to reality beyond herself constitutes the reality animal as a *personal animal*.[15]

That the human is a person does not imply that personal reality is grounded initially in self-possession or selfhood. For Zubiri and Ellacuría, the logic flows in the opposite direction. Self-possession and selfhood are grounded in human reality, both personal and social. To summarize with a characteristic Zubirian thesis, human reality grounds human being. But whereas the emergence of the personal signals a new stage in the process of realization, that is, of reality realizing and possessing itself, it does not signify an end to the process as process. My reality does not emerge as a finished fact. Personal reality *qua* reality remains constitutively dynamic. This means that, on the basis of my psychological and biological activity, I continue to gradually realize my reality, to realize myself-as-reality. Therefore, the full self-realization of humans proves anything but automatic or predictable. Rather, it is a historical realization. As such it is dynamic, open, radically free, full of danger.

> Each instant puts my entire personality into play. In every instant I can define what I now desire to be and the manner of summarizing everything that I have been up to now. And so, in every moment the personality has the constitutive possibility of being entirely renovated. And this in a radical sense. As the personality is the actuality of my reality with respect to *the* reality, it is for the same reason something absolute. Each person is a concrete figure of absolute being.[16]

Two important and interrelated themes can be initially addressed in light of this account of the personal dimension of the human. The first has to do with the individual human in relation to the totality of intramundane reality. It issues in Zubiri's curious but insightful description of the human as a relative absolute. The human is absolute insofar as he stands out from, and contrasts with, the totality of the real. He is relative insofar as he remains biogenetically linked to all the other members of the species, and materially-temporally connected to the whole of intramundane reality.[17] By virtue of his sentient intelligence, he discovers himself to be a reality among other realities. At one and the same time, he can appraise and change his environment. Yet he remains forever linked to and dependent on that same environment. For this reason, Zubiri regards him as the relatively absolute reality.

There follows a second important theme: the paradox of human freedom at once biologically conditioned and transcendentally open. The human does not merely sense stimuli. She intellectively senses realities. Likewise, she does not merely respond to stimuli, as nonhuman animals do. Instead, she chooses from among various options. "Between the naked faculty to act and her real actions, the human interjects the sketch of a project set in the context of a system of possibilities which are realized not by mere behavior, but by option."[18] The power to choose enables the human to grant preference to one possibility over another, and on that basis to transform the chosen possibility into an outcome.[19] Through the exercise of freedom, which chooses its course of action on the basis of the reality that is desired, the human stands over herself, over her nature, as it were. She makes certain possibilities available to herself which do not emerge as a result of "mere nature," that is, physical or biological dynamisms, but as the result of "human nature," that is, of freedom. In other words, in the human, nature is realized not only *in* history but *as* history, yet without ceasing to be nature. Historical reality thus constitutes her very essence. At one and the same time she is determined and open, structured and free. "The human is not only nature, because she relies on something more than potencies and potentialities. But neither is she simply history (existence, life), because her possibilities take root in potencies and her openness in a fixed 'self.' The human is both fact and result, nature and history, where the two terms are not juxtaposed, but rather are intrinsically co-structuring."[20] Freedom thus appears not only as power and gift, but also as demand imposed on the human by virtue of her being the biologically structured reality who goes beyond biology and self-possesses her own reality. Because she is the *reality* animal, the human person can appropriate possibilities. Because she is the reality *animal*, she must do so.

**The Social Dimension of the Human.** Thus far my attention has been on Ellacuría's understanding of the personal dimension of the human. However, an adequate understanding of human reality, including the role of human freedom in the shaping of historical reality, demands not only an account of individual persons but of persons in their social dimension. The reality of the human unveils itself not only in the story of each human person, but the history of human societies.[21] History and nature mutually structure one another, a fact which emerges precisely in the leap from nonhistorical to historical reality, that is, in the emergence of the human. This has important ramifications for the process of interpreting reality. Precisely because the dawn of human reality awakens history, a certain circularity accompanies the attempt to define the human in terms of historical reality. "It is impossible to interpret history without interpreting the person and society; similarly, one cannot interpret the personal and the social without interpreting history."[22] Out of this circularity two distinct but related questions emerge. How does historical reality define the human? In what ways does the human reconfigure reality as historical reality? Attention to human reality in terms of the development of individual members of the human species provides insight into the personal dimension of historical reality. Similarly, the implications of human sociality shed light on the radically new thing that the historical represents. Therefore, before considering how history functions as a constitutive dimension of human reality, it is necessary to complement the overview of the personal with a sketch of the social dimension of the human.

Following Zubiri, Ellacuría contends that materiality and biological vitality function as grounds of human reality. Specifically, they ground both the reality of the individual human as an essence and the primary natural unity of the human species. The physical reality of the species, its genetically transmitted materiality and biological vitality, does not by itself encompass the full richness of human sociality nor of the social component of history. Nevertheless, it does ground human sociality. For this reason human sociality is not, before all else, a sociological concept that we posit to explain an arbitrary or secondary penchant for living in groups. Rather, it can be traced to something far more radical. Human sociality, the reality principle that undergirds social living, emerges as an intrinsic dimension of human reality.[23]

Ellacuría begins his exposition of human sociality by observing that the distinguishing characteristic of the human is the ability and the corresponding need to grasp reality as reality. It follows that, in addition to living as a member of the species, the individual human sentiently apprehends that he belongs to a species. This is another way of saying that he does not devise sociality as a concept, but encounters and apprehends it as a reality. Consequently, in this sentient grasp of the reality of the species, the individual reaches for and begins actualizing his own human reality. "The turn to others is a biological turn, a real turn. The actualization of this turn in the intervention of some humans in the lives of others is primarily a real process, which in due course will bring about the experience."[24] This does not imply that the experience of other humans serves as a foundation of human sociality. Rather, the reality of sociality grounds the experience of it. "The apprehension by the individual of this reality of the species constitutes his own specific reality, his form of being in reality and his manner of being linked to all the other members of the same species, to whom the same thing occurs."[25] Thus, sociality, like individuality, emerges as a fundamental dimension of the human. The reality animal is a *social animal*.[26]

Ellacuría illustrates this by reference to the situation of an infant. Even before being born, the infant has a biological need for another, above all, her mother. From her first breath, driven by biological need, she seeks others and finds herself encountered by them. "It can be said, consequently, that from her primary being in reality, the reality animal discovers herself in real need. She needs the help of others. She finds herself turned toward the others out of need."[27] This "need" does not settle for the help of some abstract, generalized other, for "the other *qua* other has not yet appeared."[28] Rather, it cues in on those who are really able to lend help. However, the encounter depends on those particular, capable "others" whose willingness to help represents a matter of life or death to the infant. A simple but profound consequence attends all this: from their first encounter with the child, these others-who-help gradually insinuate themselves into her life. "It is not the child who projects her uniqueness onto others in virtue of a conscious movement from herself toward them, but rather, the others who gradually shape the child in their image and likeness."[29] The human realizes herself through the mutual bond of human sociality, and in turn this mutual bond, the radical phenomenon of actual social life which Ellacuría calls "the social nexus," is realized.[30] Thus, socialization emerges as a constitutive aspect in the process of human realization, and the link between the child and those who socialize her emerges as a real link. Building on this real link, and in conjunction with the material, biological, and personal conditions of historical reality, the social nexus gives concrete shape to that reality and does so with an astonishing degree of inventiveness.

The others-who-help initially appear to the child as something undifferentiated, not as particular human persons. Slowly, however, they begin appearing as distinctive human individuals. Gradually the child begins to recognize them and to recognize himself as one like them, as one of them. In this sense "humanness comes to the human from outside. Initially the human is something that is interiorized more than exteriorized."[31] The key point is that others really influence the shape of a child's life. This represents one of the "fundamental structures of human sociality: one discovers others as human beings only after the others have already humanized him by introducing the human . . . within his life."[32] The undifferentiated, common realm of the human appears to the child before particular persons in their differentiated otherness, prior to the emergence of the distinction itself between the personal and the social. As a result, this public face of the human influences the life of the child in powerful, largely unrecognized ways, and does so long before the particularity of any specific other, that is, the person *qua* personal, weighs in.

Ellacuría emphasizes that the very biogenetic structures and dynamisms that unite humans as a species give rise to human individuality.
That is, the radical sociality of human reality implies and demands that
the person becomes a unique person precisely in relationship with others.
"The fact that from the species itself and by reason of the species there
emerges a plurality of individuals opens the way to the individual dimension. The fact that from the individual dimension and by reason of it
there is a life shared by this plurality of individuals opens the way to
the social dimension. And the opening is in the line of an influence
flowing back and forth, that is, in the line of dimensionality."[33] Because
these two dimensions, the personal and the social, mutually determine
one another and costructure human reality, human life involves not only
an experience of life *(vivencia)* but, from its very beginning, also a sharing
of life *(convivencia)*, a life in common. "The *others* gradually configure
my own life, but what the others gradually configure is my *own* life,
which I have to embrace over and over with increasing autonomy and
in a more fully ab-solute manner."[34] With this, Ellacuría returns to the
notion of the human as a relative absolute. She is absolute because of
the reality-grasping and reality-shaping power of her sentient knowing
and choosing, relative because those powers emerge from and remain
embedded in the biologically based reality of the human species. In sum,
the reality animal is a relative absolute because she is a self in relation
to others.

This does not mean that all of one's relationships are personal relationships. Zubiri makes a further distinction between the personal and the
impersonal modes of human association, the latter serving as a technical
term to describe an aspect of human reality. The impersonal should
be distinguished from designations appropriate to nonhuman (animal)
realities. "The impersonal is a characteristic exclusive to persons. Animals
do not form 'im-personal' but 'a-personal' groups. The impersonal association of persons is what, in a limited but strict sense, should be called
'society.' "[35] These types of relationship are already operative in infancy
and remain operative throughout the person's life. The personal refers
to those moments when one encounters and engages others specifically
as persons, whether as family members or fellow workers, personal
friends or personal enemies. In this type of relationship one encounters
the other by name. By contrast, the impersonal refers to relationships
with persons treated as occupants of roles. The focus is on the role not
the unique person. The openness and flexibility of the impersonal realm
make complex social life possible. "Society is constitutively impersonal.
It has institutions, organizations, modes of functioning, etc. And in a

given society each of its members precisely has a 'place' in it. To occupy a 'place' is, in a certain way, the supreme expression of pure society."[36] To a great extent I become humanized through the mediation of the impersonal. This does not diminish the personal but only serves to emphasize that the human person is personal in a social and historical manner. Moreover, because it exercises such a tremendous influence over the constitution of each human life, the impersonal manifests the potential not only for humanization but for dehumanization. "The world offered to the human being who comes into it can be an inhospitable place, an alienating place. In such a case, the person will begin the task of becoming a person in exceedingly adverse conditions."[37] In this, traces of the historicity of human reality can be detected. I turn now to consider the interpersonal dimension of history in the makeup of the human.

**History as a Dimension of the Human.** History involves the passing of time. To be more precise, temporality serves as one of the material grounds of historical reality and of the human in history, as was already noted. Although history cannot be reduced to material temporality, it remains quite clear that if there were no temporal succession, there could be no history. Likewise, history entails biological time: not only the temporal succession of material reality, but the genetic succession of the species, without which history would not occur. But once again, although absolutely necessary, genetic transmission proves to be a radically insufficient condition of history. Because history cannot be reduced to material or biological temporality, Zubiri concludes that "there is no history except in the human. Natural History is a merely extrinsic denomination. The historical is not heredity. It is not evolution, because evolution proceeds by mutation, while history proceeds by invention, by the option of a form of being in reality."[38] To speak properly of history, according to Zubiri and Ellacuría, means to speak also of tradition. History is traditionary transmission.

When the human, the reality animal, engenders another reality animal, not only does he transmit life, that is to say, not only does he transmit to him some psycho-organic characteristics, but also, inexorably and *velis nolis*, he installs him in a certain mode of being in reality. Not only are psycho-organic characteristics transmitted to him, but a mode of being in reality as well. Embeddedness in human life is not, therefore, only transmission, but also delivery. This delivery is called *paradosis, traditio*, tradition. Concretely, the historical process is tradition.[39]

History refers to a distinct human structure comprising both transmission and tradition, or, to turn the equation around, tradition represents "a formal ingredient of history" but not "the whole of history."[40] The mutual relationship of transmission and tradition emerges in the identification of the distinct subject of each. The subject of the genetic transmission of the species is the human *phylum* itself. This conclusion flows directly from the observation that all animals genetically transmit phyletic structures to the other members of the same species. But the human animal, in contrast to all other species, transmits a structural principle of openness and indeterminacy. Humans genetically transmit something more than physical or biological structures, something more than evolutionary structures. Humans transmit the structures of history. For this reason, the human *phylum* not only provides the material body of ongoing evolution, but the material body of history as transmission.[41]

This leads to a second point, the subject of tradition. Humans transmit the genetic structures of an animal who engages reality within definite forms of being in reality.[42] Humans convey these forms to one another almost unconsciously. For example, those who care for an infant, simply by interacting with her and meeting her basic needs, insinuate themselves into her life, transmitting to her their forms of being in reality. This means that the tradition passes from individual to individual. However, this does not force us to identify "the individual" as the subject of the tradition. Rather, the subject of tradition is the irreducible unity of each-one-within-the-others, the social body. The individual and social aspects of the human remain irreducibly distinct even as they remain intrinsically connected to one another. "Individuals participate fully in the tradition, but only insofar as they are members of the *phylum*. This implies, for one thing, that the tradition always has an individual moment and at the same time a social moment. The tradition is not formally from individual to individual, even though individuals necessarily pass it on. The tradition is always social."[43] Thus, while individuals receive and hand on the tradition, they do so precisely as members of a species that by definition is open and undefined. This is not mere wordplay: to say that the human is "by definition. . .undefined" emphasizes that the dialectic of history is real: the human who shapes history is shaped by history. In this sense the human, along with being personal and social, must be considered historical. The reality animal is a *historical animal*.[44]

As a dimension of human reality, history may be defined as the traditionary transmission of possible forms of being in reality. To say that history involves tradition does not mean reducing history to tradition.

Likewise, it does not imply that history consists in conforming to what has been received.[45] The crucial point is that these forms are handed on precisely as possibilities.[46]

> Nature appears thus, in the case of the human, as a principle of history, but history appears at the same time as a principle of naturalization. In the case of the human and the social body there is a permanent influence flowing back and forth between what is natural and what is historical. When the first primitive human seized the possibility of lighting fire, he did not change his potencies and faculties, he changed his reality. His reality ended up "endowed" in a new way through this incorporated "power." This power was not transmitted genetically and thus did not constitute a potency or faculty, but it came to be transmitted through tradition, such that now the social body depends on the effective utilization of that possibility.[47]

History results not simply from the moment of handing on, but from the corresponding moment of reception, that is, of the actualization of those possibilities through the exercise of choice. This process of actualization has a definite structure: first, I consider the possibilities before me, then I design a plan that prioritizes among them, then I choose. The result of my choice is not a brute fact but an event, a historical realization with a definite result or outcome.[48] This means, quite simply, that history does not just happen. Rather, history is made. History emerges not merely out of the historical sequence of facts, but out of the dynamic progression of events, realizations, accomplishments. History dawns as a creative process. It pertains to freedom, but not a detached, ahistorical, idealistically conceived freedom for which anything is possible, nor an autonomous freedom proper to isolated individuals. As an essential characteristic of the human, freedom is shaped by the personal, social, and historical dimensions of the human and by the real possibilities from among which it chooses and which, through choice, it shapes and passes on. Possibilities become real only insofar as they are handed on by the social body of the human in history. To speak, therefore, of a discrete personal freedom detached from society or removed from history is to utter nonsense. Human freedom is personal, social, and historical.

The philosophy of historical reality, as an open material-historical realism, thus sheds new light on the ancient dilemma of freedom and necessity. By adopting Zubiri's understanding of history as traditionary transmission, Ellacuría can account for both the real continuity and the real newness of history. We have noted how material temporality and biological transmission ground historical continuity. But history also breathes newness. New things appear because newly possible forms of being in reality are actualized, and new capacities are created. For this reason, biological metaphors for history falter. History does not unfold like a pine tree from a cone. It involves more than the maturation of something previously determined but hidden, even something more than the product of a complex evolutionary schema. In and through humans, history produces something radically new, capacities that previously did not exist, and qualities or gifts that "are not given by nature, but are acquired in the course of human history or personal biography, by virtue of which something that previously did not exist is *made possible.*"[49] History, which emerges from the material and vital grounds of reality, affects and refashions reality. Radically new real things can and do appear. At the same time, what the human does in history is natural, in the sense that nature makes human doing possible. Nature, that is, physical, vital reality, transmits the very structures of openness by means of which the freedom to recreate nature appears. History emerges from nature and, from that point on, remains forever woven through it. With the human species, reality becomes historical reality.

## THE HUMAN TASK OF HISTORY

Humans not only make history, they make a mess of history. Humans not only shape historical realities, they also deform them. History, by definition, is not prefabricated. It has not been programmed in such a way that things always turn out for the better. Zubiri notes that the personal, social, and historical dimensions of human reality, although they are phyletically determined, "encompass a meaning and direction which are not univocally determined."[50] Therefore, the positive development of any given person in any of these three areas cannot be assured. We can regress or stagnate. "A human can gradually lose her individuality, can become less social bit by bit, can gradually decline in historical age, that is, with respect to those among whom she lives. A person or a community can gradually take up residence on the roadside of the human journey."[51] Human historical reality both soars to dazzling heights of achievement and sinks to terrifying depths of depravity. Moreover, neither the great accomplishments nor the dreadful failures just appears. Both bear the distinctive marks of human engineering. History occurs under the aegis not only of human responsibility but, unfortunately, human irresponsibility. Ellacuría maintains that any philosophy of history adequate to its task needs to face this troubling fact.

To illustrate the claim that humans engender history, one can cite the discussion just concluded. By their very nature as reality animals, humans select, reject, modify, create, and pass along possible forms of being in reality. They exercise the power of choice to meet the exigencies of nature. They confront necessities by actualizing possibilities. In every actualization of every possibility, they swim in a stream of tradition and make it their own. They redirect the stream and pass it on. In this way, often unconsciously and usually indirectly, they shape historical realities. Moreover, because they are essentially free and open, history can take any number of channels, channels that may or may not line up with their natural necessities as a species or with their own historical interests. Humans thus appear in nature as history-making, reality-changing reality animals. Everything they touch, take, ratify, throw away, make, remake, or name is incorporated into historical reality. A crucial implication flows from this. In every such historical realization, the human comes face to face with historical reality's moral dimension.

> The human, by virtue of her openness to reality, responds to the necessities of nature through the interposition of possibilities. Consequently, the human is subject-to appropriating possibilities, which, in being only possibilities, have to be actualized by decision, by choice. This subjection-to the need to appropriate possibilities by decision in order to go on living, and in order to be able to respond to the situations in which she is naturally, biologically immersed, makes the human a moral reality or, more exactly, a *moral reality animal.*[52]

Ellacuría's argument that humans are responsible for history follows directly from the Zubirian description of sentient intelligence in its historical-moral dimension. This moral dimension of the human extends through history and penetrates the entire social reality of humankind, but Ellacuría likewise discerns a moral dimension laced through the biographical details and personal reality of every human life. In the personal as much as in the social arena, the same crucial point emerges: the moral dimension comes to light as a dimension of historical reality.

> The human must necessarily forge her own character and appropriate her personality. In this context she can be moral or immoral, but not amoral; in this context the three key dimensions of the moral life, perfection, happiness and duty, are constructed. The possession of herself, as an ab-solute reality facing every other reality, is not given to the human once and for all; her self-possession is transcurrent and problematic. My own being is a daily question. I am an essential restlessness, and this

makes my life essentially be a mission. In this sense, prior to every "material" ethics, the human is formally and essentially moral.[53]

**The End of History.** What are the implications of the Zubirian view that the human is the reality animal? Among other things, it means that we are responsible for our lives and our history. Ellacuría underscores this point by asking where history might be headed. That is, what might constitute the end of history, the destruction of history?[54] To what extent does the possibility of the end of history affect the course of history, the forms of being in reality, and the choices of humans acting within history? From the perspective gained by viewing history through its possible end, what can we say about the way humans fashion history? Ellacuría, it should be noted, is aware of postmodern critiques of totalizing systems under the rubric of "the end of history." However, his concern in this context comes closer to what we might call "the end of the world," although he does not use this latter phrase. "The end of the world" tends to evoke dreadful images of cosmic disasters and the "natural" eradication of the human species and perhaps all life on our planet: the sun burning out, a collision with a comet, a catastrophic climatic shift, an invasion from hostile nonterrestrial beings, all the standard fare of Hollywood science fiction and fantasy literature. This is not what Ellacuría has in mind when he speaks of the end of history.

One example of what he does have in mind is the historically real possibility of a full-scale nuclear war. The discovery of nuclear energy and development of nuclear weaponry introduced this radically new fact into history: history has made the destruction of history possible.

> In the face of this [historical] eventuality, not only must measures be taken that are likewise historical, but many of the presumed metaphysical interpretations of history have to be scaled back. If many times the appeal was made to a universal conflagration or cosmic catastrophe in order to get at the ultimate meaning of history, today this ultimate meaning can be modified by the real and foreseeable possibility of the self-destruction of humanity and history.[55]

However improbable the actual use of nuclear weapons might be, the fact that they exist brings the real possibility of the end of history into history, and even the very improbability of their use lies in human hands. Another example appears: the possibility of a slow but inexorable starvation of history through the exhaustion of natural resources or the destruction of habitat. This possibility, engendered by historical, not natural, causes, also rests in human hands and represents a real human threat to history.[56] Here again the accent falls on the historically real negative capabilities of the human species in all their scope and ambiguity. Significantly, these examples bring the end of history into sharp relief in yet another way, one that proves highly relevant to liberation theology. The populations of the poor nations of the world have been and presently are growing at an accelerating rate. At the same time, the woeful capacity of those nations to supply basic necessities to their growing populations remains locked in a steep decline. Stated bluntly, the world's poor, the vast majority of our people, are already living in the neighborhood of the end. Here Ellacuría's central concerns come to light. To what extent does the possibility of the end of history affect the course of history, the forms of being in reality and the choices of humans acting within history? To what extent does it determine not only our concept of history but the reality of history? What can we learn about our historical reality and task from the victims of history?

An abyss looms before our age, the real possibility of a dramatic or gradual "historicide." Put differently, historical reality proves to be the locus of endangerment, the place where humans stand most at risk of violating and losing their humanity. Most importantly, human choices give rise to these dangers: the threat to historical reality comes from the historical reality animal. "The problem now is not, therefore, whether history can gradually exercise dominion over nature, but whether history can begin exercising dominion over itself."[57] It is in this light that Ellacuría asserts that humanity has entered upon a new epoch "characterized as much by its universal and real, historically real, unity as by the possibility, also historically real, of having to consider its own ending, an ending that in good measure depends on history itself and on what it is going to do."[58] This new epoch is not only radically characterized by the possibilities of scientific knowing, but by the radical consciousness of reality as historical reality. Ellacuría's bold logic links the end of history to this historical consciousness. First, the real proves historical just as the historical winds through reality. Second, out of their capacity for shaping historical reality, actual human choices have secured the possibility of destroying historical reality. Third, the historical reality animal is not constrained to commit "historicide." As it confronts possibilities for ending history, it encounters possibilities for reconfiguring history. The same humanity now poised to end history can educe capabilities for transforming it. But historical reality can be transformed in its configuration and direction only by means of the historical dynamisms and conditions of human freedom. Herein lies the human task of history.

History can transform its own configuration and direction. But it can do so only within the range of human freedom, the structures of traditionary possibilities, the dynamisms of historical reality itself. As we have already noted, the freedom that shapes historical reality carries the stamp of all three dimensions of the human. It is not only personal, but social and historical as well. Thus, the assertion that human freedom shapes historical reality must be nuanced by the awareness that this shaping unfolds through the traditionary transmission of possibilities and capacities that in turn condition the effective operation of that same freedom. This observation points to several things. First, the human task of history distinguishes possibilities that are concrete, historical, and real from those that are abstract, idealized and imaginary. It involves a critical moment. Second, the moral reality animal needs to move from the identification to the actualization of real possibilities. This movement depends on the adoption of a genuine moral standpoint. Third, the critical and moral dimensions need to be embodied in an adequate historical praxis, a praxis that posits and actualizes possibilities through a process of liberation. These three elements ground the connection between a liberating and critical praxis on the one hand, and the method Ellacuría outlines for liberation theology on the other. Before turning to these themes in the chapters to follow, I conclude the present discussion with a brief analysis of the logic that links the human task of history to the category of liberation.

**History and Liberation.** The Enlightenment was preoccupied with the meaning of freedom, but the preoccupation is at least as old as ancient Greece. In a certain sense, philosophy has always had to do with liberation, the freeing of individuals and peoples from ignorance, error, and mystification and with freedom, a notion that goes to the very heart of what it means to be human.[59] So, too, Ellacuría's *Filosofía de la realidad histórica* can be read in terms of the problem of freedom and the meaning of liberation. In fact, it serves as a rough draft for a Latin American philosophy of liberation.[60] But this must be understood correctly, for reductionistic versions of idealism and materialism can forcefully and disastrously disfigure the concept of freedom. On the one hand there is a temptation to treat every possibility, whether real or imaginary, as equally feasible, thus effectively negating the historical task of nurturing real possibilities. On the other hand there exists the inclination to reduce all human behavior to some type of mechanical or biological determinism, which eliminates the very notion of possibilities altogether. Steering between these minefields, Ellacuría develops the concept of liberation in terms of historical reality. This development has interesting metaphysical and critical implications.

In a general way, "liberation" describes what goes on in the ascending process of reality, where new forms of reality appear as a result of reality's intrinsic dynamism. Stated simply, "inferior forms of reality *liberate* the superior forms."[61] Liberation, in this primary sense, is virtually synonymous with realization.

> Human life is, first of all, a natural life, a life subject to all the laws of nature. This fundamental datum cannot be lightly dismissed, as if by its obvious nature it ceases to be fundamental either for philosophical reflection or for human life itself in its concrete reality. That this naturalness of life only appears to consciousness integrated with other forms less "natural," does not legitimate its being systematically overlooked. There is not a natural life, on the one hand, and a human life or human existence, on the other. Rather, there is only a single human life, and this life is always necessarily natural. Certainly, between the natural life, such as that found outside the human, and the human life, taken in its integrity, there is a profound difference *qua* life. And this is so because a process mediates between the one and the other, a process which Zubiri, from his earliest *cursos*, called a process of liberation.[62]

Liberation, in this metaphysical sense, implies not only the appearance of new forms of reality from the old, but also the fact that the old structures maintain the newly liberated ones. This enables us to see how, for example, the unfolding of human life includes elements given in natural processes along with elements forged through free decisions. Liberation does not signal the annihilation of structure or the replacement of the natural order with chaos or indeterminacy. Rather, it involves the development of increasingly complex structures. These, in turn, make possible ever more advanced realities capable of ever more autonomous activities.[63] Liberation thus operates on levels other than that of social-political history. "Ellacuría bestows on the category of liberation a metaphysical weight of the first order, inasmuch as what characterizes the whole process of the realization of reality is precisely a process of liberation."[64]

The dynamic process of reality reaches its culmination with the appearance of human freedom itself. Here, where reality realizes itself as historical reality, the notion of liberation takes on new resonances. To state this more radically, the dynamic realization of reality liberates freedom. As the product and culmination of the liberation of reality, human freedom cannot be regarded as mere indeterminacy. For one thing, it does not involve an absolute detachment from physically and biologically determined processes. Likewise, it does not imply the absence of desire and influence on the level of psycho-social structures.[65] What it does imply, as we have already noted, is the integration and elevation of these "lower" levels of activity in the appearance of something "higher," something completely new, something which determines itself. "This determination of what one wants to be and of what one wants to do as a result of what one wants to be, regardless of the stimuli which accompany this wanting, is freedom. Therefore, freedom is freedom *against* nature, but *in* and *from* nature as dynamic subtension and, above all, freedom *for* being what one wants to be."[66]

With the appearance of human freedom a twofold structure in the process of liberation also becomes manifest. On the first level, nature liberates freedom through natural processes. Within historical reality this natural dimension of liberation remains as dynamic subtension. "The fact is that one comes to freedom by a process of liberation and remains free through the dynamic subtension of the processes which intervene in liberation. Through liberation, a new realm is attained where freedom, both of personal biography and of social history, is possible."[67] However, this is not the whole story. The emergence of freedom signals the realization of reality as historical reality. Thus, on the second level, history liberates freedom through historical processes. This twofold understanding of liberation parallels a crucial anthropological distinction that Ellacuría posits between the dynamic process of hominization and that of humanization. Hominization refers to the evolutionary emergence of the human species. It results from natural, biogenetic processes that ultimately result in history. "After the vitalization of matter and the animalization of life comes the intelligization of the animal. But this process of hominization has not involved the negation of animality. On the contrary, it has been possible thanks to the perfecting of the animal structures."[68] This process of hominization capacitates freedom and serves as a material-biological condition of humanization. Humanization, in return, completes and perfects the process of hominization. "The humanization of the human species is thus presented as the ethical corrective and prolongation of the biological process of hominization. Humanization must be conceived, therefore, as that process in which one continues and prolongs the purely biological process of hominization through option and projection."[69] Hence, the liberation of human freedom includes, but cannot be reduced to, the natural processes of hominization. Freedom is ultimately liberated through the historical, humanizing exercise of freedom, the historical-ethical processes of humanization.

Human freedom is historically real freedom. It is grounded in reality but given shape by history. "The question about human freedom is . . . a question about free actions and not about freedom in the abstract, nor about each one of the component acts of a free action."[70] Therefore, it should come as no surprise that Ellacuría's philosophy of historical reality steers towards an analysis of historical liberation. After all, humans exercise their freedom within the horizon of history. Freedom must be historically liberated: it must be made possible and then actualized. Both the freedom of individuals and the structures of freedom operating in various human societies depend on the concrete historical situations of those individuals and societies. Those situations in turn are constituted by actual, historically real possibilities, or the absence of the same. The realization of human freedom does not end with its natural liberation. It begins there. From there, the liberation of freedom happens through a decision. Creating room for freedom, the liberation of freedom, constitutes the moral challenge and human task of history.

**Notes to Chapter 3**

1. *FRH*, 470.
2. See *FRH*, 91; "Antropología" (1975) 109. Ellacuría spells this out in formal Zubirian categories. There are biological notes that prove essential, that is, strictly constitutive, of human reality, although by themselves, they do not exhaust the human reality. Rather, they combine with psychological notes to form a strict structural unity. Moreover, although they are integrated into the structural unity of the human, they do not stop being biological. This means that the whole of human reality is *formally* biological. However, "the biological notes, without losing their biological characteristics, lose their substantial character and enter into the constitution of a new human substantivity, both in terms of reality and signification," "Fundamentación biológica" (1979), 419–420, trans. mine. "Substantivity" *(sustantividad)* is a Zubirian neologism that is connected to but also must be distinguished from the Aristotelian notion of substance. "Substantivity is realized in substance, but consists in the formal structure of the constitutional unity that is formally individual (and not specific or generic)," Zubiri, *OE*, glossary-appendix, 478.
3. "Hacia" (1975) 624.
4. Ibid., 624–625.
5. "Antropología" (1975) 109.
6. Ibid., 109.
7. *FHR*, 318–319. See also Ellacuría's treatment of this point in "Antropología" (1975) 109. In that earlier work he uses the same terms as Zubiri to name this threefold movement, "sensation, affection, intention." His shift in *Filosofía de la realidad histórica* to the triad "apprehension, affection, response" does not represent a break from Zubiri, but indicates the emergence of his distinctive emphasis. Most importantly, in his way of naming these three aspects of the human encounter with historical

reality, Ellacuría alludes to the threefold foundation of his theological method, a point I examine more fully in the chapter to follow.

8. "Antropología" (1975) 109. *Animal de realidades* could be literally translated "animal of realities." However, this phrase not only sounds odd and vague in English, it is slightly misleading. In this phrase, *"de"* does not connote possession either in the sense of "realities' animal" or "the animal *who has* realities." Rather, Zubiri means "the animal *oriented to* realities." One danger surrounding the translation "reality animal" involves the loss of the plural. Zubiri chooses the plural, *animal de realidades,* not the singular, *animal de realidad,* to emphasize that the human is "the animal oriented to the real *in real things,*" or again, "the animal who apprehends reality in real things." For this reason, "reality" in the phrase, "reality animal," always denotes the "reality of real things," and never an abstract (or worse, idealistic) concept of reality.

9. Because the term "transcendental" differs in classical and modern thought, and because of his need to overcome the inadequacy of idealist conceptions of the transcendental, Zubiri insinuates his own tonalities into the term. I devote greater attention to Ellacuría's use of the term in chapter 7. It suffices in this context to note that transcendental refers to "the antecedency of the real to all modes of its apprehension, or apprehension of it; it is, therefore, the antecedency toward which all thought tends but which essentially transcends all such approaches," Zubiri, *OE,* glossary-appendix, 479.

10. *FRH,* 324, author's emphasis.

11. "Fundamentación biológica" (1979) 420.

12. Zubiri, *SH,* 68, trans. mine.

13. "Antropología" (1975) 111.

14. Zubiri, *OE,* 360. Ellacuría expands on this. "The *'de suyo'* takes on a particular mode of being *'suyo'* in the human. Each real thing, through the notes that it possesses, is 'its' *[su]* reality. But in some things this character of *su* does not intervene formally either in its constitution or in the actions or reactions of its reality. These are 'closed essences.' On the other hand, essences that are 'open,' by reason of their openness to reality, act formally and are constituted in view of their selfhood *[su suidad],*" "Antropología" (1975) 110.

15. See Zubiri, *SH,* 190. Ellacuría clarifies further how the term "person" is being used here. "This constitutively self-possessing reality, in which culminates the evolutionary process that strives for greater independence and control, for a superior substantivity and individuality, is what primarily defines the person," "Antropología" (1975) 110. This discussion harkens back to Ellacuría's thesis on the dynamic character of intramundane reality; see chapter 2. For his detailed presentation of the personal dimension of the human, see *FRH,* 315–352.

16. "Antropología" (1975) 111, author's emphasis.

17. This view of the human capitalizes on the etymology of the key terms, relative and absolute (in Spanish, *relativo* and *absoluto.*) Absolute comes from a Latin root that means "to loose or detach from" (to loose *[solvere]* + from *[ab]*). Ellacuría occasionally underscores this point by hyphenating the word. Something is ab-solute insofar as it is detached from everything else. In the present argument, the human person is ab-solute insofar as he is capable of being detached from all other things, knowing himself to be *this* particular reality. Relative (along with its linguistic cousins, relate and refer) derives from a Latin root which means "to bear back" (to bear *[ferre]* + back *[re]*). The human is human precisely in reference to other real things. Apart

from the reality to which he is referred or related, he is nothing. Because he needs other things, he is relative.

18. *FRH*, 349. The importance of the phrase, "a system of possibilities," is examined below.

19. This has important existential and moral ramifications; see section two of the present chapter. Ellacuría describes freedom as "a form of self-determination, such that, properly speaking, there do not exist acts of freedom, as if freedom were one of the constitutive notes of the human structure; rather, there are free actions," *FRH*, 416.

20. "Antropología" (1979) 111.

21. "What concerns the *person* is psychology and biography; history studies the *person in society*, that is to say, the relations and progression of societies," Henri Berr, *La Synthèse en histoire. Son rapport avec la synthèse générele* (Paris, 9th edition, 1953) vii; quoted in *FHR*, 178, trans. mine, Ellacuría's emphasis.

22. *FRH*, 394.

23. Zubiri uses the term sociality *(socialidad)* to signal that humans are intrinsically (i.e., *de suyo*) social. It should be noted that he also distinguishes the *dimensions* of the human from the metaphysical *principles* that ground them. In the present discussion the focus shifts from the metaphysical principles of individuality, respectivity, and temporality, to the anthropological dimensions of the personal, the social, and the historical.

24. *FRH*, 210.

25. Pintos, 344. The relationship of reality to experience generates the operative logic here. "The first thing is the reality of the experience; after that comes the experience of the reality," *FRH*, 210. However, as Ellacuría also points out, the experience of the reality of sociality remains an essential element in the development of a coherent, theoretical account of the totality of the social.

26. See Zubiri, *SH*, 197.

27. *FRH*, 211. It should be noted that the need for others, while grounded in the biological materiality of the human, is not reducible to that dimension. Human sociality can also be traced through the person's psychological and spiritual need for others.

28. Ibid., 211.

29. Ibid., 212. "From the life itself of each individual, life already begins to be social; the self-structure of one's humanity is a co-humanization. Therefore, the first form of socialization is this humanization, if by humanization we understand the process of interiorization of the human world," ibid., 235.

30. Ibid., 227.

31. Ibid., 213.

32. Pintos, 346.

33. *FRH*, 360. "The conjunction of individuality and sociality as dimensions emerges from the phyletic character of the human reality. To appeal here to the *phylum. . .*is not arbitrary: the individual human only exists in a *phylum* and his/her pertaining to the *phylum* is absolutely essential. So the *phylum* has intrinsic characteristics which lead necessarily to individuality and sociality," *FRH*, 359–360.

34. Ibid., 213, author's emphasis and hyphenation.

35. Zubiri, *SH*, 195.

36. Ibid., 195. From this it follows that the concept of "social place" has a historically real foundation. As has been mentioned, and as will be seen more clearly below, this notion of place proves very important in Ellacuría's theological method.

37. *FRH*, 215–216.

38. Zubiri, *HD*, 69. I explore the meaning of the phrase "a form of being in reality" in the course of the present discussion; see also notes 42 and 46, below.

39. Zubiri, "Dimensión histórica," 127; quoted in *FRH*, 495, author's emphasis. The Spanish noun, *la entrega*, which I have translated as "delivery," could also be translated "surrender" or "handing over." The latter meaning is very close to the meaning of the Latin root, *traditio*.

40. *FRH*, 496.

41. Ibid., 494. Pintos spells out the elements implicit in this image. "By its pluralizing character which makes room for distinct individuals, its character as that which phyletically makes something continue, which establishes a continuity among the members of the species through their psychobiological structures, and by its character of prospective genesis which establishes a succession among the members of the same species, always originating in some and always preceding to others, by all this, the *phylum* offers what might be called the material body of history," Pintos, 350.

42. The phrase, "forms of being in reality," contains resonances of Wittgenstein's "forms of life," but with the familiar realist twist characteristic of Zubirian thought. These forms of being in reality are intimately connected to the *possibilities* of life and history. Ellacuría also utilizes Zubiri's understanding of the notion of possibilities in relation to the forms of being in reality.

43. *FRH*, 501.

44. See Zubiri, *SH*, 200.

45. "Tradition is not conformism. A community may very well modify what it has received and even smash it to bits. What I am saying is that without tradition none of this can occur, there is no history. The human is constitutively immersed in tradition. And every tradition, even the most conformist, involves a character of newness. Those who have received a tradition have, in effect, a character which the people before them did not have, because, although they might have lived the same way, the mere fact of this 'sameness,' the mere fact of repetition, has embellished with a new character the lives of those who received the tradition," Zubiri, *SH*, 204–205.

46. Zubiri distinguishes among four different meanings of the concept "possible" or "possibility." (1) "Possible" can mean *potency* (or potential) in the Aristotelian sense. (2) It can go beyond potency and refer to a *faculty*. "For example, in the human intelligence is a potency, but only the sentient intelligence is a faculty," Zubiri, *HD*, 71. (3) Zubiri reserves the plural *possibilities* for the third sense: "In potencies and faculties, Cromagnon Man is nearly as complete as the human of today. Nevertheless, in contrast to us, it was not possible for him to fly through space, because of his lack of possibilities," ibid., 71. Note that possibilities in this sense emerge historically. They are first made possible, then actualized. (4) The fourth meaning emerges when, beyond potencies and faculties, the actualization of certain possibilities requires the development of corresponding, historically acquired *capacities*. The distinction between possibilities and capacities will not concern us here; rather, it is Zubiri's fundamental distinction between potency-faculty, on the one hand, and possibilities-capacities, on the other, that allows us to see how Ellacuría handles the relationship of nature to history. The forms of being in reality through which human cultures are transmitted constitute the key example of historical possibilities. They exercise a more radical influence over the shape of historical reality than any particular event or content; see *FRH*, 545.

47. *FRH*, 547.

48. See *FRH*, 519–524, and Pintos, 349.

49. *FRH*, 545, author's emphasis; see Pintos, 352–353.
50. Zubiri, *SH*, 216.
51. Ibid., 216.
52. "Fundamentación biológica" (1979) 421, emphasis mine; author's hyphenation. "The substantive reality whose 'physical' character is necessarily to have properties by way of appropriation is precisely what I mean by moral reality," Zubiri, *SE*, 160, trans. mine. Ellacuría reminds us that "this 'having to appropriate for oneself' is, in the human, a strict biological necessity, to which the human responds unitarily as the reality animal," "Fundamentación biológica" (1979) 421.
53. "Antropología" (1975) 112, author's hyphenation.
54. Regarding Ellacuría's treatment of this theme, I am indebted to Héctor Samour, "Historia, praxis y liberación en el pensamiento de Ignacio Ellacuría," *ECA* (No. 541–542, 1993) 1109–1127, hereafter cited as "Samour."
55. *FRH*, 468.
56. Regarding this "Malthusian scenario," Ellacuría writes, "the problem cannot be posed with the simplicity with which Malthus put it, but it is a question which deserves to be revisited, because it makes patent a real situation which is of the utmost importance for history," ibid., 468.
57. Ibid., 470.
58. Ibid., 470.
59. "It can be said that philosophy always—although in diverse forms—has had to do with freedom. It has been assumed that it is the work of free humans among free peoples, free at least from those basic necessities which impede the philosophical mode of thinking. It has also been admitted that philosophy has exercised a liberating function for the one who philosophizes. As the supreme exercise of reason it has liberated those peoples from obscurantism, from ignorance and from falsehood," "Función liberadora" (1985) 45, trans. mine.
60. "The ultimate objective of the reflections of Ignacio Ellacuría in the field of philosophy was the sketch of what we can call a 'philosophy of liberation,' " González, "Prólogo," to *FRH*, 10. See also "Función liberadora" (1985), 45–64; Samour, 1113; González, 981–982; Domínguez, 74–76.
61. Samour, 1120, trans. mine, emphasis mine. Ellacuría writes: "Liberation signifies that new functions will appear from and in previous ones, yet be strictly new. It also signifies that these new functions will allow living beings, which have established certain structures, a greater autonomy, a greater play. For example, the adaptive movement of the sensitive order, with all its complexity and enrichment, would not be possible if a system of reflexes were not established," *FRH*, 413.
62. Ibid., 411–412.
63. "In general, liberation builds upon a progressive establishment of structures. This does not cause paralysis, but instead leads to the activity of a superior order," ibid., 413.
64. Samour, 1120.
65. "Without desires there would be no freedom [*libertad*]. The desires define the breadth and depth of the field of freedom, and they make of the will [*voluntad*] a constitutively intending [*tendente*] will," *FRH*, 415.
66. Ibid., 350, author's emphasis. Ellacuría adds this further observation: the self-determining human discovers that, due to his sentient character, "his determinations are driven by desire in such a way that his ecstatic *agape* always includes something of

*eros,* in each one of his options as much as in the fundamental option configuring his life," ibid., 350.

67. Ibid., 415. This discussion picks up Ellacuría's "realization" thesis. In a dense passage dealing with the structure of things realized at once on various lower and higher levels, Zubiri interrelates the three key moments of (1) necessary disengagement, (2) dynamic subtension, and (3) liberation. "In the activity of living beings, there comes a moment in which a function cannot be or continue to be what it itself is unless there enter into action other types of function. For example, there comes a moment in which . . . the human cannot maintain his 'normal' biochemical functioning except by involving himself in the situation as *reality.* The biochemical activity has thus disengaged the perceptive activity in the higher animal and the intellective activity in the human. It is a 'disengagement' because the intellective activity is not biochemical in itself. . . . The new disengaged function stabilizes the disengaging function; however, at the same time the latter has 'liberated' the superior function. . . . The unity of both aspects is found, in its turn, in the fact that this 'superior' function not only has been demanded by the 'inferior,' but also that it is sustained by it, precisely by that very thing which in this inferior function (and in order to be what it is) demands the superior function; this is what I have been accustomed to call 'dynamic subtension' of some functions by others. Necessary disengagement, dynamic subtension, and liberation, are three moments of the unity of the-thing-as-this-thing in the living being. The plenary actuation of each function 'demands,' in one form or another, appeal to the others," Zubiri, *OE,* 334–335, trans. emended, author's emphasis. These three levels in the realization of reality are, in a certain sense, recapitulated in the human encounter with reality which grounds Ellacuría's theological method.

68. "Fundamentación biológica" (1979) 423.

69. Ibid., 423.

70. *FRH,* 417.

---
†

Chapter Four

# Foundations of Theological Method

*Doing theology presupposes, although not exclusively, coming face to face with reality and elevating it to a theological concept. In that task, theology must be honest with the real.*

Jon Sobrino[1]

The last chapter sketched how Ellacuría understands the human in relation to reality. Following Zubiri, he argues that human intellection is initially and fundamentally a biological activity. The very structure and function of human sentient intelligence locates the human in reality. The relation of the human to reality is such that the human can be viewed as the "reality animal." I now turn to examine the impact of this anthropological realism on theology. Jon Sobrino anticipates this discussion when he speaks of the need to elevate reality to the status of a theological concept.[2] Among other things, this implies that theology, like every other exercise of intelligence, must avoid "the contemplative evasion and negation in practice of what is the formal condition of human intelligence."[3] Moreover, just as theology needs to encounter and reflect upon *reality* in terms of the formal structure of the sentient intelligence, it also needs to account for its own radical *historicity*. "Human intelligence is not only always historical, but this historicity pertains to the essential structure of intelligence itself, and the historical character of knowing *qua* activity implies a precise historical character of the cognitive contents themselves."[4] Given this, one could say that Ellacuría approaches liberation theology as a theology of historical reality. But what exactly does this mean? What does historical reality have to do

99

heology? What does it have to do with liberation? And what is
.... ed in the claim that theology must be honest with the real? These
questions call for an examination of Ellacuría's theological method, a
specialized area of study which—as he himself observes—emerges reflexively only after one begins doing theology.[5] In this chapter, I analyze
how the philosophy of historical reality grounds Ellacuría's theological
method. In chapter 5, I turn to the way he deploys this method and
how he expects it to influence theology itself.

## DYNAMICS OF THE ENCOUNTER WITH REALITY

Ellacuría speaks of the human encounter with reality in two different
but complementary ways. The human *apprehends* reality and reality *confronts* the human. Moreover, this human encounter with reality manifests
three interrelated dimensions which he analyzes in a key passage of the
paper he first presented in Mexico City in 1975, "Toward a Philosophical
Foundation for Latin American Theological Method."[6]

> This act of confronting ourselves with real things in their reality has a
> threefold dimension: *realizing the weight of reality*, which implies being in
> the reality of things (and not merely being before the idea of things or
> being in touch with their meaning), being "real" in the reality of things,
> which in its active character of being is exactly the opposite of being
> thing-like and inert, and implies being among them through their material
> and active mediations; *shouldering the weight of reality*, an expression which
> points to the fundamentally ethical character of intelligence, which has
> not been given to us so that we could evade our real commitments, but
> rather to take upon ourselves what things really are and what they really
> demand; *taking charge of the weight of reality*, an expression which points to
> the praxis-oriented character of intelligence which only fulfills its function,
> including its character of knowing reality and comprehending its meaning,
> when it assumes as its burden doing something real.[7]

In this dense and important text, Ellacuría utilizes his philosophical
framework to construct a theological method that mirrors the encounter
between human sentient intelligence and historical reality. First, he identifies the distinct but interconnected dimensions of the human encounter
with reality. Second, he confronts the moral dimension of that encounter,
the human capacity to shape history and the exigence to do so in a
humanizing fashion. Third, he engages the process by which the human
weaves awareness into action, tracing the braid of nature and history
running through the entire process. On the first level, he introduces the

noetic dimension of the encounter with historical reality. On the second, he accounts for the presence throughout of the ethical aspect. Finally, on the third level, he examines how the whole process is shaped by and implemented through praxis. However, each level involves the others: each reflects the operation of intelligence, each engages the person as a moral being, and each is geared to action. In other words, theology does not first conceptualize a faith content, then take up an ethical stance on the basis of that conceptualization and, as a final step, adopt a pastoral praxis in response to these first two. Neither does it simply invert this schema and begin with praxis, move to an ethical stance, and from there conceptualize the faith. Rather, Ellacuría's method starts from the integral human encounter with historical reality: when confronting the problems of existence, intelligible apprehension, ethical stance, and praxis emerge together. So too with theology: every act of theological reflection and production is simultaneously an exercise of intelligence, a deployment of one's fundamental ethical stance, and a historically real praxis. Just as Ellacuría rejects any dichotomy between sensibility and intelligence or between knowledge and reality, so he rejects any compartmentalizing of the three dimensions of method. Because the logic of the human encounter with reality informs the dynamic structure of his theological method, I begin by examining the three dimensions of that encounter.[8]

**Understanding.** The first level, realizing the weight of reality, pertains to knowing, but a knowing more basic and more profound than the mere accumulation of objective data. This noetic dimension of the encounter with reality presupposes that the human is located in reality. He or she not only stands before the real but in the middle of it. The awareness of reality is not generated by mere sentience, nor does it occur through the meditations of a detached or "pure" reason. It results from the activity of the grounded, embodied sentient intelligence of the reality animal. It results in knowledge, but neither a purely objective nor a purely subjective knowledge. Moreover, since knowing is both engaged and active, its exercise necessarily evokes the ethical character of the human.

> "Realizing the weight of reality" not only defines the primary function of the intelligence, but underlines the radically ethical character of this function. Realizing the weight of reality does not mean merely to find out about what is occurring. It is not merely to record stimuli in a well-ordered manner. Rather, it is to really come face to face with reality and to situate oneself in the world of the real in order to find the adequate response.[9]

This coming face to face with reality requires vulnerability, although it does not imply naïveté. It is receptive, but not passive. It goes beyond preconceptions and self-interest to assume the shape of a fundamental willingness to be confronted by reality, and this willingness, in turn, entails risks and gives rise to responsibilities.

Ellacuría links the willingness to know reality as it really is to the task of theology. In particular, he sees this as the parallel to the Christian obligation, articulated by Vatican II, "of scrutinizing the signs of the times and of interpreting them in the light of the gospel."[10] Such "signs of the times" manifest both a historical and a theologal density: "[T]hey not only describe reality at its most dense, but God becomes present in them."[11] An important consequence follows from this. If the material contents of theology come from historical reality and if, as signs of the times, they prove to be the place of God's self-manifestation, then historical reality itself must be considered a theological concept. In such a view, theology cannot stand alone. It needs to be integrated into the whole of historical and spiritual life. It must remain connected to both ethics and spirituality. This goes to the heart of liberation theology which "attempts to be a *real* theology, but also a *theo-logal* theology, perceiving God in reality in such a way that neither dimension tends to lose its identity, but rather, both become stronger."[12]

Ellacuría's description of the noetic dimension of the encounter with reality reflects Zubiri's epistemological tenet that "knowing and reality are, in their very roots, strictly and rigorously co-determining."[13] Individually and collectively, humans live within and among historical realities that they help construct. Their specific location and action within reality profoundly influences what and how they know. "The activity of the human intelligence, even in its purely interpretative dimension—much more in its character of projection and praxis—is conditioned by the historical world in which it finds itself."[14] To test this assertion, Ellacuría turns to the philosophy of science. He discusses the theory of relativity, an example which appears to be ahistorical because presumably its verification as "true" can be replicated at any time and in any place. He points out, however, that this theory could not have been formulated in the first place, except for the development of certain very specific, historically conditioned possibilities in the areas of mathematics and physics, to say nothing of possibilities relevant to Einstein's own biography. Moreover, it cannot be understood, much less verified, unless certain historical possibilities are actualized in the culture and biography of the individual physicist.[15] Ellacuría maintains that in a similar fashion theology, like science, can be written only on the basis of certain very precise historical circumstances which operate as conditions making its formulation possible. Thus, for example, the historical situation of Latin America—with its terrible poverty and growing consciousness of the historical injustice which that poverty represents—made possible the emergence of liberation theology.[16]

Ellacuría views the noetic dimension of the encounter with reality as deeply embedded in the dimensions of option and action. Likewise, these two dimensions also structure that encounter. On the one hand, every act of interpretation unfolds in relation to certain basic options. This involves serious implications for Ellacuría's understanding of the role of hermeneutics in liberation theology.

> Even in the most theoretical cases, the intelligence has a moment of option, conditioned by a multitude of elements which are not purely theoretical but which depend very precisely on biographical and historical conditions. Consequently, hermeneutics, even as a search for meaning, cannot be reduced to a search for what has been objectified in theoretical formulations, as if these, by themselves, give rise to the final and complete meaning of the formulations. Rather, the hermeneutical investigation should thematically and permanently ask itself, to what social world do the formulations respond, seeing that not even a purely theoretical formulation completely explains its meaning only from itself.[17]

On the other hand, knowing and action mutually determine one another, for even after history makes something possible, that possibility must be actualized as a historical reality. Historical possibilities and historical freedom thus exercise a strong mutual influence on each other. Ellacuría's detailed account of this dynamic interaction represents a crucial contribution of his philosophy of historical reality to a theological method for Latin America. At the same time, liberation theology makes one of its great contributions to Christian thought generally when it insists that the noetic moment of theology can only occur in the context of the ethical and praxis-oriented moments of option and action.

**Option of Place.** The image of shouldering the weight of reality captures the second dimension of human intellection. Ellacuría refers to this as the ethical dimension because it requires—as a underlying option—that we take upon ourselves what things really are and what they really demand. Seen from the perspective of material-historical reality, such an option involves not only the human mind, but the human person in all of his or her personal, social, and historical dimensions. The primary option involves a discernment regarding where I locate myself within historical reality. From what place can I most fully grasp what is in fact going on and, on the basis of my grasp, begin to really shoulder the weight of what is going on? Adopting this heuristic, Ellacuría gives extensive attention to the context within which theological reflection occurs. In his own words, he seeks the best possible *lugar teológico*, the most advantageous social-historical place from which to do theology. The place of theology proves crucial because human intellection can only apprehend reality in the concrete realities it encounters. The material, biological, and social-historical grounds of any encounter do not rigidly determine its outcome or contents. Nevertheless, they function as constitutive conditions of it.[18] For this reason, Ellacuría's account of theological place begins with physical spatiality. It includes the other dimensions, but never abandons this ground.[19] Each real thing has its own place within the totality of intramundane reality. Each occupies a space that is at once distinct and unique, as well as related to the spaces of all other real things, and to the spatial totality of intramundane reality. By virtue of the sentient intelligence, which allows her to relate to other realities as real, the human has a unique capacity for nonspatial presence. But this capacity retains its material and spatial roots, and these roots remain operative in theological discussions of transcendence.

In the process of encountering historical reality, humans incarnate a fundamental stance that structures further encounters. In other words, one's fundamental stance toward reality exists in a mutually conditioning relationship with the place from which reality is encountered. This has important implications for the life of faith and for theology. It means that one's faith is intrinsically conditioned by the place of faith, and one's theology by the theological place.[20] Thus, theological reflection and the social-historical location of the theologian exist in circular relation to one another. While one's primary ethical stance before reality structures the very encounter with reality (what one knows), one's choice of a physical-historical-theological place from which to encounter reality structures that primary ethical stance (who one is). It means that what one knows and who one becomes depend on where one puts one's body, understanding by *body* both the materiality and sociality of the human. The materiality of reality conditions the truth and the meaning of reality. This holds for the community as well as the individual.

Such an understanding of theological place does not dissolve the hermeneutical circle. On the contrary, it includes it, configuring it not only in terms of truth and meaning, but in relation to historical reality. It follows that hermeneutics must do more than analyze texts and traditions. It must engage in a critical, social-historical analysis which pinpoints the social origins and destinations of the forces behind the production of various texts and traditions, along with those at work in the processes of interpreting those texts and traditions. But prior to all this, it must discern the best possible place from which to engage in theology at all. This discernment goes to the heart of what Ellacuría means by "shouldering the weight of reality," although the impact of one's actual option takes shape in terms of all three dimensions of his method. The ideal theological place would be that particular, historically real location most capable of manifesting God's revelation and call to conversion (the ethical dimension), the place most likely to inspire a living faith in Jesus and a corresponding praxis of discipleship (the praxis-oriented dimension), and the place most apt to stimulate a lively, authentic theological understanding of faith (the noetic dimension).[21]

Writing from and for Latin America, Ellacuría argues that theology finds its preeminent place among the poor and the victims of violence. "The poor of Latin America are theological place insofar as they constitute the maximum and scandalous, prophetic and apocalyptic presence of the Christian God and, consequently, the privileged place of Christian praxis and reflection."[22] Shouldering the weight of reality thus corresponds to a theme that profoundly animates and distinguishes liberation theology: its preferential option for the poor.[23] The historical reality of structural poverty exhibits several dimensions that contribute to the privileged status of the poor as theological place. One of these, corresponding to the ethical exigency to shoulder the weight of reality, comes to view in Ellacuría's historicization of the Christian symbol of the Crucified One in terms of the scandal of mortal poverty. He names the victims of oppressive poverty and violent repression, both in El Salvador and throughout the Third World, the crucified people.[24] Among other things, this identification emphasizes that poverty looms as more than a gigantic and terrible tragedy. It is historical mortal sin. It results largely and directly from historical decisions and structures, and it leads to death, the slow death brought on by hunger and disease, and the violent, sudden death associated with repression. "Poverty has to do with good and evil, with justice and injustice, with the realization of the human and the structure of society. . . . Even though poverty has natural roots, as does any other individual or collective phenomenon, it is a historical reality, that is, something occasioned by historical factors and something that ought to be reversed by historical factors, in which freedom and the capacity of human persons and groups for projection and creation play a part."[25]

**Action.** Coming face to face with reality involves taking charge of the weight of reality. Ellacuría's examination of this dimension makes explicit the intrinsic dynamism of reality and, even more importantly, the ultimate realization of reality as historical reality. Just as the task of adequately realizing the weight of reality already involves opting for an adequate place from which to encounter reality, on this level the option to shoulder reality becomes incarnate in action. "Reality is given to the human as a responsibility. The essentially praxis-oriented character of the human and of human life is presented ethically as the necessity of taking charge of the weight of reality, his own and that of others, which has to be realized gradually and whose realization is his responsibility."[26] Ellacuría's emphasis on the weight of reality not only points to its metaphysical density and historical burden, but to a crime: historical reality as weighted down by sin, by murder and the coverup, by wasted lives and broken trust, by the scandal that whole peoples have been annihilated and forgotten. Fully encountering historical reality means engaging, remembering and ultimately undoing its terrible negativity. In a word, it demands conversion, a conversion of the human heart and a conversion in historical reality. From one point of view, the whole fuss about historical liberation can be taken as a way to insist that our conversion as Christians be real. From a complementary perspective, this fuss is not about "us," but about the poor person who, by definition, lives near the edge of forgetfulness and death.

Since historical responsibility demands action, the accent here falls on the transformation of reality and on Ellacuría's understanding of praxis, another central category for all liberation theologians.[27] Ellacuría defines praxis as "the totality of the social process *qua* transformer of both natural and historical reality."[28] He further qualifies this in relation to the dynamics of history. "Not every act is a praxis, but only that act which is a real act of reality; an act, moreover, which is more than a purely natural act, because history, being always made, is always more than made, and this 'more' is the *novum* which the human adds to nature, from it, but above it. If one wishes to speak of transformation, the transformation that would define praxis would be the intromission of human activity, as the creation of capacities and appropriation of possibilities, into the dynamic course of history."[29] As an exercise of sentient intelligence and freedom, praxis encompasses an activity that springs from choice. It denotes a doing, creating, or shaping which grasps realities as realities. As the very dynamism of historical reality, praxis "embraces all the forms of human activity, whether speculative, social, aesthetic, religious or technical."[30]

Because human intelligence emerges from and remains attached to praxis, the search for truth is exercised from a network of interests and projects. Intellectual activity needs to recognize its praxis-oriented nature and objectify the character of its historical interests. It does not need to break free from praxis in order to achieve some idealized objectivity. Human knowing, Ellacuría maintains, "needs praxis not only for its scientific verification, but also to put it in touch with the source of many of its contents. The necessary reference to reality as principle and ground of all realistic activity, takes on a special character when we attend to the necessarily dynamic character of the cognizant reality itself and the reality in which we exist."[31] Likewise, theology cannot separate itself from the praxis-oriented faith context that gives rise to it without gravely disfiguring that same faith. It, too, begins and ends with praxis. Because of this, the primary goal of theology is not to rationalize or explain the faith; its apologetic task encompasses more than changing minds. To repeat, Christian theology participates in the evangelical call to conversion. It aims to transform hearts, to liberate oppressed peoples, and humanize historical reality. Consequently, only by *taking charge* of the weight of reality can theology *realize* and *shoulder* the weight of reality. Only as a praxis of liberation, which grounds the exercise of intelligence in the dynamics of historical reality, does theology fulfill its mission to interpret and actualize the Christian gospel. "Reality will not come to be what it should be with respect to the human, if the reality animal does not positively take charge of it."[32]

In summary, then, Ellacuría's theological method is driven by the noetic, ethical, and practical imperatives which orient the reality animal to the ever more complete realization of reality. Moreover, the realization of historical reality *qua* historical occurs in and through concrete historical liberation. Therefore, theology achieves its end not in an abstract search for truth, but in an active commitment to liberation. This claim resonates with Marx's famous eleventh thesis on Feuerbach: "The philosophers have only *interpreted* the world, in various ways; the point, however, is to *change* it."[33] But Ellacuría's insistence on liberative transformation does not simply represent a reworking of Marx. Philosophically grounded in Zubirian realism, it functions as a practical correlative of the conviction that reality has priority over meaning. "Precisely because of this priority

of reality over meaning, no real change of meaning occurs without a
real change of reality; to attempt the first without intending the second
is to falsify the intelligence and its primary function, even in the purely
cognitive order."[34] The fundamental logic of Ellacuría's theological
method thus appears in his starting point, the human in social-historical
reality. He does not start by objectifying the cognitional processes of the
thinking, theologizing subject, or by correlating existential questions with
theological answers.[35] Rather, like other liberation theologians, he views
theology as a second act that reflects on liberative faith praxis. Furthermore, he locates the methodological foundations for theological reflection in historical reality and the praxis that shapes it. His method of
historical reality and liberation thus generates the theological correlative
of the philosophical turn to reality. It completes the movement away from
idealistic reductionism and locates the believer, the faith community, and
the faithful theologian in reality. To make this concrete, that is, to show
how Ellacuría engages the expectation that Latin American liberation
theology reflect Latin American historical reality, I turn now to his treatment of those critical factors that constitutively condition theological
method.

## CONSTITUTIVE CONDITIONS OF METHOD

Although Ellacuría never produced a systematic, book-length treatment
of theological method, the final section of his address at the Mexico City
conference in 1975 sketches the main lines that such a treatment might
have taken. He briefly discusses four critical conditions constitutive of
method that would enable Latin American theology to encounter Latin
American reality.[36] These conditioning factors parallel the fundamental
demands which a theology must address in order to respond to the
historical reality of Latin America. The general shape and operation of
these constitutive conditions derives from the view that the human being
is oriented to reality and shaped by historicity. The particular shape and
operation of this method can only be determined in relation to the
specific historical realities that give rise to it and to which it responds.

**Human Activities and Areas of Reality.** Ellacuría begins with a general
reflection on the human activities that theology employs and the areas
of reality that theology attempts to address. "Every human activity and
every area of reality has its own scientific nature and critically requires
its own method, which should comply with the structure of that activity
and that area."[37] Hence, articulating the proper method for any given

discipline will depend on a prior identification of the type of reality with which it is concerned and the kind of activities by means of which it probes and deals with that reality. This means, broadly, that Latin American theologians must reflect carefully on the methodological issues implicit in the procedures and operations they use to arrive at theological affirmations. Likewise, they need to be clear about the area of reality to which they direct their reflections.

The area of reality that Latin American theology probes is not God *in se*, but the self-communication of God in history. This distinction informs Ellacuría's entire project.[38] It also immediately gives rise to the acute, practical question, who or what should set the agenda for theology? Ellacuría argues that the real issues to be addressed by theology should not be defined primarily by the administrative concerns of bishops, nor by the academic pretensions of theologians. Rather, the real concerns of theology are forged by the historical reality of the people of God in their concrete need of salvation. "The salvation of God and the salvific mission of the church and the faith concretize their universality here and now in very precise forms. The theologian should inquire reflexively, in a first moment, about the signs in which are revealed and concealed the salvific presence of God in a Jesus who continues becoming flesh throughout history."[39]

Turning to the actual activities of the theologian, Ellacuría insists above all that theology is not a pure science. It does not start with a univocal, scientific self-definition and then force theological activity to fit that definition.[40] Instead, after identifying the area of reality with which it is dealing, the self-communication of God in history, theological activity must discern what concrete issues it needs to address and how it aims to address them. Theological method flows from the reality of its real situation. The historically real context of a theology serves as a critical and constitutive condition of its method.

> In our case, it is necessary to decide what we understand by Latin American theology, because the fundamental presupposition regarding what should constitute a Latin American method for doing theology springs from that. It is also necessary to decide what historical mode of living the faith and of perceiving its proper reality the person of Latin America possesses in his or her present situation. Finally, it is necessary to decide what is expected or what can be expected of theology in Latin America in order that the continent live its own style of faith in relation to its own historical situation, and work for this historical situation from an adequate mode of living its faith.[41]

Significantly, regarding both the historical sphere of God's self-revelation and the activities necessary for approaching the reality of one's faith in God, Ellacuría emphasizes the crucial importance of perceptively attending to popular religiosity. As the living faith of the poor, popular religiosity hallows the theological place from which Latin American theology works. At the same time, it safeguards theologians from the temptation to elitism, as real a danger in academic and ecclesiastical circles as in the world of politics.[42]

**Social Interests behind Theological Activities.** The second constitutive condition of Latin American theological method arises out of its need to uncover and evaluate the social interests behind its own activities and production. If the particular social character of theology is not recognized and critically correlated with an effective social praxis, then profound theological deviations inevitably will follow. Ellacuría develops this argument with several crucial observations. (1) *Theological activity not only serves the faith, it conditions and serves an ecclesial institution.* At the same time, it is configured by that ecclesial institution. Moreover, the ecclesial institution springs from and remains profoundly configured by various other social-historical forces and structures. Hence, through the ecclesial institution that it serves, theological activity is transformed into an ally or adversary of certain social forces. (2) *The production of theology is influenced by a variety of social forces and agendas.* "Theological activity is not only subject to the multiple pressures of the social order, which, if not unmasked, mystify their results, but it has to make use of theoretical resources that can stem from ideologizations that are more or less concealed."[43] (3) *Theological activity has a multilayered social-historical character.* The historicity of theology stems, on one level, from the fact that it is produced in history by human beings who exercise a historically conditioned freedom. However, at an even deeper level, it springs from the formally social character of the area of reality to which it responds, the self-communication of God in history.

Ellacuría identifies the social interests behind theological activities by asking, for what and for whom is a theology produced? The point here is not to ascertain what kind of people engage in theological activity and produce theological works. As a general rule, theologians belong to a class of highly educated cultural elites. Although significant, this does not represent the only relevant issue. Something even more radical emerges. Who reaps the social-economic-political benefits of this or that theological activity, once it has penetrated the structures of the social order that receives it? Who stands to profit from this or that particular way of handing on or reinterpreting a theological tradition? Ellacuría consistently confronts the tendency toward anti-intellectualism that can emerge in tandem with social activism. He argues forcefully that theology needs careful, profound, and, at times, technical academic scholarship in order to pursue its task. But, at the same time, he is acutely aware of the dangers that face academic theologians, including the covert attempts of historically concrete interests affected by theological production to coopt that production. Therefore, before deciding which particular themes to address, the theologian first must conduct a thorough inquiry into his or her relationship with those interests.

**The Social-Historical Dimension of Hermeneutics.** A third constitutive condition of Ellacuría's theological method emerges around the social-historical dimension of hermeneutics. He does not deny the need for or minimize the importance of the hermeneutical moment in theological method. On the contrary, his method deploys a hermeneutical strategy, but it resists the idealistic and reductionistic tendencies characteristic of some theories of interpretation. The hermeneutical circle utilized by Latin American theological method involves a real, historical, and social circularity. Dismissing the idea of a hermeneutical circle that exists between a purely theoretical horizon and the comprehension of a corresponding conceptual meaning, Ellacuría introduces and enters the hermeneutical circle between historical reality and the socio-historical sentient intelligence. "The fundamental circularity which actually occurs in human knowing, to say nothing about the other dimensions of human activity, is not that of a theoretical horizon and some theoretical contents which are understood from that horizon and in part reshape it; rather, it is that of a historical-practical horizon and some social-historical structural realities which flow from it and also reshape it, if in fact there is a real transformation of the concrete realities."[44]

Once again, Ellacuría stakes a basic methodological claim on the nature and function of the sentient intelligence and the multilayered social-historical character of theological activity. His hermeneutical strategy capitalizes on the anthropological premise that the sentient intelligence apprehends and confronts itself with social-historical reality. Reality generates the contents of knowledge. In a similar fashion, reality constitutes the horizon within which those contents disclose their real meaning.

> Therefore, before pondering the theoretical horizon of my comprehending and my opting, however existential it be, it is important to ponder the real horizon from which any type of human function is exercised. This

can appear a repudiation of the very character of horizon, but it points to the fact that the horizon, technically understood, is not explained from itself as the result of a presumed, purely transcendental openness. Rather, in its turn, it is preconditioned by a series of elements which stretch from the biological structures themselves to the farthest social-political conditioning factors, while passing a long line of other types of conditioning factors.[45]

Thus, the interpretation of symbols and texts must go beyond a purely conceptual or even existential understanding of meaning. It must devise strategies for uncovering the way particular meanings are first rendered possible and then actualized by particular social-historical situations. It must account for the historicity of theological activity itself, of the interests it serves, and the area of reality it probes, as well as the historicity of the texts, symbols, and concepts that it seeks to interpret. This results in a social-historical hermeneutics that not only interprets reality in a historically conscious way, but directly affects social-historical praxis.

**The Critical Analysis of Theological Language.** Fourth, Ellacuría argues for the need to constantly and critically analyze the language that theology employs "not as a pure investigation of linguistic analysis . . . , but as an investigation of what the terms employed uncover or cover up."[46] At stake here are questions about whether and how theology can make use of such disciplines as the social sciences, especially when these might have a Marxist or revisionist Marxist orientation. Ellacuría appeals to the traditional relationship between theology and philosophy to situate his answer to this question. "As philosophy has been an interpretative mediation of reality in classical theology, Latin American theology needs the mediation of the social sciences. This does not imply the negation of the philosophical contribution, but its qualification."[47] In that relationship he discovers a general principle of theological mediations. The specific logic that justifies the application of that general principle to this case, thus permitting the mediation of the social sciences in theological production, flows from his analysis of the multilayered historicity of theology. Given the intrinsic historicity of the area of reality that theology probes, and given the historical conditioning of all theological activity, a theology of historical reality urgently needs accurate interpretations of the historical situations from which it emerges and for which it is produced in order to discharge its proper task.

> The reason for this necessary connection between theology and the social sciences arises from the unity of historical reality and the social body to

which both disciplines direct themselves. It also arises from the praxis-oriented character of both sociology and theology in Latin America today. Finally, this necessity arises from the ideologization which afflicts the interpretation of the faith as much as the interpretation of historical reality.[48]

To assert the existence of a necessary connection between theology and the social sciences does not imply that theology attempts to evaluate the adequacy of the social analysis. Nor does it mean that sociological theory determines the course of theological reflection. Sociological analysis of data does not function like a premise in deductive reasoning. It may shed light on the concrete reality of a particular historical situation, and it may lend impetus to the demands arising from the problematic character of a historically real situation. But the situation itself, uncovered and clarified by the analysis, serves as the place where the self-revealing God may be encountered by faith, which, in turn, provides the grist for theological reflection. It is not sociological theory which drives theological reflection, but communal faith lived in historical reality and historical reality encountered by the community's faith.

Ellacuría regards sociological theory as a necessary and effective mediation between Latin American theology and Latin American historical reality. "Theoretical mediations, as much as practical mediations, are necessary for interpreting and transforming the world along Christian lines. Theology is not a pure reflection upon faith from faith itself (one must not forget that faith itself is not pure faith), nor can Christian activity be discharged without operative supports."[49] He recognizes that social analysis makes a crucial contribution not only to the ecclesial praxis of the Latin American Church, but also to the production of a distinctive and useful Latin American theology. It is also obvious, from his perspective, that Latin American theology can and must make use of Marxist and revisionist Marxist thought, both in its critical and constructive moments.[50] However, he recognizes that distortions can enter into Christian thought and praxis through the uncritical deployment of such mediations. For this reason, historically constituted mediations must not be converted into absolute norms of either Christian faith or praxis. "If the medium is absolutized, it becomes idolatrous; consequently, it is converted into the negation of that which it wants relatively to mediate."[51] So Ellacuría affirms the value to theology of theoretical mediations such as Marxism. At the same time, theologians must guard against any use of language which might "disfigure the purity and the fullness of the faith, and see to it that theology not be converted into a sacralized version of a particular secular discourse."[52] For this reason, the critical analysis of mediating systems serves theology as a fourth constitutive methodological condition that limits, directs and evaluates the use of such mediations.

Because the explicit attention given to questions of method in the modern period results directly from the epistemological orientation of modern thought, it comes as no surprise that Ellacuría's idea of method has epistemological resonances. However, his approach to method parallels his overall approach to the modern problematic. His assertion that the dynamic structure of theological method recapitulates the human confrontation with reality embodies both the critical structure of the modern turn and the constitutive conditionings of its being a turn to reality. Linking theological production to the area of historical reality, he examines the interests behind that production, develops a historically critical hermeneutic, and argues for an attentive analysis of theological language. Each of these conditioning factors embodies and completes the turn to reality as historical reality. In responding to the exigencies that emerge with these constitutive conditions, Ellacuría formally connects theology to the task of history, and incorporates the ethical implications of that task in theological method itself.

### Notes to Chapter 4

1. Jon Sobrino, "De una teología sólo de la liberación a una teología del martirio," *RLT* (No. 28, 1992) 32, trans. mine, hereafter cited as "Sobrino, Teología del martirio."
2. Along these same lines, Sobrino also coins a unique description of the liberation theologian: "If allowed to paraphrase Zubiri—who called the human being 'the reality animal' *(animal de realidades)*—we could say that the theologian of liberation is above all 'the reality theologian' " *(teólogo de realidades)*. Jon Sobrino, "La teología y el 'principio liberación,' " *RLT* (No. 35, 1995) 118, trans. mine, hereafter cited as "Sobrino, Principio liberación."
3. "Hacia" (1975) 625.
4. Ibid., 626–627.
5. "Contrary to what Descartes and his followers thought, the questions of method are not prior to the intellectual task which is occupied with resolving specific problems. Even temporally, they assume a certain posteriority: after having realized a productive intellectual work, one raises the question about how one went about it, whether by critically justifying it, by correcting what went before or by starting over," ibid., 609. While keeping this important point in mind, I examine Ellacuría's method before turning to his "prior" theological reflections on issues of salvation, church, and the like, in order to highlight the internal logic by which he links historical reality to liberation theology.
6. See "Hacia" (1975).
7. "Hacia" (1975) 626, author's emphasis. Ellacuría titles the section of the essay in which this text appears, "Some fundamental affirmations for a correct conception

of human intelligence in order to determine Latin American method in theology," ibid., 624–629. See the table on page 127, chapter 5, for a schematic outline of the elements of Ellacuría's theological method and the corresponding dimensions of human intelligence which he outlines here.

The full text in Spanish reads: "Este enfrentarse con las cosas reales en tanto que reales tiene una triple dimensión: *el hacerse cargo de la realidad*, lo cual supone un estar en la realidad de las cosas—y no meramente un estar ante la idea de las cosas o en el sentido de ellas—, un estar 'real' en la realidad de las cosas, que en su carácter activo de estar siendo es todo lo contrario de un estar cósico e inerte e implica un estar entre ellas a través de sus mediaciones materiales y activas; *el cargar con la realidad*, expresión que señala el fundamental carácter ético de la inteligencia, que no se le ha dado al hombre para evadirse de sus compromisos reales sino para cargar sobre sí con lo que son realmente las cosas y con lo que realmente exigen; *el encargarse de la realidad*, expresión que señala el carácter práxico de la inteligencia, que sólo cumple con lo que es, incluse en su carácter de conocedora de la realidad y comprensora de su sentido, cuando toma a su cargo un hacer real." For a different English translation of this paragraph, see Sobrino, *Liberator,* 34. For an especially insightful commentary, see Sobrino, "Principio liberación," 115–140. Other useful reflections include José María Mardones, "La historización de los conceptos teológicos," in J. Gimbernat and C. Gómez, eds., *La pasión por la libertad: Homenaje a Ignacio Ellacuría* (Navarra: Ed. Verbo Divino, 1994) 189–212, hereafter cited as "Mardones"; José González Faus, "Mi deuda con Ignacio Ellacuría," *RLT* (No. 21, 1990) 255–262, hereafter cited as González Faus, "Mi deuda"; Sobrino, "Ignacio Ellacuría," 146–147. Ellacuría himself further develops this triple dimension of the confrontation with reality in "Fundamentación biológica" (1979) 422–423.

Both Whitfield and Lassalle-Klein comment on the wordplay that Ellacuría uses to describe these three levels. Both also acknowledge the difficulties involved in translating it; see Whitfield, 205–206, and Lassalle-Klein, *Jesuit Martyrs,* 125–126. "The three phrases play on the noun *cargo*, in Spanish a physical load, a duty, burden, or accusation, and its related verbs *cargar* and *encargarse*, to develop distinctions in the different forms in which the human intelligence should apprehend reality if it is to be fully human in that apprehension," Whitfield, 205. *Hacerse cargo* can mean "to take charge of" or "to see about," but in this context it means "to become acquainted with," "to understand," "to realize," or "to perceive." I choose "realizing" (in the sense of "knowing," not in the specialized Zubirian sense of "actualizing") to evoke a profound sense of understanding; see below, n. 9. *Cargar con* may be translated "to pick up," "to carry or take away," "to shoulder," "to take upon oneself," "to assume," "to take on," or "to bear," as in "to bear a burden," "to take on a responsibility." *Encargarse de*, may be translated "to take charge of," "to look after," "to see about," "to attend to," "to take [something] over," or more loosely, "to actually transform" (Lassalle-Klein, *Jesuit Martyrs*). It, too, *may* be translated "to take responsibility [for something];" see the translation in Sobrino, *Liberator.* While the shades of meaning between the second and third dimensions appear quite subtle at first, Ellacuría emphasizes that the third level has to do with praxis, the moment of transformative action, while the second has to do with a fundamental option regarding one's place.

I use the formula "the weight of reality" to translate all three phrases, choosing "weight" from among the various meanings of *cargo* because of its multivalence. This approach has the merit of emphasizing the profound interrelations that link these dimensions. However, besides being slightly awkward, it also tends to obscure the shades of difference which Ellacuría evokes at the same time, the shifts in accent from weight perceived more or less neutrally as "mere" weight, to weight as "burden" (or even "accusation") and, finally, weight as "responsibility."

8. Compare this approach with Lonergan's: "[T]ranscendental method is concerned with meeting the exigences and exploiting the opportunities presented by the human mind itself," *Method in Theology*, op. cit., 14. Compare also with Sobrino, whose description of theology clearly makes use of Ellacuría. "To do theology is to exercise one's intelligence. The latter has its own structure, yet we reach the conclusion that its exercise is configured historically by a specific *pathos*. To accent the primary point, we recall that the formal structure of intelligence consists in 'the apprehending and facing of reality.' This occurs on a *noetic* level, which presupposes being incarnated in reality, on an *ethical* level, which presupposes that the intelligence is addressed by reality and should respond to the demands of that address, and on a level of *praxis*, which presupposes that it should take responsibility for a real task," Sobrino, "Principio liberación," 116–117. Ellacuría himself makes use of an initial distinction between this fundamental *method*, which parallels the dynamic structure of human intellection, and the variety of useful *methods* that can and should be employed by theology as well as by other disciplines. *Method* (singular) refers to "the reflexively considered, critical and operative aspect of a system of thought," while *methods* (plural) constitute any and all of the various instruments by means of which all theoretical labor is made possible and actualized, "Hacia" (1975) 609.

9. "Fundamentación biológica" (1979) 422. González Faus further elucidates the depth and intensity of the "realizing" that is involved here. " 'Realizing the weight' of reality involves a conception of knowing more profound than the mere objective accumulation of data. Spanish expressions such as ¡*ahora me hago cargo!* (now I get it!) or *hazte cargo* (you must understand) allude to a comprehension which goes far beyond mere objective knowing and links knowing and empathy," González Faus, "Mi deuda," 256.

10. Second Vatican Council, "Guadium et Spes," No. 4, in W. Abbott, ed., *The Documents of Vatican II* (New York: Guild Press, 1966) 201–202. To put this another way, *really realizing the weight of reality* involves discerning in history the "authentic signs of God's presence and purpose," ibid., No. 11, 209.

11. Sobrino, "Principio liberación," 120. In order to read the signs of the times, theologians need to guard against the presumption that they can always use previously adequate categories to analyze new realities. This does not mean, of course, that they can approach each new situation with no presuppositions, with nothing but "new eyes" for seeing reality. But they do need to be critically aware of what categories, constructs, and terms they are using, how they are using them, and how those categories may guide or skew their investigations of reality. These issues come up repeatedly in the discussions to follow, in relation to such themes as theological place, liberative hermeneutics, theological usage of nontheological language, and the historicization of concepts.

12. Sobrino, "Principio liberación," 119; author's emphasis and hyphenation.

13. Zubiri, *IS*, 10; see above, chapter 2, n. 8.

14. "Hacia" (1975) 627.

15. In this discussion, Ellacuría gives his own articulation to a theme that many recent philosophies of science, following in the footsteps of Thomas Kuhn, have addressed; see Thomas S. Kuhn, *The Structure of Scientific Revolutions* (Chicago: University of

Chicago Press, 1962, 1970), 2nd edition; see also Richard Bernstein, "Philosophy, History and Critique," in *The New Constellation: The Ethical-Political Horizons of Modernity/Postmodernity* (Cambridge: MIT Press, 1991) 15–30.

16. "What seminal experience and intuition has given rise to the theology of liberation? Purely and simply, the daily experience of the unjust poverty in which millions of our fellow Latin Americans are obliged to live. In and from this experience emerges the shattering word of the God of Moses and of Jesus: this situation is not the will of that God," Roberto Oliveros, "History of the Theology of Liberation," *MLT*, 5.

17. "Hacia" (1975) 627. I take up a more detailed discussion of Ellacuría's hermeneutics below.

18. See below, n. 39, for the definition of "constitutive conditions."

19. As noted above, Ellacuría identifies *spaciality* as one of the material foundations of historical reality; see above, chapter 2, section four.

20. Ellacuría distinguishes theological place *(lugar)* and source *(fuente)*, taking as " 'source' or deposit that which in one form or other maintains the contents of the faith." However, he notes that this distinction must not be applied in a way that views the two as mutually exclusive. "In a way, the place is a source insofar as the place makes it possible for the source to present one thing or other, so that, thanks to the place and by virtue of it, certain specific contents are actualized and made really present," Ignacio Ellacuría, "Los pobres, 'lugar teológico' en América Latina," *CIRD*, 1984 168; originally published in *Misión Abierta* (No. 4–5, 1981) 225–240; hereafter cited as "Lugar teológico". See also, Sobrino, *Liberator*, 23–24.

21. See "Lugar teológico" (1981) 165–168.

22. Ibid., 163.

23. The "preferential option for the poor" is crucial to liberation theology and prominent in recent Catholic social thought. In Latin America, the episcopal conference brought this option to explicit articulation at the meeting in Puebla in 1979. "We affirm the need for conversion on the part of the whole Church to a preferential option for the poor, an option aimed at their integral liberation," CELAM, "Evangelization in Latin America's Present and Future," No. 1134, in J. Eagleson and P. Scharper, eds., *Puebla and Beyond* (Maryknoll: Orbis, 1979) 264. For a good overview of official church teaching, see Donal Dorr, *Option for the Poor: A Hundred Years of Vatican Social Teaching* (Maryknoll: Orbis, 1983). A key theological voice has been that of Gustavo Gutiérrez; see, for example, *A Theology of Liberation: History, Politics and Salvation*, trans. by Caridad Inda and John Eagleson (Maryknoll: Orbis, 1973, 1988); "Theology from the Underside of History," in *The Power of the Poor in History* (Maryknoll: Orbis, 1983) 169–214; "Option for the Poor," *MLT*, 235–250. See also Juan Luis Segundo, *The Liberation of Theology*, trans. by John Drury (Maryknoll: Orbis, 1976); "The Option for the Poor: Hermeneutic Key for Understanding the Gospel," in *Signs of the Times: Theological Reflections* (Maryknoll: Orbis, 1993) 119–127; John O'Brien, *Theology and the Option for the Poor* (Collegeville, Minn.: The Liturgical Press, 1992).

24. Ellacuría's writings on this theme include "El pueblo crucificado" (1978) 189–216; *MLT*, 580–603; "Las Iglesias Latinoamericanas interpelan a la Iglesia de España," *ST* (No. 826, 1982) 219–230; "Quinto centenario de América Latina ¿descubrimiento o encubrimiento?" *RLT* (No. 21, 1990) 271–282. Jon Sobrino has also written extensively on this theme; see *Liberator*, 254–271; "The Crucified Peoples: Yahweh's Suffering Servant Today," *The Principle of Mercy*, op. cit., 49–57. I explore the importance of this notion for Ellacuría's theology below, chapter 7.

25. Ignacio Ellacuría, "Pobres," in C. Floristán and J. J. Tamayo, eds., *Conceptos fundamentales de pastoral* (Madrid: Editorial Trotta, 1983) 789, trans. mine.
26. "Fundamentación biológica" (1979) 422.
27. Like the preferential option for the poor, the theme of praxis receives extensive treatment in most liberation theologies. Some important and representative works include Clodovis Boff, *Theology and Praxis: Epistemological Foundations* (Maryknoll: Orbis, 1987); Gustavo Gutiérrez, *The Theology of Liberation*, chapter 1; "Liberation Praxis and Christian Faith," in R. Gibellini, ed., *Frontiers of Theology in Latin America* (Maryknoll: Orbis, 1972) 19–22; José Miguez Bonino, *Doing Theology in a Revolutionary Situation* (Philadelphia: Fortress Press, 1975) 86–105; from a Hispanic and Latino/a perspective, see Roberto Goizueta, "Rediscovering Praxis: The Significance of U.S. Hispanic Experience for Theological Method," in *Mestizo Christianity: Theology from the Latino Perspective* in Arturo Bañuelas, ed., *Mestizo Christianity: Theology from the Latino Perspective* (Maryknoll: Orbis, 1995) 84–103; Ada María Isasi-Díaz, "*Mujerista* Theology's Method: A Liberative Praxis, A Way of Life," ibid., 177–190; see also Matthew Lamb, "The Theory-Praxis Relationship in Contemporary Christian Theologies," *Proceedings of the Catholic Theological Society of America* (Vol. 31, 1976) 149–178; John Markey, "Praxis in Liberation Theology: Some Clarifications," *Missiology* (Vol. 23, 1995) 179–195; Craig Nessan, *Orthopraxis or Heresy: The North American Theological Response to Latin American Liberation Theology* (Atlanta: Scholar's Press, 1989).
28. "Función liberadora" (1985) 57.
29. *FRH*, 594.
30. Domínguez, 72.
31. "Hacia" (1975) 628–629.
32. "Fundamentación biológica" (1979) 422.
33. Karl Marx, "Theses on Feuerbach," in R. Tucker, ed., *The Marx-Engels Reader*, 2nd ed. (New York: W.W. Norton, 1978) 145; see also "The German Ideology: Part I," ibid., 146–200.
34. "Hacia," (1975) 626. Recall the manner in which Zubiri distinguishes between intellection and comprehension. The latter operation follows the former, the primordial apprehension of reality, and builds upon it.
35. On the genesis and ground of method, interesting contrasts can be drawn between Ellacuría's approach and those of Lonergan and Tillich; see Bernard Lonergan, *Method in Theology*, op.cit., 3–25; Paul Tillich, *Systematic Theology*, Vol. I (Chicago: University of Chicago Press, 1951) 3–68.
36. "*Condicionamientos críticos del método teológico latinoamericano*" is the title of the final section of "Hacia una fundamentacíon filosófica del método teológico latinoamericano." The term, *condicionamientos*, proves somewhat difficult to translate. It is related to the term, *condiciones* (conditions), and some translators simply use "conditionings." However, "conditionings" does not readily convey the forceful, shaping and constitutive character of the *condicionamientos* through which a historical reality is what it is. Therefore, in the present context, I intersperse "conditionings" or "conditioning factors" with the slightly more cumbersome circumlocution, "constitutive conditions," in an effort to evoke the dynamic, structural influence of the *condicionamientos* of theological method.
37. "Hacia" (1975) 629. I translate *actividad* with its English cognate, "activity." However, it is very close in meaning to "operation" or "enterprise," that is, a structured, directed complex of sentient, intellectual and volitional activities, in this case, everything that

goes into producing theology. Ellacuría adds that "the activity itself should conform to the exigencies of the area of reality to which it is directed," ibid., 629. He defines the area *(ámbito)* of reality in relation to the human activities that probe it. "By area of reality we understand here not an object or series of objects but the concrete, historical totality with which a specific activity is confronted," ibid., 629. Thus, the activity and the area mutually condition and define one another.

38. Of course, this way of identifying the area of reality which theology probes is not limited to Latin American theology. For example, compare with Karl Rahner, *Foundations of Christian Faith: An Introduction to the Idea of Christianity* (New York: Crossroad, 1984) 51–68; Paul Tillich, *Systematic Theology,* Vol. I, op. cit., 211–218; Roger Haight, *Dynamics of Theology* (Mahwah, N.J.: Paulist Press, 1990) 51–67.

39. "Hacia" (1975) 630. I explore the extent to which the concern for salvation in history proves decisive for all of Ellacuría's theological reflection in chapters 6 and 7.

40. In his contribution to the Rahner festschrift in 1975, Ellacuría states, "the theoretical determination of what Latin American theology should be cannot be made as an *a priori* determination from the formal analysis of what theology is and what Latin America is. Neither can it be made in an *a posteriori* mode starting from the present results of Latin American theology. The *a priori* determination can offer a certain formal framework, outside of which Latin American theology is not realizable. But this is insufficient, because one cannot have a positive determination of a theology prior to the historical realization of distinct theologies. . . . The *a posteriori* determination is also useful, but does not contribute sufficiently critical formal criteria," "Tesis sobre teología," No. 9.1, No. 9.1.1, No. 9.1.2 (1975) 336–337.

41. "Hacia" (1975) 630.

42. "Popular religiosity is not simply the faith of the people. Even less is it a certain popularized form of theology. But we should not, for this, stop needing to be aware of it as a theological place of inspiration and verification," ibid., 630. Some very early works of liberation theology viewed popular religiosity pejoratively, but a more nuanced appreciation of this rich and complex reality quickly emerged; see, for example, Segundo Galilea, "The Theology of Liberation and the Place of Folk Religion," *Concilium* (No. 136, 1980) 40–45; Diego Irarrazuval, "Religión popular," *ML,* Vol. II, 345–375 (unfortunately this essay does not appear in *MLT*); Juan Luis Segundo, *The Liberation of Theology,* chapter 7. For a careful study of popular religiosity in Latin America, see Daniel H. Levine, *Popular Voices in Latin American Catholicism* (Princeton, N.J.: Princeton University Press, 1992); for a spirited discussion of popular religiosity from the perspective of Hispanic and Latino/a theology, see Virgilio Elizondo, *The Future Is Mestizo: Life Where Cultures Meet* (New York: Crossroad, 1988); Orlando Espín, *The Faith of the People: Theological Reflections on Popular Catholicism* (Maryknoll: Orbis, 1997); "Tradition and Popular Religion: An Understanding of the *Sensus Fidelium,*" in A. Bañuelas, ed., *Mestizo Christianity,* op. cit., 148–174.

43. "Hacia" (1975) 631.

44. Ibid., 632. For an interesting comparison, see the important work by Juan Luís Segundo, *The Liberation of Theology,* op. cit., 7–38.

45. "Hacia" (1975) 632.

46. Ibid., 633. Ellacuría introduces this theme with a caution for his audience of Latin American theologians which makes pointed references to this underlying issue. He notes, for example, that "the Aristotelian language has advanced the intellection of the faith along roads which today appear partial and debatable. For the same reason,

we may ask ourselves whether the Marxist language cannot bring us to similar mistakes unless it is used critically," ibid., 633.

47. "Tesis sobre teología," No. 9.2.3.1 (1975) 338. For a strong critique of the type of argument that Ellacuría develops here, see John Milbank, *Theology and Social Theory* (Oxford/ Cambridge, Mass.: Blackwell, 1995), especially chapter 8. Milbank does not explicitly mention Ellacuría. However, given his general attack on the use of the social sciences in theology and his particular criticism of other liberation and political theologians (C. Boff, Gutiérrez, Metz), one must assume that he would strongly disagree with Ellacuría on this point and in general. It should be noted that, while Milbank's works have rightfully earned him the respect of other theologians, his sweeping critique of modern social science and its use by theology has in turn been sharply criticized on a number of grounds; see, for example, Anthony Godzieba, "Fear and Loathing in Modernity: The Voyages of Capt. John Milbank," in *Philosophy and Theology* (Vol. 9, No. 3–4, 1996) 419–433; Paul Lakeland, "Mysticism and Politics: The Work of John Milbank," ibid., 455–459; Gregory Baum, "For and Against John Milbank," in *Essays in Critical Theology* (Kansas City: Sheed and Ward, 1994) 52–76. I believe that Ellacuría's analysis of the human encounter with historical-theologal reality provides further resources for a fruitful engagement with Milbank's thought and a convincing rebuttal of his central thesis.

48. "Tesis sobre teología," No. 9.2.3.3 (1975) 338.

49. "Hacia" (1975) 633.

50. "The affirmation that Christianity does not need to have recourse to Marxism in order to develop itself as Christianity is in itself mistaken, and disregards the intellectual tradition of the Christian faith. Christianity does not receive revealed truth from Marxism, just as it does not receive it from any other system. But it needs to intelligently apprehend the faith and give a rational account of it. For this reason, it needs Marxism, at least for the questions it raises," "Teología de la liberación y marxismo," No. 2.2.3 (1990) 126, trans. mine; see also, ibid., 118–126; "Hacia" (1975) 63; "Estudio teológico-pastoral de la 'Instrucción sobre algunos aspectos de la teología de la liberación' " (1984) 158–165.

51. "Hacia" (1975) 633.

52. Ibid., 633.

*Chapter Five*

# Operations of Theological Method

*The prevailing tendency today of measuring the truth by the way it functions, rather than making it more difficult to recognize the theoretical validity of theology, reminds theology to elaborate anew the meaning of Christianity in terms of historical validity. With this there appears a principle of theological historicization which compels theology to refer to historical reality as the place of verification.*

Ignacio Ellacuría[1]

In *Sacramentum Mundi*, Karl Rahner begins his reflections on the nature of theology with the following definition. "Theology is the *science* of faith. It is the conscious and methodical explanation and explication of the divine revelation received and grasped in faith."[2] Ellacuría does not follow this tack.[3] Rather, as we saw in the last chapter, his view of theology links the noetic moment which Rahner's definition emphasizes—theology as an exercise of rational intelligence—to two other dimensions, the ethical and the praxis-oriented. Regarding the ethical dimension, theology must make an option to embrace reality from within reality, an option for a particular and optimal theological place. Therefore, he seeks to shoulder the weight of reality by embracing and reflecting on the Christian vision from the place of the crucified people of El Salvador. Theology also entails praxis. It aims not merely to understand reality from a faith perspective, but to transform reality. It desires not only to transform individual persons and social groups, but the very structures of social-historical reality. It seeks a transformation that occurs not by accident, but through an intentional process of liberation, a liberation at once historical and theological. The issue of liberation thus touches the very heart of theology. This liberation can be described "in theological terms as a liberation by degrees from sin, from the law, and from death," and also "in historical terms as liberation from everything that oppresses people and prevents them from enjoying their call to be God's free children."[4] As a theology grounded in historical reality, liberation theology manifests a clear historical and even political vocation.

In Ellacuría's view, the turn to historical reality supplies liberation theology with the radical source of its most pressing concerns, along with the dynamic intellective structure of its method. Similarly, he insists that the object of theology, the Reign of God, can only be apprehended in terms of historical reality, "for ultimately the Reign of God, the central point of Jesus' message, alludes to the reigning presence of God in this world, to the God who becomes history so that history can rise up to God."[5] But while liberation theology mediates between the theological and the historical, it never seeks to be anything other than theology or less than a total theology. For this reason, it finds its identity in the theological tradition. It turns to revelation, tradition, and the magisterium as its primary sources. It takes its central symbols, concepts, and principles from the sources. However, it turns to these sources and makes use of their resources aware that all theology stands in danger of falling into idealistic reductionism. For all their power to reveal transcendent reality, the sources of theology—including the Bible, creeds, doctrines, sacramental traditions, conciliar decrees, and teachings of the magisterium—never cease being historical realities.[6] When they are treated like ahistorical ideals, as in biblical fundamentalism or magisterial traditionalism, they degenerate into common worldly powers. In the worst cases, they operate as idols. Likewise, when theological concepts operate as ahistorical and abstractly universal truths, they begin to conceal reality, not reveal it. Sensitive to these threats, liberation theology battles the temptation to remove theological sources and concepts from their historical ground. Precisely here, with his critical method for the historicization of concepts, Ellacuría makes a seminal contribution to this theological enterprise.

## HISTORICAL REALITY AND
## THE METHOD OF HISTORICIZATION

Ellacuría uses the term "historicization" to designate two different but correlative processes that his philosophy of historical reality interprets.[7] First, the *historicization of nature* names the dynamic by which nature becomes history. In this phrase, historicization is synonymous with realization, the realization of reality at its highest level, that is, as historical reality. "In the final analysis, the historicization of nature consists in the fact that humans make history from nature and with nature, that is, with everything that is given to them. At the same time, the naturalization of history consists in the fact that, in one way or another, all of history ends up reverting to nature or being incorporated into nature."[8] Among other things, the historicization of nature articulates the Zubirian view that history cannot be considered in an integral fashion apart from its material grounds. Ellacuría points to human work, especially that kind of work that involves direct, transforming contact with material realities, as an excellent, everyday example of this historicization of nature/naturalization of history. As this example indicates, historicization educes the determinative influence of human praxis upon historical reality.[9] Furthermore, the example underscores the importance of the material, spacial, temporal, and biological grounds of history that serve as the dynamic subtension for historical reality, reality at its highest level of integration. In short, historicization describes the ascending process that characterizes reality and leads to the appearance of historical reality.

Second, Ellacuría speaks of the *historicization of concepts*. While the historicization of nature refers to the very dynamism of historical reality itself, the historicization of concepts investigates, validates, invalidates, unmasks, or otherwise clarifies how closely concepts used to describe historical realities actually correspond to those realities. "Demonstrating the impact of certain concepts within a particular context [*determinada realidad*] is what is understood here as their historicization. Hence, historicization is a principle of deideologization."[10] This second type of historicization may appear to have little in common with the first but is, in fact, its epistemological counterpart. It, too, focuses attention on the material and biological grounds of historical reality and the apprehension of reality. Insofar as conceptualization appears after and out of the primordial apprehension of historical reality, even apparently abstract and universal concepts—from those deployed by theoretical physics to those of transcendental theology—are grounded in historical reality. "To state that concepts are historical, above all when they refer to historical realities, is almost a tautology. Historical concepts are placed here in opposition to abstract and universal concepts."[11]

Ellacuría maintains that strictly speaking there are no abstract and universal concepts. Human concepts are historical realities. The historicization of concepts springs from this claim and opposes the various attempts of idealistic reductionism to subvert it. For example, in three different essays Ellacuría historicizes the socio-political concepts of property, common good, and human rights. He shows how these notions can be trumpeted as true, good, or just without adequately accounting for the actual historical situations to which they are being applied and, what is worse, without attending to the scandalous fact that they can be employed to bring about circumstances that utterly contradict the truths they proclaim.[12] Among other offenses, the destructive use of concepts implicitly ignores the fact that historical reality grounds intellection. Ellacuría develops his method of historicization to explicitly account for the material and biological grounds of intellection.

> The biological or material character of human knowing is at the root of ideologizations: individual and group survival, with their necessary tendency toward superiority and domination, determine and condition the possibilities of objective knowing, above all, when that survival is endangered. In this sense, all knowing is interested knowing, and the fundamental interest of knowing is life, and the direction one wants to give that life.[13]

Ellacuría's appropriation of Zubirian epistemology lies behind this claim. Humans utilize intelligence not only to understand reality, but to survive. In their efforts to survive, they understand and change historical reality. As with other animals, human survival implies conflict and struggle. But with the human animal an important difference appears: the struggle for survival is conscious as well as self- and group-referential. In the historical process of apprehending, evaluating and affecting reality, humans construct concepts, rationalizations, ideologies, etc. Once generated, concepts and ideologies bend back on their human makers, shaping them both as individuals and groups by conditioning their historical possibilities. The necessity for the critical historicization of concepts arises in response to this tendency.

Because human intelligence never completely abandons its material, biological, and historical foundations, and because ideologies maintain links with different social forces powered by various real interests, the encounter with historical reality is never neutral, never merely objective.

Even the most scientific concepts contain elements of interest. Moreover, precisely because concepts can be abstracted from concrete, material reality, they tend to be highly manipulable. This conceptual pliability proves useful in the apprehension of complex and hidden aspects of reality. One can hardly imagine the development of such disciplines as theoretical mathematics or quantum physics without it. However, it also grounds the manipulability of concepts in the pejorative sense. It may not necessitate but it does facilitate the possible misuse of concepts and ideologies. Among other things, the powers of abstraction, rationalization, and conceptualization enable humans to lie, to falsify their apprehension of reality, to introduce the ahistorical, the unreal, and the inhuman into the human heart of historical reality. Even the most legitimate example of ideology (ideology in the neutral sense) can degenerate into a destructive, idolatrous form (ideology in the pejorative sense).

Ellacuría develops the distinction between the neutral and pejorative senses of ideology in the context of his reflections on the critical function of a philosophy of liberation.[14] He refers to a nonpejorative and necessary sense of ideology that clearly operates in the social and human sciences, in philosophy, theology, and related areas and can be found at work even in the so-called hard sciences. Ideologies make use of concepts, symbols, images, references, and the like to transcend the mere reporting of facts and provide a coherent explanation of some historical reality.[15] But, of course, this process can be mutilated and even cannibalized. When groups use ideologies to hide and distort reality, above all, when they interpret and justify certain historical realities by appealing to some abstract, universal, or necessary characteristics, all the while hiding the interests that really motivate their interpretation, the ideologies become twisted.

> This phenomenon of ideologization proves really dangerous because it has strict connections to social realities profoundly configured by both collective and individual consciousness. Therefore, any social system or social subsystem seeks ideological legitimation as a necessary part of its existence and/or good functioning. It is obvious that when this system is unjust or simply inert, its ideological apparatus surpasses the character of ideology and falls into that of ideologization.[16]

While historicization has an obvious utility in relation to socio-political concepts, it is Ellacuría's use of this method in relation to theological concepts that most concerns us here. Writing on such dogmatic themes as salvation and sacraments, he observes that "it is necessary to purge them of self-interested sacralization in order to recover their full meaning.

That is best done by *historicizing* them, which does not mean reciting their history but establishing their relationship to history."[17] The languages of faith and theology, and all other religious constructions of reality, make use of ideologies. Moreover, real partisan interests link theological ideologies to a variety of historical influences, including those exerted by various social forces. As a result, theologians can deploy ideologies in such a way that they mutate into idolatrous forms. This tends to happen precisely when those interests that make use of the ideology give the appearance of being detached from history and historical interests. In other words, the destructive uses of religion and its theological ideologies proliferate precisely where those who deploy them feign divinely authoritative immunity to the threat of falling into idolatry. But even when it falls short of actual idolatry, theology can deploy ideologies in such a way that their historical character becomes obscured. This proves toxic for a living faith. Because of these dangers, Ellacuría underscores the importance of attending to the social historical factors that constitutively condition theological discourse. With his method of historicizing concepts, he develops a philosophically rigorous way to respond to this formal exigence. Several general characteristics of historicization emerge consistently from these examples. I conclude this discussion and summarize Ellacuría's use of historicization by viewing these characteristics through the lens of the threefold encounter with reality. It will be helpful to refer to the table on the facing page.

First, in terms of the noetic level, *the process of historicization seeks to establish what is the relationship of a concept to historical reality.* Concepts themselves only exist in process, constantly shading their meanings and modulating their connotations. Hence, historicization engages them as historical concepts.

> The historical concept, because it refers immediately to historical realities, to changing realities which depend on the structural and conjunctive situation in which they are found, acquires a distinct meaning in accordance with the moment of the process and in accordance with the context in which it is found. Historical concepts refer to distinct realities in process: they refer to the same reality, but in a distinct mode of the process. In this they are like the analogous concepts of classical philosophy which maintain a certain unity of meaning although they refer to distinct realities.[18]

These dynamic realities must be engaged through a dynamic process. Historicization does not remove the concept from its history or fix its meaning once and for all. Rather, it reflects the open and open-ended

# Table 1: Schematic Outline of the Elements of Ellacuría's Theological Method

| | Realizing the weight of reality el hacerse cargo de la realidad | Shouldering the weight of reality el cargar con la realidad | Taking charge of the weight of reality el encargarse de la realidad |
|---|---|---|---|
| **Foundations of Method** | **Noetic Dimension** The noetic dimension entails being among the reality of things in their active and material dimensions. | **Ethical Dimension** The ethical dimension has to do with taking upon ourselves what things really are and what they really demand. | **Praxis-Oriented Dimension** The praxis-oriented dimension involves taking responsibility for doing something to actually transform reality. |
| | **Understanding** Understanding is conditioned by the actual possibilities of historical reality. | **Option of Place** What one knows and who one becomes both depend on where one chooses to place oneself. | **Action** Human activity creates capacities and actualizes possibilities; in this way it leads to transformation. |
| **Operations of Method** | **Historicization of Concepts** Historicization establishes what is the relationship of a concept to historical reality. | **Place of Historicization** Historicization derives from the turn to reality, but effects a return to reality via the place that affords greatest access to the real. | **Historicization as Praxis** Historicization deploys a modified dialectic both in theory and in praxis; it finds verification in the moment of praxis. |
| | **Utopia/ Propheticism** Propheticism animates the critical contrast between particular historical situations and the anticipated Reign of God that utopia historicizes. | **Persecution/ Martyrdom** Persecution and martyrdom are the verification that theology shoulders the weight of reality; hence, the task (as well as the content) of theology is soteriology. | **Theology/ Ecclesial Praxis** As the ideological moment of ecclesial praxis, theology guides that praxis to its proper place within the larger historical praxis by discerning where and how the church ought to incarnate itself. |

manner in which concepts emerge and live. Its results can be revised at a later time or in a different situation. Its application in one context might require a different set of criteria in a distinct setting. Thus, one must guard against historicizing a concept and then absolutizing the historicized product. All this follows from the simple observation that concepts manifest historicity both in their origins and in their ongoing use: every concept not only has a history but *is* historical. The process of historicization thus enables theology to discharge its interpretative task. It continually renews, clarifies, and purifies the connections between theological concepts and the historical-theologal realities to which those concepts refer. In this way historicization helps make possible both historical liberation and soteriological faith, but by itself it neither fully effects the former nor fully expresses the latter.

Second, regarding the ethical moment, *historicization derives from the turn to reality, but effects a return to reality via the place that affords the greatest access to the real.* The question of place is endemic to the process of historicization for the same reasons that theological place proves important to theological production. Some places prove helpful and others harmful to the authentic deployment of historicization. Ellacuría's examination of degenerate forms of ideologies sheds further light on why this is so and why the place of the poor is a privileged place both for theology as well as for the process of historicization. In his article on the historicization of human rights, he observes that "the human is not a univocal and abstract generality, repeated over and over in concrete humans, but, especially with regards to problems having to do with the law, it is a reality split between those who enjoy rights and those deprived of them. Even more to the point, humanity is a reality dialectically divided between the strong and the weak, the master and the slave, the oppressor and the oppressed."[19] In a divided world, where certain interests can only be pursued by suppressing or thwarting opposed interests, and where dominant ideologies reflect the interests of those with the greatest power and influence, the impulse toward destructive and even idolatrous applications of ideologies becomes virtually inexorable. Moreover, both neutral and destructive ideologies operate as forms of being in reality which come to constitute the collective consciousness of divided societies. Even those whose interests are frustrated by the dominant interpretations, internalize and passively accept them as if they represented the whole truth of reality.[20]

Just as the place of the poor represents the privileged *lugar teológico*, in the face of these socio-historical dynamics it appears as the best locus for historicization as well. Historicization requires a dialectical, critical moment. Moreover, it elicits a way of being in reality that seeks the priorities and interests of reality itself over one's own self- and group-interests. This recommendation appears counterintuitive for the same reasons that the Christian gospel scandalized Jews and struck Greeks as madness (1 Cor 1:23). Its logic comes to light in the relationship between truth and power. The capacities of conceptualization unleash real power, including that violent power which advances self- and group-interests by distorting the truth. The power to distort the truth about reality lays the foundations for the oppressive domination of reality and ultimately tends to destroy both community and self. In the tradition of the prophets, Ellacuría links the actualization of truthfulness to the renunciation of that domineering power which deception nurtures. The deideologization and historicization of concepts from the place of the poor steps courageously and concretely in the direction of embodying this renunciation.

Third, looking at the dimension of praxis, *historicization, which deploys a modified dialectic in both its theoretical and praxis-oriented moments, finds its verification through the moment of praxis.* By probing the interests underlying the formulation and use of particular concepts, historicization exercises a critical function. It also implies a negative moment, although it does not take up residence in negativity but pushes on to a concrete affirmation. More specifically, it actively seeks to negate a negation, to denounce and help reverse a negative contrast experience.[21] An obvious example makes this clear: if the concept of national security is deployed, not to protect the people of a nation but to rationalize the massacre of a village of unarmed peasants, the negativity of the process that exposes this fact achieves a positive end. It functions in favor of life.[22] As such, historicization must not only be ongoing but, in a real though limited sense, dialectical. "It attempts to look for the most profound roots of that negativity, without failing to remember that the real negativity, however real it may be, does not demonstrate all of its negativity except in contrast with some positivity which is more or less pre-thematically grasped."[23]

The massacre of innocent people is a ghastly and utterly negative thing. Likewise, the manipulation of a real (albeit limited) value like national security to cover up, rationalize, and justify such a crime is ghastly and negative. Where good journalistic or legal investigation aims to expose the original crime, the exercise of historicization seeks to prevent the ideological manipulation of it. The exposure of the ideological moment of dehumanizing praxis through the exercise of historicization must touch both the level of theory—revealing those on whose faces the truth of national security and insecurity is etched—and the level of praxis. Having historicized a concept, one must act accordingly. The critical component of historicization uncovers what has been covered up, including the historicity of the concept itself and the real historical interests to which the concept is linked by its use. It seeks to recover and restore the vital meaning of the concept by reestablishing its relationships to a humanizing historical reality. Conversely, the inappropriate universalization of concepts, the abstract, ahistorical use of ideas, leaves them impoverished. This implies that ideologization, not historicization, poses the real threat of reductionism. Historicization, as the negation of reductionism, represents the enrichment of concepts through the restoration of their relationship to historical reality and historical praxis.

## HISTORICIZING THE CHRISTIAN VISION

Ellacuría makes use of the process of historicization to help theology employ concepts and ideologies in a critical, ethical, and efficacious way. What happens when this method is applied not only to discreet theological concepts but to the Christian vision as a whole? An implicit answer to this question starts to emerge by turning to the eschatological-historical vision of Christian faith. Ellacuría reinterprets theology's horizon and method in terms of utopia and propheticism. As historicization enables theology to retrieve its historical concepts, place, and praxis, so too this dialectic contributes historical concreteness to the task of relating God's world and its future to actual historical reality. However, Christian theology cannot ground itself in the academy alone, nor in some privatized spirituality.[24] Because theology springs from, finds verification in, and returns to historical-ecclesial faith, commitment, and action, it needs to be an ecclesial theology. This realization underlies Ellacuría's view of Christian theology as the ideological moment of the ecclesial praxis which it serves. Finally, this theology engages its tasks in a bitterly divided world. As Christian, it is called to embrace the burden and the reproach of a sinful history where the real causes of division and oppression are covered up. Shouldering the weight of reality means directly confronting idols. For that reason it may involve literally bearing the cross.[25]

**Utopia and Propheticism.** Several months before he was assassinated, Ellacuría wrote his final theological essay, "Utopia and Propheticism from Latin America: A Concrete Essay in Historical Soteriology."[26] This dense and provocative title practically summarizes the intent and logic of his theological method. He calls this a *concrete* essay to indicate that it comes from and returns to an explicitly historical experience and place, Latin America. Hence, this is not an attempt to render a timeless, universal interpretation of the Christian vision. Instead, Ellacuría offers a historicized approach to a central theological discipline, soteriology. In so doing he introduces propheticism, a prophetic praxis or way of life, and links it to a utopia that incarnates the salvific content of the Christian vision. In his own words, he aims to depict "propheticism as method and utopia as horizon from the historical context of Latin America and from a perspective that is explicitly Christian with regards to both prophecy and utopia."[27]

Ellacuría insists that the object of theology—as understanding, as option, and as praxis—is the Reign of God. "The very thing that Jesus came to announce and realize, namely, the Reign of God, is what should become the unifying object of all Christian theology, including moral theology and pastoral practice. The greatest possible realization of the Reign of God in history is what the true followers of Jesus should pursue."[28] But how does theology make God's Reign its object? What does this look like in concrete, realistic terms? To begin with, Ellacuría argues that theology must historicize the Reign of God in order to apprehend, opt for, and serve it. He then adds that only a historical concretion of the Christian utopia can adequately historicize the Reign of God. "Up to a certain point, Christian utopia and the Reign of God can be considered the same, although when one speaks of Christian utopia one accents the utopian character of the Reign of God and not its other characteristics. But the concretion of utopia is what historicizes the Reign of God, both in the hearts of humans and in the structures without which that heart cannot live."[29]

The phrase, "the concretion of utopia," appears strange and paradoxical. This is due, in part, to the common view of utopia as nothing more than an impractical, unrealistic plan for social and political reform. Ellacuría critiques and rejects this view as idealistic and reductionistic. At the same time he avoids the counteractive impulse to simply banish all utopianism. In place of these two extremes, he retrieves an understanding of utopia grounded in historical realism. In the course of this retrieval, he also qualifies and deepens historical reality's openness.

> To think that utopia in its own intrinsic formality is something outside of every historical place and time supposes an emphasis on a single characteristic of utopia to the neglect of its real nature as it is found in the thought of those who have been true utopians in one form or another.

There is no escape from the historicity of place and time, although neither
is it inevitable to remain locked into the limits of a certain place and a
certain time.[30]

Ellacuría constructs his approach to utopia on this important realization.
The historical concretion of utopia cannot be worked out ahead of time
by appealing to an a priori, ahistorical ideal. Nor can it be reproduced
in a purely academic retrieval of a biblical concept such as Reign of God.
Rather, the historically embodied religious imagination must fashion
concrete ideals, that is, historically real possibilities capable of responding
critically and prophetically to the restless desire for the Reign of God.
This can only be done from a real historical situation and through the
critical praxis of a people working to actualize these ideals. Only in this
way can one overcome both the idealistic caricature which removes
utopia from historical reality and the anti-utopian reaction that eliminates
its theologal openness.

Ellacuría does not treat utopia as a mere concept. Here, too, place
and praxis prove integral to his constructive approach. One begins to
apprehend the general and undefined Christian utopia in relation to
God's Reign as one makes an option for the Reign and its values, and
as one unleashes the Reign by acting to establish that which historicizes
it, namely, the concrete Christian utopia. Significantly, this argument
reflects a basic thread running through the entire Christian tradition.
The church in every age has sought at least implicitly to historicize the
eschatological thrust of the Christian vision and to embody that vision
in its moral teachings and spiritual life.

Although liberation theology has historicized the Reign in its own way,
all of the church's tradition has always tried to do this. If one reads, for
example, *Gaudium et Spes* or the various papal encyclicals on the church's
social teaching, one sees there the need to historicize, if not the Reign,
at least the faith and the Christian message. Whether this be done with
greater or lesser prophetic and utopian vigor, the need to do it is still recognized.[31]

Thus, in seeking to historicize the Christian vision, Ellacuría stands in
continuity with the whole Christian tradition. Explicitly historicizing that
vision in terms of the Reign of God elicits the biblical tradition that
perhaps most closely reflects the preaching of Jesus himself. It also
connects him to one of the more spirited theological debates of the last
century and a half. However, Ellacuría develops a distinctive voice within
that debate: he insists that the best possible concretion of the general

Christian utopia appears only in conjunction with propheticism, and he undertakes to retrieve the Reign of God in that light.[32]

Ellacuría defines propheticism as "the critical contrasting of the proclamation of the fullness of the Reign of God with a specific historical situation."[33] Like the method of historicization, propheticism adopts the dynamic structure implicit in the encounter with reality in order to operate as a critical, dialectical, and praxis-oriented method. Like utopia, with which it emerges and operates, propheticism springs from and acts upon historical reality in the light of Christian faith.

> Propheticism, rightly understood in its complexity, is at the origin of the universal and general utopia. . . . Without propheticism, there is no possibility of making a Christian concretion of utopia and, consequently, a historical realization of the Reign of God. Without an intense and genuine exercise of Christian propheticism, the concretion of Christian utopia cannot be arrived at theoretically, much less practically. Here too the law cannot replace grace, the institution cannot replace life, established tradition cannot replace radical newness of the Spirit.[34]

A historically concrete utopia can represent the Christian utopia only if it exists in concert with a propheticism grounded in the Reign of God. At the same time, propheticism needs utopia grounded in the Reign of God to help it remain Christian. "Christian propheticism lives on Christian *utopia*, which, as utopia, largely lives and feeds on the summons issued by the Spirit throughout history, but as *Christian*, largely lives on the proclamation and the promise that are explicitly and implicitly expressed in the revelation already given."[35] Without propheticism, which animates the critical contrast between the anticipated Reign of God and the particular historical situation, that Reign cannot be adequately historicized as a general utopia. This does not mean, on the one hand, confusing or conflating the religious symbol of God's Reign with any given historical arrangement. But, on the other, neither does it allow that Reign to be utterly divorced from history. The dialectic of utopia and propheticism produces the concrete horizon of a historicized ideal which allows the negative contrast experience to appear in all its negativity. Without propheticism, utopia tends to be little more than a romantic fantasy, an attractive, abstract evasion of historical commitment. Without propheticism grounded in historical reality, the Christian vision, and utopia, to say nothing of theology, have no case against the famous indictment associated with Marx. But prophetic religion is not opium.

> If [religion] is more a protest than a mere expression, if it is more a struggle than a mere comfort, if it does not remain a mere sigh, if the

protest and contrast become historical utopia which negates the present and impels into the future; if, in short, prophetic action is initiated, then history is made by way of repudiating and surpassing and not by way of evading. Thanks to its propheticism, utopia does not fail to be efficacious in history, even though it is not fully realizable in history, as is the case with Christian utopia.[36]

Ellacuría grounds the dialectic of utopia and propheticism in the Reign of God which Jesus preached and which the Holy Spirit continues to animate. Drawing on a trinitarian understanding of revelation, he links the foundational Christian revelation disclosed in the historical Jesus with the ongoing revelation that takes flesh in human efforts to construct concrete utopias under the inspiration of the Spirit. "Priority in the fullness of Christian action is to be attributed to the revelation and the promise of Jesus, even in the destructive phase of the propheticism. This is yet more valid when what is sought is to realize God's will or designs, for whose discernment both the Spirit of Christ and the historical outlines of Jesus of Nazareth's journey through history are indispensable."[37] In the play of possibility and actualization, the dialectical interplay of utopia and propheticism critiques, corrects, and forges the emergent historical reality. Likewise, the conjunction of utopia and propheticism unveils history as the place of real transcendence. God elects to make history the theophanic place, although Scripture offers no direct reasons or explanations for God's choice. "History is the arena of novelty, of creativity. God's self-revelation comes by making *more* history, that is, a greater and better history than existed in the past."[38] But if history serves as the place of God's self-revelation, it does not do so mechanically. As with the unfolding of history itself, the revelatory moment occurs through the exercise of human freedom in collaboration with God.[39] Moreover, for history to be revelatory it must also be read with the aid of the Spirit. When humans read history under the guidance of the Spirit, they discover there the signs of the times. These signs, first read in history as possibility and promise, must then be acted on. They must be actualized in the strict Zubirian sense.[40] But the human actualization through which God is revealed in history, while fully human, remains strictly grace.

What propheticism gathers and expresses is the historical-transcendent intercession of the Spirit, which makes present the utopia already offered and contrasts it with the signs of the times. Thus, propheticism and utopia, history and transcendence, nourish each other. Both are historical and both are transcendent, but neither becomes what it is meant to become except in relation to the other.[41]

**The Ideological Moment of Ecclesial Praxis.** Sentient intelligence orients the human to reality while unleashing the reality-transforming processes of history. Building his theological method on this anthropological foundation, Ellacuría identifies the factors which condition theological production and situates that production against a prophetic-utopian horizon. At the same time, theology explicitly embraces praxis, the social-historical creation and actualization of possibilities by means of which human ingenuity, courage, cooperation, and persistence, or the lack thereof, shape historical reality. This dimension appears concretely in his descriptions of theology as "the ideological moment of ecclesial praxis," and as "the reflection from faith on the historical reality and action of the people of God, who follow the work of Jesus in announcing and fulfilling the Kingdom."[42] Stated negatively, theology is not the ahistorical contemplation of unchanging verities, nor is it a form of absolute knowing completely above the vicissitudes of history, completely superior to all other forms of knowing. "It takes a more or less biased naïveté to believe that theology, at least when it does not refer explicitly to practical questions, enjoys a special status which makes it immune from every disfiguring conditioning factor."[43]

This historicization of theology makes bold claims on the ecclesial community and striking demands on theologians. Any theology that ignores or denies its own conditioning factors risks exposing religious faith to manipulative uses of ideologies and becomes itself a form of ideological opium, if not manifest idolatry. For this reason, Ellacuría explicitly relates theological production, on the one hand, to the conflict-ridden dynamics of social-historical praxis that shape historical reality and, on the other, to the dynamics that incarnate the Reign of God in history. To effect this move, he also articulates the internal connections between theological production and ecclesial praxis, along with the methodological starting point of the former and the frame of reference of the latter.

> If historical praxis is a divided praxis, if in this divided historical praxis the Reign of God and the reign of evil become present and operative, if the ecclesial praxis cannot be neutral with respect to this division and this operative presence, if the theological task receives its truth, its verification, from its incarnation in the true ecclesial praxis, in a truly Christian ecclesial praxis, then it must be asked, in what form of ecclesial praxis

should its ideological moment of theological production incarnate itself? Appealing to the Reign of God is not quite enough. Rather, it is necessary to determine the place in which the truth of the Reign of God is most accessible.[44]

To address the question about the form that ecclesial praxis should take, Ellacuría again draws upon the essential logic of his theological method. His manner of doing this can be summarized as a thesis dealing with the task and goal of theology. *Theology, operating from a concrete historical place, conceptualizes the link between historical reality and the Reign of God which ecclesial praxis incarnates.* A set of parallel, subordinating relations lie embedded in the logic of this thesis. On the one hand, theology appears as a moment of ecclesial praxis. "Theology should place itself at the service of ecclesial praxis whenever that praxis is Christian or in order that it be so."[45] This identification of theology within the wider framework of ecclesial praxis elicits the awareness that the theological task constitutes a form of ministry. On the other hand, ecclesial praxis shows up as a moment in the larger historical praxis to which it brings the Good News of the Reign of God. Thus, theology serves the mission of the church, not the church as an end in itself. Put another way, theology serves the Reign of God to which the church itself is oriented. At its best, ecclesial theology maintains a critical, prophetic edge and a creative, utopian urgency.

> Establishing theology as a moment of ecclesial praxis highlights the fact that theological production is not an autonomous theoretical undertaking, but an element within a broader structure. Ecclesial praxis is taken here in the broad sense which includes every undertaking of the church that is in some fashion historical, understanding by the church a community of humans who, in one way or another, realize the Reign of God. This latter referent is chosen in order to stress the aspect of praxis, that is, of transformative action, which the church necessarily assumes in its historical pilgrimage.[46]

When viewed as a moment of ecclesial praxis, theology avoids turning in on itself. However, it cannot serve just any ecclesial praxis. Theology retains its Christian character precisely insofar as the ecclesial praxis which it serves renounces self-centeredness in favor of a wholehearted commitment to the horizon of Jesus. Therefore, for theology to be authentically Christian, the ecclesial praxis that it serves must incarnate itself in history on behalf of the Reign of God.

To incarnate itself in history, ecclesial praxis needs to conceptualize its relationship to historical praxis. Ellacuría maintains that Christian ecclesial praxis enjoys a relative autonomy vis-à-vis the historical praxis within which it is ultimately embedded. Both elements in this claim prove significant. The relative autonomy of ecclesial praxis, which rests epistemologically on the singularity of its object and sociologically on the specialization of its functions, finds its theological ground in the theologal dimension of reality, a dimension that allows theology to postulate the "more" of historical reality. But however much one might insist on the uniqueness and extramundane focus of theology, of faith, and of ecclesial praxis, all three are distinctively located within the horizon of historical reality and function as part of historical praxis. This fact cannot be denied without an idealistic reduction that disfigures them. The moment of ecclesial praxis unfolds as part of the total praxis of universal history, not as the totality itself, nor even its central determining element. This assertion, which can be further linked to and illuminated by a theory of secularization,[47] recognizes that ecclesial praxis lacks the material conditions to dominate the course of history. At the same time, the recognition that ecclesial praxis cannot dictate the course of history corresponds to the inner exigence of Christian faith itself. As the parable of Jesus would have it, the Christian moment within history represents the leaven, not the loaf.

> The church does not have sufficient corporeality or materiality to bring about the immediate fulfillment of this political order, which extends to everything from collective knowledge to social organization, from the structures of power to social forces; other entities exist for that purpose. But the church does have the function of leavening, that is, the ferment that transforms the dough to make of it the bread of life, human bread that gives life to human beings; the dough of the world and its organization is a necessary condition for the church, while the church's appropriate role is to become salt which inhibits corruption and leavening which transforms the dough from within.[48]

Theology guides ecclesial praxis to its proper place within the whole of historical praxis by discerning where and how the church ought to incarnate itself. It discharges this responsibility not by centering on timeless truths, nor even on the church alone, but by taking as its primary object the Reign of God and the relationship of the church to God's Reign. Ellacuría arrives at this central affirmation by turning to the historical Jesus and arguing that every ecclesial praxis should stem from the church's primary mission to follow him. "If the fundamental object of the mission of Jesus was the Reign of God, then it should be so as well for ecclesial praxis and for the ideological moment of that praxis."[49] But precisely here discernment is needed, for ecclesial praxis must align itself with no other Reign of God than the one announced by Jesus. "Theological production is not an end in itself, nor does it have roots in itself, but neither can it subordinate itself to just any ecclesial praxis. For while ecclesial praxis as a whole and to the end cannot fundamentally separate itself from the following of Jesus, it can do so in particular moments and in large sectors of what makes up the ecclesial structure."[50] On the basis of this crucial observation, and with an implicit appeal to the tensively related Christian doctrines of grace and sin, Ellacuría outlines a fundamental ecclesiology that views the church in terms of its praxis, a praxis that both fashions history and mediates the Reign of God. On the one hand, the Spirit guides and abides in the church. On the other hand, human beings, including those who make up the church, sin. They do so not only individually, but corporately, through the very institutions that structure the church. For this reason, simply being linked to a particular ecclesial structure cannot insure that theological reflection will be true or even Christian. Rather, ecclesial praxis must measure itself according to the demands of the Reign of God that appear in any given historical situation. "There exists, therefore, a hermeneutical circulation which goes from the Reign to praxis but returns from praxis to the Reign, where both poles are gradually reinterpreted through the presence and influence of the Spirit of Christ."[51] Because history embodies a division between oppressors and the victims of oppression, the option for the latter creates the way into this hermeneutical circle delineated by ecclesial praxis in service of the Reign of God.

Ellacuría emphasizes that, while the Reign of God cannot be separated from God, neither does it function here as a cipher for God. Although the Reign "formally includes God, it formally includes God's reigning in history, [and] includes them in intrinsic unity."[52] This articulation of the parameters for speaking about the Reign of God bears a structural similarity to the christological formula of Chalcedon. There is the divine element, the Reign of *God*, which "appeals to the totality of God revealed by Jesus and in Jesus, but appeals to this totality according to the very mode of the revelation of Jesus."[53] Paradoxically, the Reign manifests the unbounded openness of transcendence that is, at the same time, limited to the framework proposed by Jesus. This framework is captured, though not exhausted, by the tradition that revelation constitutes. Moreover, as the reigning of God in history, the Reign of God points to the dynamic action and the real place where the presence of God in Jesus Christ is realized: the realm of the human, the sphere of the historical. "By being the *Reign* of God it appeals to history and humanity as the

place of the presence and action of God in Jesus Christ. It is not easy
for theology to demonstrate how this Reign should be in order to actually
be the Reign of God, but it is a task as fundamental as that of showing
who the God of the Reign is."[54] Finally, the Reign of God is *one*. It
represents a radical unity both as a reality and as a historical structural
concept. "For this reason, Latin American theology does not agree with
those who refer to its proper object as social praxis, such as the social
doctrine of the church formulates it. . . . Liberation theology is concerned
about historical praxis, but this does not mean that, formally, its object
or theme is social justice. On the contrary, its theme and its object is
the Reign of God."[55]

From this analysis it follows that the Reign of God takes on historical
reality as a dynamic mediation between the historical and transhistorical.
"The reality of the Reign of God implies in itself the problem of its
realization: it is a reality in the process of being realized. Theological
reflection, therefore, has to confront itself directly with what constitutes
the realization of the Reign of God. As the fundamental object of theological reflection is not God but the Reign of God, the aspect of realization
turns out to be decisive."[56] Hence, by inserting itself within the totality
of historical praxis through the mediation of ecclesial praxis, theology
does more than reflect on the Reign of God. As a response to grace it
participates in the historical realization of that Reign. Once again, this
does not mean that theology should take responsibility for economic or
political tasks. Nor does it imply a denigration of the theoretical or
academic elements in the theological task.[57] But it does mean that theology can only engage its proper tasks in dialogue with historical experience. It implies further that theology must make use of the social sciences
to help it concretize, clarify, and deepen its grasp of the historical praxis
within which it is embedded at any given moment.

In light of the church's appropriate function and role, the importance
of theological place once again comes into view, now in relation to
theological praxis. Even while historical place conditions praxis, historical
praxis constructs place. As a concrete instance of historical *reality*, place
serves praxis as one of its necessary conditions and intrinsic components.
As a moment in *historical* reality, every place appears in a process of
praxis-oriented reconfiguration. Consequently, the praxis-oriented place
of theology proves both historically constructed and history-making.
Likewise, as a moment within the totality of historical praxis, ecclesial
praxis is determined to a great extent by the particular place from which
it encounters that totality. This observation assumes a special importance
insofar as the divisions that afflict the totality of human history condition

every historical praxis. This means that theology's historical horizon is a fractured whole.

**Persecution and Martyrdom.** If the notion of theological place informs Ellacuría's understanding of theology in relation to ecclesial praxis, it similarly influences his view of the dialectic of utopia and propheticism. It was noted above that a theology of historical reality highlights the critical relationship between theological place and theological reflection and between the place of historicization and the effective use of that deideologizing process. So, too, with the dialectic of utopia and propheticism.

> To achieve an adequate conjunction of utopia and propheticism. . .it is necessary to situate oneself in the proper historical place. Every conjunction of these two human and historical dimensions, if it is to be realistic and fruitful, must "situate itself" in precise geo-socio-temporal coordinates. Otherwise the unavoidable thrust of the principle of reality disappears, and without it both utopia and propheticism are mental games, more formal than real.[58]

The sobriety with which Ellacuría searches for an adequate theological place also animates his search for the place of utopia and propheticism.

> It is said that in cultures that have grown old there is no longer a place for propheticism and utopia, but only for pragmatism and selfishness, for the countable verification of results, for the scientific calculation of input and output, or, at best, for institutionalizing, legalizing, and ritualizing the spirit that renews all things. Whether this situation is inevitable or not, there are nonetheless still places where hope is not simply the cynical adding up of infinitesimal calculations; they are places to hope and to give hope against all the dogmatic verdicts that shut the door on the future of utopia and propheticism and the struggle. One of these places is Latin America.[59]

Ellacuría deploys the prophetic-utopian dialectic not only from Latin America but for Latin America, and for a reordering of global structures and relations that reflects what the view from Latin America discloses. The emphasis on the particularity of place does not lead to relativism or the rejection of moral principles with a universal applicability. On the contrary, it is precisely in terms of the unity of historical reality that Ellacuría critiques the present global order and rejects its false utopias:

> The offer of humanization and freedom that the rich countries make to the poor countries is not universalizable and consequently is not human,

even for those who make it. Kant's keen way of putting it could be applied to this problem. Act in such a manner that the maxim of your will can always serve, at the same time, as the principle of a universal law (*Critique of Practical Reason*). If the behavior and even the ideal of a few cannot become the behavior and the reality of the greater part of humanity, that behavior and that ideal cannot be said to be moral or even human, all the more so if the enjoyment of a few is at the cost of depriving the rest. In our world, the practical ideal of Western civilization is not universalizable, not even materially, since there are not enough material resources on earth today to let all countries achieve the same level of production and consumption as that of the countries called wealthy, whose total population is less than 25 percent of humanity.[60]

Ellacuría argues that a genuine universalization can be achieved only through a preferential option: the option for the poor. Although this argument appears counterintuitive, it capitalizes on the fundamental logic of his description of historical reality. The partiality of the option for the poor does not contradict the universality which reason seeks. Rather, it makes that universality possible and capable of being historically realized. Through this option a world order that extends support to all people, including the poorest, can become a historically real possibility.

Ellacuría further details the logic of the option for the theological place of the poor by linking the dialectic of utopia and propheticism to the distinctive mission which the church fulfills through its evangelical praxis. Ecclesial praxis needs to assume an evangelical conjunction of utopia and propheticism because it finds itself embedded in a larger historical praxis that is fragmented and riven with conflict. Like Christian theological understanding, Christian theological praxis finds itself lodged amidst the historical divisions of this fractured totality. It may enjoy a certain degree of autonomy, yet it remains configured ultimately by what it takes from other moments of historical praxis, as well as by the inner logic that impels it to put itself at the service of historical reality as a whole. The conjunction of these two elements, being configured by historical particularity and being called to serve history as a whole, proves significant for ecclesial praxis. It means that theology's fundamental discernment involves this question of place.

> If theology understands itself as the ideological moment of ecclesial praxis, if, within the universal historical praxis, ecclesial praxis takes the side of those who suffer the sin and injustice of the world, if this ecclesial praxis is that of a church of the poor which seeks, by its own means, the realization of the Reign of God in history, then theological production,

whose fundamental object is the Reign of God and whose radical objective is the realization of this Reign, will generate the optimal conditions for realizing its own undertaking in a Christian manner.[61]

Ellacuría insists that the discernment regarding theological place fundamentally affects ecclesial praxis. This is negatively confirmed by efforts to bypass such a discernment. When ecclesial praxis pretends to serve the whole of history by assuming an impartial stance toward all of history's conflicting interests, it only deludes itself. Ahistorical attempts to rise above all divisions tend to generate an idealized *notion* of the church in history, a hollow *ethics*, and a covert, possibly dishonest, *praxis* that in fact contributes to one side or the other. As an alternative, Ellacuría proposes that "the historical mode of situating oneself in the totality involves incorporating oneself reflexively on one of its opposing sides in order to take on the opposition and in this way manage to overcome it."[62] This strategy acknowledges the possibility of detecting the operation of structural principles of evil and good in concrete circumstances. At the same time it recognizes the profound extent to which every theology is political theology. Yet it does not necessitate a Manichean dualism that locates all the good on one side and all the evil on the other. Rather, Ellacuría's view of historical reality once again comes into play: where history is divided, historical praxis serves the whole through the part. Moreover, in this divided history, the theological place of the victims and an option on their behalf situates ecclesial praxis within the orbit of the Reign of God.

A corollary attends the Christian discernment which places ecclesial praxis and theology at the service of history's victims. Because historical reality is divided by oppression, interpreting reality in the light of God's Reign and, above all, actively transforming reality into that Reign, necessarily implies unmasking and fighting against the anti-Reign. Stated bluntly, a real theological commitment to the realization of the Reign of God almost inevitably leads to conflict, often brings on persecution and, in the extreme, ends with martyrdom. Theology and ecclesial praxis find their real place at the foot of the cross. For many, this language evokes little more than the pious images associated with certain devotional traditions. For Ellacuría it points to the historically real cost of discipleship. By definition, a theology that "shoulders the weight" engages the terrifying depths of human history with bold faith and sober historical realism.

> A Reign of God which does not enter into conflict with a history configured
> by the power of sin is not the Reign of God of Jesus, however deeply

spiritual it may appear, just as a Reign of God which does not enter into conflict with the malice and evil of personal existence is not the Reign of God of Jesus. We have, thus, a historically verifiable criterion, a verification much more certain and profound than that of a presumed and partial conformity with theoretical formulas. This is not simply a problem of orthodoxy and orthopraxis, because the praxis which is sought here is the *true* and complete realization of the Reign of God.[63]

In the final analysis, ecclesial praxis and theology seek the realization of the Reign of God, the full revelation of the mercy of God. Therefore, the theologian, as a person of faith really affected by the negativity of historical reality, must incarnate theology in a very specific praxis. Sobrino calls it the praxis of mercy. "Theology becomes converted in its very task and not only in the contents which it offers, into soteriology. It becomes compassionate reason."[64] In a brilliant development of Ella-curía's insistence that theology must shoulder the weight of reality, Sobrino calls this dimension "the principle of mercy." To the traditional understanding of theology as faith seeking understanding, *intellectus fidei*, he adds the image of theology as *intellectus amoris*, love seeking understanding.

The theology of liberation insists that there are not only limitations and tragedies in reality, but there exists *sin*, personal and structural, as a form of death. In this manner it emphasizes the radicality of the negative dimension of reality, in both the subjective and objective realms. And it affirms that the *intellectus* must shoulder the weight of this reality *qua* burden. In fact, if the *intellectus amoris* really "carries the weight of reality," it immediately comes face to face with the dialectical and dualistic dimensions of reality. Reality *qua* sin fights against anyone who wants to transform it into grace. In the language of the synoptic gospels, the anti-Reign fights against the Reign. Therefore, sin is not only there, but it lashes back, and it presents theology with the dilemma of taking on this backlash in the form of persecution and martyrdom, of "shouldering the weight of reality" or "allowing oneself to be carried along by reality."[65]

The principle of mercy involves a principle of justice and a principle of liberation, too.[66] But mercy, justice, and liberation become historically concrete only at great cost. The willingness to apprehend, embrace, and transform reality invites the disciple of Jesus into the fate of Jesus. "Persecution and martyrdom are the greatest verification that the *intellectus* has shouldered the weight of reality. But this, at the same time, has helped the *intellectus* to better perceive the weight of reality and apprehend how to take charge of it."[67] In the case of Ellacuría, the implications of theology as *intellectus amoris* appear with stunning clarity. As a theologian, he articulated the connections between perceiving, shouldering, and transforming historical reality. As a martyr, he verified them.

### Notes to Chapter 5

1. "Tesis sobre teología," No. 2.5 (1975) 326, trans. mine.
2. Karl Rahner, "Theology," in K. Rahner, ed., *Encyclopedia of Theology: The Concise Sacramentum Mundi* (New York: Crossroad, 1975, 1991) 1687, author's emphasis.
3. In "The Church of the Poor, Historical Sacrament of Liberation," Ellacuría writes: "The theology of liberation understands itself as a reflection from faith on the historical reality and action of the people of God, who follow the work of Jesus in announcing and fulfilling God's Reign," "Sacramento histórico" (1977) 127, trans. Wilde, emended; *MLT*, 543. I examine this definition at greater length in chapter 7, section three.
4. "Teología frente al cambio" (1987) 241, trans. Brockman; *TSSP*, 19.
5. Ibid., 242, trans. Brockman, emended; *TSSP*, 20–21.
6. I return to this assertion and its theological implications when I examine Ellacuría's treatment of historical transcendence; see chapter 6.
7. I consistently translate *historización* with its English cognate, "historicization," even though this term has no fixed meaning in English. Some authors use it with pejorative intent to denote a reductionistic process. For Ellacuría, by contrast, historicization represents a positive, practical step toward unveiling the truth of some historical reality. I explore this claim in relation to his philosophy of historical reality in the pages to follow. For additional secondary sources that devote serious attention to the theme of historicization, see Schubeck, *Liberation Ethics*, op. cit., 116–126; Mardones; Sajid Alfredo Herrera, "Aproximación al método de historización de Ignacio Ellacuría," in A. González, ed., *Para Una Filosofía Liberadora* (San Salvador: UCA Editores, 1995) 31–39, hereafter cited as "Herrera"; Omar Serrano, "Sobre el método de la historización de los conceptos de Ignacio Ellacuría," ibid., 41–50, hereafter cited as "Serrano."
8. *FRH*, 169.
9. Commenting on this same point, Robert Lassalle-Klein observes that "Ellacuría uses the term historicization to refer to the incorporative and transformative power which human praxis exerts over the historical and natural dimensions of reality. . . . Praxis appropriates from historical tradition its concepts, values, practices, and other ways of being in reality, simultaneously being shaped by and transforming them. In its primary sense, then, historicization refers to this process," Lassalle-Klein, "The Body of Christ," 68.
10. "Propiedad" (1976) 591; *TSSP*, 109. Ellacuría often plays off of the rich multiplicity of meanings at work in the term, *realidad*. Insofar as it serves as a "primary term" in his philosophical vocabulary, I almost always translate it by its English cognate, "reality." However, in this instance Ellacuría speaks of a *determinada realidad* to stress the specificity of the actual setting, the determinate situation or particular context, in which a concept is used. Thus, I follow Berryman's translation of this idiomatic text; see also Lassalle-Klein, "The Body of Christ," 68.

11. "Propiedad" (1976) 590, trans. mine; *TSSP*, 108. See Schubeck, *Liberation Ethics*, 119.
12. See "Propiedad" (1976); "Bien común" (1978); "Derechos humanos" (1990). In the last of these articles, "The Historicization of Human Rights from the Oppressed Peoples and Popular Majorities," Ellacuría focuses on the concept of human rights from the context of El Salvador near the end of the terrible civil war (and shortly before his own assassination). Various vested interests on all sides of the conflict were appealing to "human rights" to validate their particular agendas and behaviors. In response, Ellacuría sets out to (1) verify the actual extent to which various appeals to human rights bring about truth or falsehood, justice or injustice, social order or disorder, (2) establish whether the alleged rights serve the minority in power or the marginalized majority, (3) examine the real conditions to be met so that implementing the rights might at least become an actual possibility, (4) deideologize the idealized approaches that hinder the substantial changes that must occur if the right is to be effectively implemented and not only affirmed as possible or desirable, and (5) introduce a timeframe that quantifies by which time the proclaimed ideals should have achieved some acceptable degree of realization. It is significant to note that the first of these five steps explicitly links historicization to the three dimensions of the human confrontation with reality. A concept must be historicized in terms of whether it is true or false (the epistemological issue), whether it is just or unjust (the ethical issue), and whether it promotes order or disorder (the praxis-oriented or political issue). See "Derechos humanos" (1990) 590.
13. "Propiedad" (1976) 588, trans. mine; *TSSP*, 106.
14. See "Función liberadora" (1985). Ellacuría's distinction comes across more directly in Spanish where he uses two related but different words, *ideología* and *ideologización*. A similar distinction appears in the work of Juan Luis Segundo; see, for example, Juan Luis Segundo, *The Liberation of Theology*, op. cit.; *Faith and Ideologies*, trans. by John Drury (Maryknoll: Orbis, 1984).
15. See "Función liberadora" (1985) 48.
16. Ibid., 49.
17. "Sacramento histórico de la liberación" (1977) 128, trans. Wilde, author's emphasis; *MLT*, 544. I focus extensively on the content of Ellacuría's historicization of salvation in chapters 6 and 7. I examine his historicization of the church-as-sacrament in the final section of chapter 7.
18. "Propiedad" (1976) 590, trans. mine; *TSSP*, 108.
19. "Derechos humanos" (1990) 590.
20. Ellacuría contends that "to challenge the role played by ideology, we must first define what the predominant ideology is, and how it is the ideology of society itself as it is structured at a particular moment. When Durkheim spoke of a collective consciousness as a body of beliefs and feelings shared by most of the members of a society, he was recognizing a fundamental social fact. However, this group consciousness, although reflective of most people, is constituted by the interests of the concrete form of that society, based on the interests of the ruling class. This is another social fact that it would be unfortunate to overlook. We must ask how this group consciousness is shaped and whom it serves. The answer is not difficult if we can find out what purposes the educational system serves and who controls the media," "Propiedad" (1976) 589–590, trans. Berryman; *TSSP*, 107.
21. This dialectic of negation and affirmation reappears below in the discussion of propheticism and utopia. Ellacuría observes that "there exists a mutually empowering relationship between utopia and denunciation. Without a certain, at least pre-

thematic, estimate of an ideal that is possible and necessary, one will not be aware that something can be surmounted. But without the effective verification. . .that a negation exists which is a privation and a violation, awareness will not be converted into a real exigence and dynamism in the struggle [to overcome it]," "Derechos humanos" (1990) 592. Regarding the importance of negative experiences of contrast for theology, see Edward Schillebeeckx, *God the Future of Man*, trans. by N. D. Smith (New York: Sheed and Ward, 1968) 136, 153–154, 164; Roger Haight, *Dynamics of Theology*, op. cit., 158.

22. For example, see Mark Danner, *The Massacre at El Mozote*, op. cit; Ricardo Falla, *Massacres in the Jungle: Ixcán, Guatemala, 1975–1982*, trans. by Julia Howland (Boulder: Westview Press, 1994).

23. "Derechos humanos" (1990) 592. For the "real though limited" way that historicization must be dialectical, recall Ellacuría's thesis on the dialectic in his analysis of the structure of reality.

24. See J. Matthew Ashley, *Interruptions: Mysticism, Politics, and Theology in the Work of Johann Baptist Metz*, op. cit., 1–26; "A Post-Einsteinian Settlement? On Spirituality as a Possible Border-Crossing between Religion and the New Sciences," in M. P. Aquino and R. Goizueta, eds., *Theology: Expanding the Borders* (Mystic, Conn.: Twenty-Third Publications, 1998) 80–108.

25. This reference to the cross "does not have to do with an expiatory masochism of a spiritualizing sort, but with the discovery of a historical reality. Consequently, it does not have to do with mourning and mortification, but with rupture and commitment," "El pueblo crucificado," (1978) 196, trans. mine; *MLT*, 587.

26. The original title of this essay in Spanish, "Utopía y profetismo desde América Latina: Un ensayo concreto de soteriología histórica," was edited for the *ML* version. Likewise, the English translation of this article, "Utopia and Prophecy in Latin America," omits the subtitle completely. A note on the translation: in the title and throughout this essay, Ellacuría uses a somewhat rare Spanish word, *profetismo*, which Brockman translates "prophecy." However, the Spanish equivalent of prophecy is *profecía*. I consider the most accurate translation of *profetismo* to be "propheticism." This somewhat archaic word comes very close to the meaning Ellacuría intends: a prophetic way of life, a life imbued with a prophetic vision, option, and praxis. To remain consistent, I emend "prophecy" to "propheticism" when I quote from Brockman's translation.

27. Ibid., 394; trans. mine; *MLT*, 290.

28. "Religiones abrahámicas" (1987) 9, trans. mine; quoted in Sobrino, *Liberator*, 105.

29. "Utopía y profetismo" (1989) 395, trans. mine; *MLT*, 291. Ellacuría's unusual Spanish term, *concreción*, and its equally rare English cognate, "concretion," speak of something being made concrete, of its being embodied. Hence, concretion is close in meaning to embodiment. While this latter term might make for a smoother English translation, I follow Brockman here, mainly because his term achieves what Ellacuría intends, the direct linking of theological content, method, and genre (recall that this is a *concrete* essay in historical soteriology).

30. Ibid., 394, trans. mine; *MLT*, 290.

31. Ibid., 395, trans. mine; *MLT*, 291.

32. Ellacuría's approach to the Reign of God has been adopted and amplified in the later christological writings of Jon Sobrino; see, for example, Sobrino, *Liberator*, 67–134; "Central Position of the Reign of God in Liberation Theology," in *MLT*, 1993, 350–386. Instructive contrasts can be drawn between Ellacuría's historicization

of the Reign of God and the important works of Rudolf Bultmann and Wolfhart Pannenberg. While Bultmann radically recovers the eschatological and critical dimensions of Christian revelation, the Reign of God itself does not factor strongly into his interpretation of these. Likewise, his heavy emphasis on the existential and subjective acceptance of the kerygma practically ignores the irruption of God's Reign in history and renders his theology virtually asocial and ahistorical. See Rudolf Bultmann, *Theology of the New Testament*, trans. by Kendrick Grobel (New York: Charles Scribner's Sons, 1951) 3–32; Mark Chapman, "The Kingdom of God and Ethics: From Ritschl to Liberation Theology," in R. S. Barbour, ed., *The Kingdom of God and Human Society* (Edinburgh: T&T Clark, 1993)153–156; Sobrino, *Liberator*, 110–112. Pannenberg's reflections on the Reign of God go beyond Bultmann's ahistorical existentialism, for he attempts to view the Reign as bearing not only on eschatology but on Christian ethics as well; Wolfhart Pannenberg, *Theology and the Kingdom of God* (Philadelphia: Westminster Press, 1969, 1977) 79–80; *Jesus, God and Man* (Philadelphia: Westminster Press, 1968, 1977) 225–235. However, he attempts to affirm the social-historical-ethical function of God's Reign without explicit attention to its being for the poor, its opposition to the antiReign, and its relation to a salvation in and of history; see Sobrino, *Liberator*, 112–117.

33. "Utopía y profetismo" (1989) 396, trans. mine; *MLT*, 292; see also Ignacio Ellacuría, "Diez afirmaciones sobre 'Utopia' y 'Profetismo,'" *ST* (no. 917, 1989) 889.

34. "Utopía y profetismo" (1989) 395–396, trans. Brockman, emended; *MLT*, 291.

35. Ibid., 397–398, trans. mine, emphasis mine; *MLT*, 293.

36. Ibid., 397, trans. Brockman, emended; *MLT*, 293.

37. Ibid., 398, trans. mine; *MLT*, 293.

38. "Historicidad de la salvación cristiana" (1984) 334, trans. Wilde, author's emphasis; *MLT*, 259.

39. On the theological view of the world and history as the place and medium of divine revelation, see Roger Haight, *An Alternative Vision: An Interpretation of Liberation Theology* (Mahwah, N.J.: Paulist Press, 1985) 56–60, 86–89.

40. "To *actualize* means to give present reality to what is formally a historical possibility and, as such, what can be taken or left, what can be read in one way or another. What must be actualized, then, is what is given, but the reading and interpretation of what is given, the option for one part or other of what is given, depend on a historical present and on historical subjects," "Utopía y profetismo" (1989) 398, trans. Brockman, author's emphasis; *MLT*, 293.

41. Ibid., 399, trans. Brockman, emended; *MLT*, 294. I return to this point below, chapter 7.

42. See "Teología como praxis" (1978); "Sacramento histórico de la liberación" (1977) 127, trans. Wilde; *MLT*, 543.

43. "Teología como praxis" (1978) 458.

44. Ibid., 473.

45. Ibid., 466.

46. Ibid., 460–461.

47. Ellacuría describes the central elements of secularization in his early theological work, *Teología política*. "It is not just that the world is becoming a larger factor in personal subjectivity and socialized objectivity. It is not just that it is exerting more and more attractive and configurative force over our lives. The world is also *worth more* and *valued more highly*. The higher valuation of the world is not only proper; it should also be promoted more earnestly as a historical sign of Christian salvation.

... At the same time the classic realm of 'the religious,' as something over against the world with its growing value, is *worth less* and *valued less*. Here I am not referring to the Christian faith nor to the church as a community of authentic Christian faith. ... [Rather], the socio-cultural efficacy of 'the religious' is diminishing in value and people's evaluation, and so is the force of 'religious' motivations in prompting people to accept and live the faith," "Historia de la salvación y salvación en la historia" (1973) 2–3, trans. Drury, author's emphasis; *FMF*, 6–7. Secularization and theology was a burning issue when Ellacuría was completing his theological and philosophical formation. A large bibliography has grown up around this theme; for a representative treatment, see Peter Berger, *The Sacred Canopy* (Garden City, N.Y.: Doubleday, 1967); see also, Johann Baptist Metz, *Theology of the World*, trans. by William Glen-Doepel (New York: Herder & Herder, 1969).

48. "Sacramento histórico" (1977) 140–141, trans. Wilde; *MLT*, 553–554.

49. "Teología como praxis" (1978) 467. While Ellacuría's theological argument for the need to turn to the historical reality of Jesus is both praiseworthy and sound, the way he uses historical Jesus research in his theological writings is dated and flawed. He was critiqued on this point by other liberation theologians. Segundo writes, "I think that Ignacio Ellacuría (*Freedom Made Flesh*) and Jon Sobrino (*Christology at the Crossroads*) are the Latin American theologians who did most to focus theology and exegesis on the historical Jesus and the political key as the tool of interpretation. I think it is unfortunate, however, that Ellacuría seems to follow the lead of European exegetes in seeking the historical significance of Jesus in his possible connection with the Zealots," Juan Luis Segundo, *The Humanist Christology of Paul* (Maryknoll: Orbis, 1986) 223. Segundo's criticism seems even more accurate today, in the wake of two decades of vibrant Jesus research. For example, the important criticism by New Testament scholar John Meier of the use of Jesus research by systematic theologians—he singles out Segundo and Sobrino—would certainly apply to Ellacuría's writings as well; see John Meier, "The Bible As a Source for Theology," in *Proceedings of the Catholic Theological Society of America* 43 (1988) 1–14.

50. "Teología como praxis" (1978) 466.

51. Ibid., 468.

52. Ibid., 468.

53. Ibid., 469.

54. Ibid., 469, author's emphasis.

55. Ibid., 469.

56. Ibid., 470.

57. Ellacuría judges that the "immediatism of the political activist which demands from every theological agent and undertaking an immediate reference to action, or which attains only a partial, superficial praxis, is the ruination of theological praxis and, in the final analysis, of theology's relative autonomy in the totality of historical praxis," ibid., 471.

58. "Utopía y profetismo" (1989) 393, trans. mine; *MLT*, 289.

59. Ibid., 393–394, trans. Brockman, emended; *MLT*, 289–290.

60. Ibid., 406–407, trans. Brockman; *MLT*, 299–300.

61. "Teología como praxis" (1978) 476.

62. Ibid., 464.

63. Ibid., 472, author's emphasis.

64. Sobrino, "Principio liberación," 127. In an earlier article Sobrino argues that this soteriological dimension proves constitutive of theology because sin and suffering

are constitutive of historical reality. "Every theology must confront suffering, determine the fundamental form of suffering, and ask what can be done about it. I would suggest that the development of every Christian theology has been determined, explicitly or implicitly, by the way it has responded to suffering, for in one way or another, all theology claims to be a form of soteriology. This makes sense insofar as salvation stands at the heart of Christian faith," "Theology in a Suffering World: Theology as *Intellectus Amoris*," in *The Principle of Mercy*, op. cit., 29.

65. Sobrino, "Principio liberación," 134, author's emphasis.

66. Ibid., 127; see also Sobrino, "Theology in a Suffering World," 27–46.

67. Sobrino, "Principio liberación," 138. He continues, "reality is like a book to be read. Shouldering reality's weight is not the only possible reading, and there are other very necessary forms. But it is a very real and, in certain respects, irreplaceable reading," ibid., 138. See also Sobrino, "Ignacio Ellacuría," 232–238; "The Legacy of the Martyrs of the Central American University," in *The Principle of Mercy*, op., cit., 173–187; "Epilogue: A Letter to Ignacio Ellacuría," ibid., 188–189.

*Chapter Six*

# Salvation in History

*A historical understanding of salvation cannot
theorize abstractly on the essence of salvation.
Not only is that abstract theorizing more
historical than it appears, and as abstraction it
can deny the real meaning of salvation, but it is
also impossible to speak of salvation except in
terms of concrete situations. Salvation is always
the salvation of someone, and of something in
that person.*

Ignacio Ellacuría[1]

In the introduction I proposed in summary fashion the conclusion
for which I would argue: Ellacuría grounds theological method in
historical reality and praxis in order to show how Christian salvation
is salvation in and of history. Chapters 2 and 3 provided the background
sketch of historical reality and the human task of history. In chapters 4
and 5 I traced how Ellacuría crafts a method for Latin American liberation
theology on the basis of this philosophy of historical reality. Now begins
the final major stage of this inquiry. In chapters 6 and 7 the focus
shifts to what Ellacuría calls the fundamental vantage point of all of
his theological work, the relationship between Christian salvation and
historical liberation.[2] He describes this relationship under the rubric of
historical soteriology. In negative terms, he aims at an understanding
of Christian salvation that is free of every idealistic temptation to sever
the world of God from the human world. Put positively, he seeks to
articulate anew the relationship of transcendence to history, arguing that
the presence of God's salvation becomes manifest in and through history.
Because the logic of Ellacuría's historical soteriology corresponds with

the threefold dynamism of his theological method, I attempt to capture that broad correspondence through the overall structure that unifies these two chapters. I begin by developing a theological interpretation of the relationship of transcendence to history, which underscores the noetic dimension of Ellacuría's method. Then I return to the place of theology, the foot of the cross, and examine the ethical option that characterizes Ellacuría's salvation theory, that of taking the crucified peoples down from their crosses. I conclude with a reflection on the ecclesial praxis that participates in God's saving action and constitutes God's people as a historical sacrament of liberation.

## BEYOND OBJECTIVISM AND SUBJECTIVISM

In *Freedom Made Flesh*, a collection of some of his earlier theological works, Ellacuría introduces a thesis to which he subsequently returns over and over: salvation history is a salvation in history.[3] This thesis addresses the relationship between Christian salvation and human history by unifying two basic propositions: the belief that salvation has a history and the expectation that salvation influence history.[4] The first, salvation history, points to the historical character of salvific acts. It articulates the Christian conviction that "the great salvific, revealing and communicating acts of God have taken place in history, even though their critical justification cannot achieve or be reduced to proofs from historical science."[5] The second, salvation in history, highlights the salvific character of historical acts. The questions raised from this perspective "are especially concerned with which historical acts bring salvation and which bring condemnation, which acts make God more present, and how that presence is actualized and made effective in them."[6] These two perspectives are neither exclusive nor identical. They remain different yet are closely related. "Salvation in history is not to be equated completely with salvation history; but the former is the body of the latter, its visible aspect, the thing which enables it to be operative."[7] Salvation in history thus mediates salvation history. Ellacuría's understanding of reality as historical reality is at work and at stake in this fundamental affirmation of historical soteriology.

> There is not only a salvation history, but salvation must be historical. This implies two things: salvation will differ according to the time and place in which it is realized, and it should be realized in history and in historical human beings. That is, salvation should not be understood univocally, nor should it be understood as if the human being were a spirit without

history, without incarnation in the world, nor as if salvation in the hereafter were not supposed to be signified, to be made into a sign, in the here and now.[8]

In his effort to underscore the rationality of Christian salvation, Ellacuría develops a historical soteriology. He wants to present faith in a way that appears credible both for those outside of Christianity and for believers living in an increasingly secularized world. This does not mean that he worries above all about making faith credible. On the contrary, his priority is that faith be real and salvific, as his constant emphasis on faith praxis makes clear. However, the accent on praxis does not remove faith's apologetic thrust, but rather deepens it and renders it genuine. Ellacuría's effort thus manifests an apologetic motivation not unlike that of earlier fundamental theologies. At the same time, his method represents a new strategy that enables him to avoid the pitfalls of those prior theologies. Drawing on Zubiri's analysis of idealistic reductionism, Ellacuría critiques the two most prominent approaches to fundamental theology so as to avoid the objectivism of some traditional approaches and the subjectivism of certain transcendental interpretations of Christian salvation.

The objectivist approach sought to secure the credibility of faith through a demonstrative apologetic of natural reason. "Objectivity was based on the historically proven interruption of the laws of nature: the historical interruption of physical laws of nature would confirm the irruption of the supernatural."[9] This approach, operating from a dehistoricized paradigm of nature, tends to reduce the actions of God in history to objective intellectual formulas. At the same time, it proves "alien to transforming praxis, to the historicity of reality, and to the personal immanence of God in human history."[10] The subjectivist approach appealed to personal subjectivity as the basis for verifying every other reality. "By showing the openness of subjectivity to something above and beyond the immanent limitations of nature, and even of the world in its totality, it felt it had a solid basis for ultimately proving the coherent connection between the Christian message and personal or interpersonal subjectivity."[11] This approach also leads to a truncated view of the connection between the world of God and the human historical world. "It has value insofar as it attempts to give an immanent base to God's presence among humans, but it tends to conceive human transcendence in individual terms, and by itself it does not lead to a social and historical praxis."[12]

In Ellacuría's view, these two approaches not only impoverish soteriology, but also diminish history. He examines this latter consequence with special attention to the form it takes in the objectivist paradigm. A deductive fundamental theology, although it uses the revealed words and deeds of God as a starting point, eventually abandons the very place from which those divine actions arise. "In the move from a fundamentally biographical and historical experience with its own theoretical interpretation to a metaphysical formulation, historicity was diluted in favor of a static theory of essence."[13] Although this tendency never achieved absolute ascendancy in Catholic theology, its pervasiveness in some periods left salvation profoundly dehistoricized. It suggested that human consciousness and freedom, to say nothing of the history of peoples, are but mere accidents having little to do with the essential mechanics of salvation. The irony, of course, is that this completely contradicts the manner and content of salvation in the biblical tradition, and never more so than when it leaves us with a dehistoricized Jesus whose humanity is only a shell. Of course, this approach formally recognizes the life and death of Jesus as a human, but it heavily emphasizes those events that occur outside or beyond history. It uses the details of Jesus' historical life to situate the mystery of salvation, but in a way that denies any metaphysical and theological significance to these historical facts as historical. As a result, the historical as such hardly functions as a theological category. "The historical data or, more precisely, the historical, biographical and social course of the life of Jesus is stripped of real density and salvific significance and, in exchange, questions regarding the metaphysical constitution of his person, of his double nature, of the hypostatic union take on absolute importance."[14] The process may be subtle, but its effect is disastrous. The urge to sever the historical from reality accompanies a christological tendency to minimize the historicity of Jesus. It leads ultimately to Docetism.

    In contrast to both objectivist and subjectivist approaches to soteriology, Ellacuría's apologetic for the rationality of Christian salvation does not sidestep historicity, but capitalizes on it. History retains both its intramundane integrity and its theologal character. It emerges not only as historical reality, but as the locus of a simultaneously final and open revelation. "There is a history of revelation, not only because revelation has been gradually given to humankind as it slowly fashions itself in history, but also because God's revelation continues to be given to us in our history."[15] The Christian Scriptures testify that history is the privileged place of revelation and salvation, and the theological anthropology which Ellacuría grounds in historical reality elicits the same conclusion. "Surely the fundamental presupposition of revelation strictly speaking, and of the faith that responds to it, is the existence of an intelligence and a will, of an apprehension of reality and of an option from it."[16] At the same time, revelation and salvation appear as God's free gift of grace added to the fundamental gratuitousness of creation. "Both because of the metaphysical density and the essential openness of historical reality, biographical and social history is converted into the *best place* (metaphysical density) and the *unique place* (openness) *for the possibility of a doubly gratuitous revelation and salvation.* This allows human individuals and humanity as a whole to participate in the very trinitarian life of God."[17]

The gratuitous newness of God becomes known to humanity through specific prophets and whole peoples. For Christians, the historical revelation of God reaches its apex in Jesus, although this revelation includes both his forerunners and those who followed him. "Jesus lives from the Jewish tradition and, through it, from many other traditions, and he continues living in the traditions of many other persons and peoples."[18] Jesus, who lived in a specific place and time, did so in and from various other tradition-laden strands of human history. Regardless of how little or how much we might know about the details of his life, we do know this: Jesus is a historical reality. Therefore, christology must seek to encounter and depict Jesus as a historical reality.[19] Ellacuría sustains this assertion by making use of the pivotal christological category of the *logos*, understood both as word and as principle of rationality.

> We must move on to an historical *logos*, without which every other *logos* will remain speculative and idealistic. This new historical *logos* must start from the fact, indisputable to the eye of faith, that the historical life of Jesus is the fullest revelation of the Christian God. It must also operate methodologically as a *logos* of history which subsumes and goes beyond the *logos* of nature, the latter often having neglected the being and reality of the former. Only a *logos* which takes into account the historical reality of Jesus can open the way for a total christology, a christology capable of dealing with the changing face of history. Only such a christology can reveal to us that there is salvation in history at the very roots of salvation history.[20]

Ellacuría's historicization of Christian salvation—salvation history is a salvation in history—invites a parallel approach to the doctrines of revelation and incarnation. "God's word to humanity is a historical Word of salvation."[21] The Word of God is not merely a natural Word, something deduced from the natural essence of the world, but a historical Word that irrupts into history and configures it as a history of revelation. That the Word became flesh does not mean primarily that the Word became nature. Rather, Ellacuría insists, the Word became history, or better, historical reality. This view of the incarnation corresponds to and deepens the insight that history is the place of revelation. At the same time, the doctrine of the incarnation itself is rescued from abstract, ahistorical interpretations that threaten to reify and render it impotent. Finally, if the Christian understanding of salvation, along with the revelation and incarnation of that salvation, are all best understood and made operative by first historicizing them, it follows that the concept and practice of faith must likewise be historicized.

> If faith were merely the acceptance of a fixed deposit of dogma by some universal human being, then the only accommodation or adaptation required would consist in the correct translation of certain texts whose distinctive history and language had somehow been forgotten in the past. But that is not what faith is. There is no universal human being; nor is the deposit of dogma formed by items of intellectual content which are learned, accepted, and then simply transmitted. Faith is a personal relationship, which takes its start from a personal God and is personally addressed to a person who is conditioned by his time and place, his people and his history. The original communication took place at a specific point in history, but this communication continues on as a living, personal reality through the mediation of the church.[22]

Faith is a personal relationship, but not, for this reason, something private. For his part, Ellacuría vigorously opposes any attempt to make salvation the object of a privatized faith. Salvation concerns both the entire human as personal, social, and historical and the entire history of humanity taken as a whole. By contrast, the privatization of soteriological faith acts like a cancer. It ravages the practice and understanding of the faith while hideously assuming faith's external form. Historicization provides a remedy for this malignancy. As a living response to the saving Word of God, authentic faith takes shape in a community of believers. Only a people can mediate Christian salvation in such a way that it proves personal, social, and historical. At the same time, the implicit pneumatology that undergirds Ellacuría's theologal conception of historical reality allows the full impact of the incarnation to be apprehended. The Word became history through the power of the Spirit, and the Word continues to become history in the community that that same Spirit gathers, animates, and sends to the world. Ellacuría's historicization of the incarnation thus highlights the profound impact that ecclesiology and soteriology have on one another.

Having discussed the contention *that* salvation entails salvation in history, it still remains to be considered *what* this salvation is. I take up this issue in the last section of chapter 7, exploring more deeply the connection between historical soteriology and ecclesiology. First, however, I sketch the way Ellacuría historicizes the concept of transcendence in order to situate the discussion of the content of salvation. I follow the argument he develops in his essay, "The Historicity of Christian Salvation," beginning with his treatment of historical transcendence in the Old and New Testaments, then summarizing his view of transcendence and historical reality. In this discussion the real benefit of the philosophy of historical reality comes to light: historicizing the Christian conception of salvation breathes new life into this otherwise exhausted concept.

## THEOPHANY OF A LIBERATING GOD

Through his insistence that salvation history is salvation in history, Ellacuría does several things at once. First, he rescues Christian salvation from interpretations that idealize and dehistoricize it, thus impoverishing both the theology of salvation and the praxis of salvific faith. Second, he reaffirms the positive value of history: "[H]istory is a reality of extraordinary metaphysical density and the relations of the human with God, founded in freedom, are constitutively historical."[23] Third, once again using language that echoes the christological formula of Chalcedon, he insists on the fundamental unity of history, a "unity without separation and without confusion."[24] He thus rejects the philosophical dualism that splits history into sacred and profane, and insists instead that "there is a single historical reality in which both God and humans intervene, so that God's intervention does not occur without God's presence in some form."[25]

The apprehension of a unified, divine-human history rests upon the theologal dimension of reality. Recognizing this, Ellacuría seeks to get beyond overly simplified characterizations of the relationship between the natural and the supernatural, where transcendence "is identified with separateness, and it is thus assumed that historical transcendence is separate from history; the transcendent must be outside or beyond what is immediately apprehended as real, so that the transcendent must always be other, different, and separated, whether in time, in space, or in its essence."[26] In contrast, he views transcendence "as something that transcends *in* and not as something that transcends *away from*; as something that physically impels to *more* but not by taking *out of*; as

something that pushes *forward*, but at the same time *retains*."[27] At work
here is a basic insistence that the historical and the spiritual not be
dichotomized, an attitude that calls to mind the way both the Old and
New Testaments approach salvation.

> The attempt to extract from the Old Testament only its religious spirit,
> while completely abandoning its historical flesh, and likewise the attempt
> to emphasize the spirit of the New Testament without considering what
> it contains of historicity, or to use its sense of historicity only to support
> its spirit, would in both cases represent a mutilation. In both cases there
> is spirit and flesh, God and history, inseparably united in such a way that
> the disappearance of one would result in the disfigurement, if not the
> destruction, of the other.[28]

Ellacuría turns to Scripture to develop his theology of historical transcendence. Beginning with the Old Testament, he looks at the way God's
action in history is presented in the account of the Exodus. He then
examines historical transcendence in the New Testament with special
attention to the New Moses christology at work in the Gospel of John.
In this way he addresses the charge that liberation theology relies too
much on the Hebrew Scriptures. More importantly, he refutes the impre-
cation that a historicized understanding of salvation implicitly undermines the "spiritual salvation" revealed in the Christian Scriptures
and tradition.

**The Exodus Narrative.** Ellacuría's examination of historical transcendence begins with the paradigmatic Hebrew account of salvation, the
story of the Exodus. In his view, the crucial question does not concern
the historical status of the events behind the scriptural account, for
regardless of where one stands with the results of historical-critical
scholarship, this revelatory text presents salvation in historical terms.[29]
Rather, the crucial question is theological: it involves a theological understanding of reality and revelation. What does it mean to say that human
history is presented as the place where God's salvific will and liberative
action becomes manifest? Ellacuría identifies the tensions that this question evokes by summarizing four historical-theological affirmations implicit in the Exodus narrative.

> (1) The departure of the people of Israel from Egypt is a historical event
> or is presented as a historical event. (2) The departure from Egypt is a
> salvific event of transcendental importance for the fulfillment of God's
> plan for the chosen people. (3) Moses is a human who uses human and
> political means to carry out that historical-salvific event. (4) Israel does

not hesitate to believe, despite the demonstrable presence of humans in the action, that it is God who is liberating them.[30]

History is presented as the place of salvation, not to ground the rationality of faith nor to symbolically express subjective religious convictions, but to show that God acts in and through the historical actions of people.[31] History appears as the place where God meets humanity and humanity meets God. Far from reducing it to the mechanical unfolding of a preset divine plan, this account views history as radically open to the future.[32] At the same time, history appears as the "place" of a people. The people discover that God works on their behalf by reflecting on their sociopolitical experience of slavery and their sociopolitical action of leaving that slavery. The place of salvation is neither an abstractly conceived history nor an individualistic conception of experience. It is the historical experience and action of a people.

> Only the whole people, which does not exclude the singular richness of a personage like Moses, can manifest the true God, who is not enclosed in the solitary subjectivity of the great heroes, but becomes present in the sorrows, struggles, and hopes of the popular majorities. For good reason the fundamental article of Israel's faith is the liberation of a whole oppressed people. . . . Thus, this fundamental article of faith refers not to God alone, to a God apart from human history, nor even to a God who gives meaning to individual life and whose fullness is projected beyond history. On the contrary, it is from and in history itself that God becomes present as the fundamental and foundational religious event, not only not separated from the sociopolitical process but established and re-lived in that process.[33]

God's self-communication appears to and through a people, a historically constituted and history-making people. Israel begins to take shape as a people, to understand itself precisely as God's chosen people, exactly insofar as God comes to be known as Israel's God through Israel's history. This insight, which underlies the rich biblical image, people of God, grounds Ellacuría's theology of revelation.[34] The name of God is revealed in and through the historical experience of a people. The particular action of a people, that of leaving their slavery in Egypt, becomes the privileged "historical place" of a new revelatory experience of God. "The theophany arises from a theopraxy and leads to a new theopraxy: the God who acts in history, in a very specific history, can be discovered and named in a more explicit, and even a more transcendent, way."[35] This praxis-oriented revelation connects God's transcendence to God's mercy: the God of the theophany is a God who witnesses the affliction of God's people and decides to act on their behalf (Ex 3:6–7). The logic of mercy moves God to act *in* history as the Lord *of* history.

> If God is not understood in history as the Lord of history, that is, as God who intervenes in history, then God is not understood as the whole, rich and free, mysterious and accessible, scandalous and hope-giving God. Rather, God would be understood as the mover of natural cycles, as a paradigm of eternal sameness; there might be an after, but not an open future, so God remains as the mover and perhaps the end or goal of a necessary evolution. But Moses invokes Yahweh and the acts of Yahweh not to repeat the sameness but to break the process, and that break in the process is where something more than history becomes present in history.[36]

Clearly the experience of transcendence mediated by this theophany is not an experience of distance and separation. Far from abandoning the people to their pain, God becomes involved in their struggle and empowers them to leave the situation of oppression. This historical experience of transcendence introduces the Hebrew people to a whole new sense of God, even while it enriches their traditions, memories, and celebrations of the covenant God made with them.[37] Moreover, while the Old Testament concepts of "the people" and "the reign" elicit immediate associations to the historical reality of the relationship between God and humanity, they also underscore the indispensable materiality of the human pole of that relationship. The identity of the people comes to be mediated by the land they occupy and live in. Similarly, the reign represents their political reality, the historical structures of possibility that enable them to meet their concrete needs and humanize their history, while doing so in a context of freedom and self-determination. As a consequence of these material associations, the theologically enriched concepts of "people of God" and "Reign of God" stand in diametrical opposition to every form of historical exploitation and material oppression.

In this meditation on the Old Testament view of historical transcendence, Ellacuría remains focused on the radical unity of history. It is simultaneously the work of human hands and the place of God's revelatory action. God does not act except in and through Moses and the people. Similarly, Moses only acts in response to God's command and inspiration, and the people leave Egypt only because God guides and empowers them. This connection is crucial.

Yahweh appears as the transcendent moment of a single praxis of salvation, the moment which breaks the limits of human action and/or redirects the deepest meaning of that action. This does not mean reducing God to history; on the contrary, it means elevating history to God, an elevation that becomes possible only because Yahweh has previously descended to it through Moses. Yahweh intervenes because he has heard the cry of the oppressed people.[38]

With an eye to the radical unity of history, Ellacuría rejects interpretations of the Exodus as only a sacred event or merely a profane occurrence embellished by religious mythology. His approach reflects the attitude of the text itself. "The believing authors of the Exodus accept it as evident that God is the principal author of these deeds, but they also report it as evident that Moses is the arm of Yahweh and that his historical action is simply a salvific action."[39]

It follows that the attempt to separate out which actions are those of God and which are human actions is pointless. The salvation effected by the God of the Exodus appears in history as liberation, while the liberation of the people from their oppression is the revelatory place of God's gracious salvation. It is one historical act of salvation-liberation. This does not mean that all divisions disappear. Although it proves impossible to positively separate the contribution of God from that of Moses, this does not mean that their contributions can be simply conflated. More important, a real dichotomy appears within history between the actions of Moses and those of Pharaoh, between actions that embody God's will and favor God's people and those that do not. I quote Ellacuría's examination of this point at length.

> There is a historical praxis of salvation and a historical praxis of perdition; a historical praxis of liberation and a historical praxis of oppression. The salvation and liberation are material, sociopolitical, fully real, and demonstrable in the first place; only in a second moment do they appear as the privileged locus of the revelation and presence of God. Certainly this second moment is not a purely mechanical reflection of the first; it required God's special but intraworldly intervention in order to go beyond the historical action. God has become freely present in history, in a way that is peculiar to a people and their state of prostration; whoever makes contact with that people and their state of prostration makes contact with the God who acts in history. They are in contact with grace and justification if they are in the line of justice and liberation; in contact with sin if they are in the line of oppression and limitation. Theopraxy is the starting point of the process of salvation, just as the rule of sin and evil is the

starting point of the process of condemnation. Moses enters fully into God's theopraxy, while Pharaoh enters fully into the denial of the God of life and freedom, perhaps in the name of the god who upholds his form of domination. Just as their starting points in the history of salvation are different, so is the corresponding theophany: for Moses and his people it is the theophany of a liberating God; for Pharaoh and his people it is the theophany of a God of punishment. But the liberation and the punishment come through historical events. Only by reaching this theophany is the theopraxis completed and the fullness of history demonstrated, the fullness of God in history. And this constantly renewed theophany is the measure by which to regulate what should be the historical praxis of salvation.[40]

As the measure according to which the historical praxis of salvation should be judged, the revelatory theophany thus manifests an ethical dimension. However, neither the theophany nor the historical praxis can be reduced to purely ethical terms or identified simplistically with the politics of the human sociodrama. Ellacuría's historicization of salvific faith does not reduce salvation to the mere transformation of oppressive social structures. However, it does illustrate that salvation only attains its fullness when it includes and embraces historical, sociopolitical structures. In this the full import of Ellacuría's method can be observed. The historicization of salvation that characterizes the Exodus narrative does not simply single out "ethical consequences" that should be drawn from faith but that are no longer directly related to faith. Faith praxis is ethical praxis. It is the historical praxis of salvation. Because it reflects "the dual unity of God *in* humanity and of humanity *in* God," this historical praxis of salvation does not represent "a merely political, or merely historical, or merely ethical praxis, but a transcendent historical praxis, which makes manifest the God who becomes present in the acts of history."[41] Moreover, this transcendent historical praxis is remembered and expressed in the cult of Sinai, but the cult draws its meaning from the liberative event, not visa versa.[42] All of this supports Ellacuría's thesis that salvation history is salvation in history. The history of Israel manifests that history itself is the special place of the divine salvific action. The ramifications of this are significant. The life, faith, and action of a people is the place where God is truly encountered. This basic point does not disappear in the New Testament approach to transcendence, although the revelation of Jesus as the Christ does inaugurate a new stage in the realization of historical reality in its transcendent depths.

**The New Moses.** The Christian Scriptures represent a qualitatively new step in the one historical process of salvation, but they do not cause a radical break in that process. Ellacuría's theology of revelation makes good use and good sense of this doctrinal affirmation. In particular, the New Testament "surpasses what has gone before by giving new concreteness and realization to what in the prior stage was a somewhat indeterminate weighing up of both the historical and the transcendent aspects."[43] He also notes that although the appearance of Jesus and the sending of the Spirit render the revelation of God as the Lord of history more definitive, at the same time that history paradoxically remains open to the future, to the "more" of the transcendent God who acts in history. As a result of the Spirit given to them, the followers of Jesus have the capacity to "discover, discern and realize" the presence of this "more" in historical reality.[44] These three actions correspond to the threefold exigence of his fundamental method in theology. At the same time, these tasks clearly involve more than merely translating or even interpreting "truths" that have already been given. As a salvific exercise of compassionate reason which aims to discover, discern, and realize new advents of ecclesial praxis in ever new historical situations, theology must be creative.

The incarnation represents one of the New Testament's most creative and sophisticated theological reflections on historical transcendence. However, Ellacuría does not focus on it in the present context, nor does he exhaustively survey the variety of other ways the inspired Christian authors address this issue. Instead, he limits his discussion to one early layer in the christology developed by the Gospel of John, that of Jesus as the New Moses. It appears that he focuses on the fourth gospel, at least in part, because it serves as a prime example of the New Testament's tendency to "transcendentalize" salvation. From this example he argues that the New Testament, far from abandoning historical transcendence, in fact retains and deepens it. Jesus, like Moses before him, comes to be recognized as God's representative because of the signs that he works, signs which have the function of unifying the signifier and the signified, the historical event that points to salvation and the salvation made present in the historical event. However, in contrast to the Exodus narrative, the historical medium remains virtually hidden behind the theological design that predominates in the Gospel of John. "History has almost completely disappeared, becoming a purely theologal, and at most, religious, reality. But not because history is negated. History is to be lived with a different spirit in the new eon; the law prevailed in the old eon, and love is to predominate in the new. And in love one sees an even greater demand for commitment to others and historical commitment, because God's love is a love of total self-giving unto death."[45] So, while it is evident that the movement from the Old to the New Testament involves a real shift with regard to the theological understanding of transcendence, the shift is not from "historical" transcendence to "spiritual" transcendence. The spiritualization characteristic of the New Testament does not mean that history has been surpassed as the medium of revelation and salvation; the transcendent and the historical remain intrinsically connected to one another.

> In speaking of historical transcendence in the New Testament, we cannot overlook the dehistoricization of the Mosaic character of Jesus, the archetypal realization of what was only a prototype in Moses, in other strata. But the fact that the historical has been transcendentalized does not detract from the need to emphasize that the first level is historical and refers to historical events and corroborations in the past, present and future; without them that transcendentalization would be unfounded and even to a certain extent meaningless. The clear historicization to which the Gospel of John subjects all Jesus' polemics with the Jewish religious and political authorities—the "Jews"—and especially his trial, crucifixion and death clearly proves that the transcendentalization is not an escape from historical realities but another way of confronting them, a way no less effective and polemical than that of a confrontation in terms of political power.[46]

The historicization of transcendence not only affects the New Moses. It implicitly calls attention to the new Israel, the new people of God. The ethnic particularity that defines Israel as the chosen people gives way to a new understanding of salvation, which conceives the whole world as embraced by God's salvific will. Although prefigured by the prophets, the New Testament articulation of this universal salvation represents a new stage in the history of revelation. At the heart of this shift lies the extraordinarily rich image that forms the core of Jesus' preaching, the Reign of God. "Reign of God and people of God are two concepts and realities which operate absolutely on the same plane. There will be a Reign of God because and to the extent that there is a people of God. There will be a people of God when and to the extent that there is a Reign of God."[47] These assertions impose a certain ecclesiological reserve. They imply that "the concept, people of God, is more closely related to the concept and reality of the Reign of God than the concept and reality of the church."[48] Hence, prior to the formal questions of ecclesiology, Ellacuría seeks out the pre-ecclesial qualities of those who most closely resemble the people of God in history.

The Old Testament conviction that God is a God of the people remains a fundamental part of the New Testament revelation, despite the impression that the New Testament appears more interested in spiritual and personal salvation. In fact, the spiritualization of salvation can only remain true to its foundations if the people of God remain a historical people and God remains the God of the people. Likewise, the personal revelation of the salvation that comes through Jesus, while it must be interiorized by every believer, depends upon this same foundational connection between God and the whole people. The people must be a true people for God to be revealed to them, while God's historical self-communication to the people is a fundamental condition of the people becoming a true people. Ellacuría's concept of historical transcendence embodies and employs this divine-human dialectic of revelation.

> (1) The one we call God is known and experienced above all from his free relationship with the people. (2) The people cannot reach their fullness as a people without reference to the true God who is constituted as the God of the people. (3) All of this is achieved through a historical mediation which definitively pertains to the oppression and domination of a people seeking their liberation and struggling historically to make themselves into a free people. (4) This historical mediation, without abandoning its historical materiality, should be transcended and interiorized by each member of the people, for God is the God of all but also of each one. God is the God of the here and now, as well as the God of all places and all times.[49]

Ellacuría moves from this brief analysis to several conclusions regarding historical transcendence as it appears in the Johannine New Moses christology. Although the fourth gospel ends up emphasizing the transcendence and divinity of Jesus, it begins by seeing him as another Moses, that is, as one whose mission involves liberation for his people. Insofar as Jesus is presented to his people as someone who responds to their need to be liberated, this liberation is both religious and historical. Therefore, the fundamental proposition that salvation is constitutively historical is clearly affirmed, even though the historical presence of salvation *qua* liberation does not assume the same concrete shape in Jesus' praxis as it does in that of Moses. In the praxis of Jesus, the historical plan of salvation that links faithfulness to God and the fullness of life is no longer based on a theocratic political arrangement, but on a new conception of the relationship between holiness and the good of the world. "The liberating presence of God no longer takes the form of a theocracy, but becomes a force without political power, which aims to transform historical reality from the viewpoint of the people, precisely against the powers that presented themselves as theocratic, and consequently, as idolatrous, insofar as they claim dominion in God's name."[50] This difference in praxis is linked to a further crucial difference between their respective fates. Like Moses, Jesus cannot enter into the promised land with his people; however, unlike Moses, who dies as an old man, Jesus is murdered by idolatrous worldly powers stung by his liberating praxis. In the light of his resurrection, historical salvation comes to be formulated in terms of an eschatology that is personal as well as collective. Meanwhile, Christian historical transcendence retains and surpasses the historical transcendence revealed to Israel. "The historical praxis of Jesus reveals in him a new and definitive presence of God, which in turn lends new perspectives and new dimensions to transcendence in its specifically and fully Christian sense."[51]

## HISTORICAL REALITY AND HISTORICAL TRANSCENDENCE

Ellacuría interprets transcendence from the perspective of historical reality in order, first, to address the general relationship between profane history and salvation history, and, second, to identify the specific contribution of the Christian vision to the notion of historical transcendence. Along with these two points, a third proves relevant to the present discussion, the dialectic of historical sin and grace.

**Profane and Sacred History.** The philosophy of historical reality provides grounds for arguing that profane history and salvation history are part of one great history. "Salvation history and the so-called profane history both belong to a single history which they serve: the history of God, what God has done with the whole of nature, what God is doing in human history, and what God desires as a result of God's constant self-donation, which can be imagined as stretching from eternity to eternity."[52] This does not mean identifying salvation history with the autonomy of the profane, nor should it be explained dualistically. The key to correctly conceiving this one history of God is correctly conceiving the doctrine of creation. Ellacuría does not view creation as an effective act placed by God in which the created object stands apart from God as a separate effect. Drawing on Zubiri, he proposes a quite different conception. "Creation can be seen as the inscription *ad extra* of the trinitarian life itself, a freely desired inscription, but of the trinitarian life itself. Therefore, it would not involve an idealistic exemplary causality, but a communicative and self-donative action of the divine life itself. This inscription and self-communication has degrees and limits, by which each thing, according to its own limits, is a limited way of being God; this limited way is nothing other than the nature of each thing."[53]

This theology of creation complements Ellacuría's metaphysical understanding that intramundane reality gives of itself more and more, such that ever higher forms of reality emerge from, retain and elevate those forms which go before them. Because his theory of reality is theologally open and thus capable of being complemented by a trinitarian theology of creation, it does not degenerate into a merely Promethean account of the dynamic structure of reality. At the same time, his thesis regarding the realization of historical reality indicates how this creative inscription of the triune life appears in a particularly dense way with humanity and history. "The human, as a formally open essence, and history in its essential openness, are the realities where this inscription of the trinitarian life can give of itself more and more, although always in a limited way: open but limited, limited but open."[54] The importance of what Ellacuría means by the theologal dimension of historical reality appears once again.

> It would not simply be that God is in all things, as essence, presence and potential, depending on the character of those things; it would be that all things, each in its own mode, have been inscribed according to the triune life and refer essentially to that life. The theologal dimension of the created world . . . would reside in that presence of the trinitarian life, which is intrinsic to all things, but which in the human can be apprehended as real and as the principle of personality. There is a strict experience of this theologal dimension and through it there is a strict personal, social and historical experience of God. This experience has different degrees and modes; but when it is a true experience of the real theologal dimension of the human, of society, of history, and in a different measure, of purely material things, it will be an experience, a physical probing of the trinitarian life itself, however mediated, incarnated and historicized.[55]

**The Christian Vision.** To underscore the particular contribution of Christianity to the conception of historical transcendence, Ellacuría focuses on the salvific preeminence of the Christ event. He reflects on the dogmatic assertion that the fullness of salvation has appeared in history in the person of Jesus of Nazareth. This move presupposes the turn to historical reality, but it complements the theologal element of that turn with the theological perspective afforded by Christian revelation. It does not sanction "a caesaropapist and/or religionist subjection of profane history to the specificity of Christ as head of the church, and therefore to the church as the continuation of the work of Christ."[56] However, it does maintain that, at the level of its richest and deepest manifestation of reality, history is open to transcendence. Moreover, authentic liberation includes both historical and transcendent elements. From a christological perspective, this takes the form of extending *in* history the ongoing incarnation of Christ as Lord *of* history. In terms of Ellacuría's theology of creation, authentic liberation involves drawing human history into the history of God by building the Reign of God on earth. However, the Reign of God can serve as an adequate symbol of Christian transcendence only if it is built on earth.

> To devote oneself solely to the religious aspect of the Reign, without concern for its essential reference to the world and history, would mean, in the final analysis, betraying the history of God, leaving the field of history to the enemies of God. This does not reduce the history of God to the history of Christian salvation in its restricted sense, much less reduce the history of God to the history of political, social, economic, cultural, etc., events. Rather, it involves an attempt, through Christian faith and action in the midst of the world . . . to build the history of God, in which the action of Christ and the action of humans, the dictates of faith and the dictates of reason, flow together in a distinct way and with a distinct, real density.[57]

Ellacuría's philosophy of historical reality, which argues so insistently for the unity of reality, finds its theological correlative in this affirmation of the unity of profane and sacred history. To repeat, this unity does not involve the collapse of salvation history into profane history or the confusion of divine and human realities. In fact, Ellacuría argues that the very opposite would hold true: to *separate* "the things of God and the things of humanity . . . would mean *confusing* God with humanity."[58] Therefore, the history of God does not refer to some third reality that is formed by joining human history and divine history. Rather, it represents the structural unity of salvation history and world history. So one must analyze the history of the world to discern the concrete dimensions and tasks that must be undertaken if salvation history is to fulfill its mission. Conversely, "the history of revelation," in Ellacuría's view, "tries to orient the history of the world to the demands of God's history."[59] Thus, the self-communication of God appears not only in salvation history in the strict sense, but in the whole of history and, to some extent, in every instance of authentic salvation in history.

**Sin and Grace.** Ellacuría understands and appreciates the purpose of the traditional distinctions between nature and grace, the natural and the supernatural, but he downplays this language.[60] He signals why with an incisive question. "Is the diversity which arises because of the distinct modes of God's self-donation greater than the unity that arises from the fact that it is one God who gives himself in distinct manners?"[61] He returns to the scriptural examples of Moses and Jesus and poses three further questions in order to augment his point.

> Are Moses' action in bringing the oppressed people out of Egypt and God's presence in that action different from their respective action and presence in giving the law or celebrating religious rites? Are Jesus' action in the feeding of the hungry multitude and God's presence in that action different from their respective action and presence in expelling the merchants from the temple or proclaiming the Reign of God and institutionalizing the eucharistic supper? Are we right to describe the more "profane" cases as God's natural intervention and the more "religious" cases as supernatural intervention?[62]

The philosophical foundations and thrust of Ellacuría's theology constrain him to answer all these queries in the negative. The accent must fall on the intraconnectedness (respectivity) of historical reality, and the theologal unity (religation) between historical reality and God. Therefore, he sets out to explain the profound divisions of history using an intrahistorical line of demarcation. That line falls between sin and grace.

> The fundamental difference is not between nature and the supernatural; since they are part of the whole history of God, who in creating humans raises them to personal participation in God's own divine life, the difference is between grace and sin. Some actions kill (divine) life, and some actions give (divine) life; some belong to the reign of sin, others to the reign of grace. Some social and historical structures objectify the power of sin and serve as vehicles for that power against humanity, against human life; some social and historical structures objectify grace and serve as vehicles for that power in favor of human life. The former constitute structural sin; the latter constitute structural grace.[63]

The structural character of history and the structural opposition between historical grace and sin assume the dimensions of a mortal conflict between the Reign of God and the sin of the world. Theology seeks to objectify this conflict in order to discern God's active presence in history and embody God's desire to save humanity. A liturgical parallel can be found in the prayer which begs the Savior to take away the sin of the world. "Speaking generally, the realization of the Reign of God in history implies 'taking away the sin' of the world and making the incarnate life of God present in humans and their relationships. It is not simply a matter of taking away sin where it is (in the world), but of taking away the sin-of-the-world."[64] Ellacuría observes that no special talent for discernment is required to identify the presence of the sin of the world in the situation from which he writes. It can be found all around: where injustice and oppression reign; where ideologies and lies suffocate truth; where idols demand human victims while dishonoring the place of the living God; where human dignity is disgraced and the poor die prematurely simply for being poor. The sin-of-the-world manifests certain universal features. Yet, as a historical reality, it must be discovered, named, and combated at the concrete or "local" level where history is encountered and realized. "What that worldly sin is, the sin which condemns the world, must be determined in each case. The other sins must be interpreted in terms of that sin-of-the-world, without forgetting that all sin leads to the destruction of the sinner and is objectified in one way or another in structures that destroy humanity."[65]

Within the complex weave of history, the conflict between the sin-of-the-world and the Reign of God is enjoined most fiercely in the place of the poor. From this Ellacuría draws a striking theological allusion. "The death of the poor is the death of God, the ongoing crucifixion of the Son of God. Sin is the negation of God and the negation of sin moves, sometimes along unknown paths, toward the affirmation of God, toward God being made present as the giver of life."[66] The discussion now shifts to Ellacuría's historicization of salvation—including his focus on historical crucifixion and his view of the bearers of salvation in history—and the real weight which his interpretation lends to the Christian symbol of the cross.

### Notes to Chapter 6

1. "Sacramento histórico" (1977) 128, trans. Wilde, emended, author's emphasis; MLT, 544.
2. See "Sacramento histórico" (1977) 136–137; MLT, 550–551. Besides this article, the collection of essays that make up Freedom Made Flesh all touch on this thesis, either directly or indirectly; see especially "Historia de la salvación y salvación en la historia" (1973) and "Liberación: misión y carisma de la iglesia latinoamericana" (1971). Two later articles also focus primarily on this theme: "Historicidad de la salvación cristiana" (1984) and "Salvación en la historia" (1993). In addition, see "El pueblo crucificado" (1977); "Monseñor Romero, un enviado de Dios para salvar a su pueblo, RLT (No. 19, 1990) 5–15, published originally in ST (No. 811, 1980) 825–832; "Verdadero pueblo" (1981); "Religiones abrahámicas" (1987).
3. "Historia de la salvación y salvación en la historia" (1973) 8, trans. Drury; FMF, 15.

4. See "Religiones abrahámicas" (1987) 6–7; "Historicidad de la salvación cristiana" (1984) 323; *MLT*, 251; "Historia de la salvación y salvación en la historia" (1973) 8; *FMF*, 15; "Liberación: misión y carisma de la iglesia latinoamericana" (1971) 74; *FMF*, 134.
5. "Historicidad de la salvación cristiana" (1984) 323, trans. Wilde; *MLT*, 251.
6. Ibid., 323, trans. Wilde; *MLT*, 251.
7. "El anuncio del Evangelio y la misión de la Iglesia" (1973) 50, trans. Drury; *FMF*, 94.
8. "Liberación: misión y carisma de la iglesia latinoamericana" (1971) 74, trans. mine; *FMF*, 134–135.
9. "El anuncio del Evangelio y la misión de la Iglesia" (1973) 49, trans. mine; *FMF*, 90.
10. Ibid., 49, trans. Drury; *FMF*, 92.
11. Ibid., 49, trans. Drury; *FMF*, 91.
12. Ibid., 49, trans. mine; *FMF*, 92. For a detailed, insightful examination of these two approaches under the rubrics of "traditional" and "transcendental" fundamental theology, see Francis Schüssler Fiorenza, *Foundational Theology: Jesus and the Church* (New York: Crossroad, 1992). His analysis of these two paradigms closely resembles Ellacuría's critique.
13. "Salvación en la historia" (1993) 1252.
14. Ibid., 1254–1255. Ellacuría does not deny that questions of nature and essence are important. He only rejects the view that such questions are more important or more theological than existential, historical questions. He likewise resists the suggestion that these two types of questions are mutually exclusive. Addressing both sets of questions together, he seeks the real in the historical and the historical in the real.
15. "Historia de la salvación y salvación en la historia" (1973) 7, trans. Drury; *FMF*, 14. Ellacuría is careful not to compromise the finality of the revelation that appears in Christ. "We can acknowledge that the deposit of faith is closed *as a system of possibilities*, as Zubiri does for example; but history is precisely the actualization of possibilities," ibid., 7, trans. Drury, author's emphasis; *FMF*, 14. It should be added that these possibilities become actualized precisely through the faith praxis of the followers of Christ.
16. "Salvación en la historia" (1993) 1256.
17. Ibid., 1258, author's emphasis.
18. Ibid., 1258.
19. "Today it would be absolutely ridiculous to try to fashion a christology in which the historical realization of Jesus' life did not play a decisive role. The 'mysteries of Jesus' life,' which once were treated peripherally as part of ascetics, must be given their full import, provided, of course, that we explore exegetically and historically what the life of Jesus really was," "Carácter político de la misión de Jesús" (1973) 13, trans. Drury; *FMF*, 26.
20. Ibid., 13, trans. Drury; *FMF*, 26–27.
21. "Liberación: misión y carisma de la iglesia latinoamericana" (1971) 73, trans. mine; *FMF*, 132.
22. Ibid., 78, trans. Drury; *FMF*, 141–142.
23. "Salvación en la historia" (1993) 1255.
24. "Historicidad de la salvación cristiana" (1984) 328, trans. Wilde; *MLT*, 254.
25. Ibid., 328, trans. Wilde; *MLT*, 254. This, in turn, leads to an important question regarding how human and divine intervention in history are to be distinguished and related. Ellacuría's response to this question mirrors the Ignatian "rules for the discernment of spirits," in which different spiritual motions are identified in

accordance to whether a person is fundamentally moving toward or away from God (*Spiritual Exercises*, No. 313–317). "What we need to discern is the different ways in which God and humans intervene, and the different types of relationship between those interventions. God's intervention and God's presence in human intervention are of different types when the human intervention occurs in the context of sin and when it occurs in the context of anti-sin, or grace," ibid. 328. There exists no essential conflict between God and humans; the essential conflict involves those powers in favor of God's Reign and those opposed to it. Thus, theology's most basic dividing line does not run between nature and supernature but between sin and grace. This point is developed in further detail below.

26. Ibid., 328, trans. Wilde; *MLT*, 254.
27. The Spanish text reads, "Este modo consiste en ver [la trascendencia] como algo que trasciende *en* y no como algo que trasciende *de*, como algo que físicamente impulsa a *más* pero no sacando *fuera de*; como algo que lanza, pero al mismo tiempo retiene," ibid., 328, trans. Wilde; *MLT*, 254; both author and translator contribute to the emphasis in this sentence.
28. Ibid., p. 330, trans. mine; *MLT*, 256.
29. "It does not matter for our purposes if the scientific and critical historicity of the events narrated in Exodus is denied, because the question remains valid, from a theological viewpoint, why the revelatory tradition saw a need to give historical flesh to the supposedly nonhistorical content: God's revelation and self-giving. We do accept that what happened in that history or in that historification, as the inspired author expresses so explicitly, is something that must be faithfully accepted as the salvific presence and action of God. ... Whether or not it happened as narrated, the narration itself, in what we might call its revelatory internal logic, is sufficient to demonstrate what we mean here. To acknowledge only a purely extrinsic relationship between the medium and the message does not do justice either to the text or to the intention and purpose of the writer," ibid., 331, trans. Wilde; *MLT*, 256–257.
30. Ibid., 330, trans. mine; *MLT*, 256.
31. "One might say that history encompasses and surpasses both the natural and the subjective, personal arenas; far from excluding them, it frames and empowers them. But without history the arena of God's revelation and self-giving would be drastically reduced," ibid., 333–334, trans. Wilde; *MLT*, 258–259.
32. "The *Deus semper novus* is one of the ways we encounter the *Deus semper maior*. Thus, history is the fullest place of transcendence, of a transcendence that does not appear mechanically, but only appears when history is made, and which irrupts in novel ways in the constant disestablishment [*desinstalación*] of the determining process," ibid., 335, trans. Wilde; *MLT*, 259.
33. Ibid., 336, trans. Wilde; *MLT*, 260.
34. "There is a people of God because there is a God of the people and not, for example, a God purely of the cosmos or a God of the hierarchical structures, or simply an abstract and rational God who would be the origin, creator and conserver of all that is," "Pueblo de Dios" (1983) 841.
35. "Historicidad de la salvación cristiana" (1984) 336, trans. Wilde; *MLT*, 260.
36. Ibid., 333, trans. Wilde; *MLT*, 258.
37. "The experience and memory of the departure and the journey would keep alive their experience of God in the generations to come. Even when the re-living became fundamentally cultic, they would seek to nourish the re-living by recalling and invoking that history," ibid., 337, trans. Wilde; *MLT*, 261.

38. Ibid., 338, trans. Wilde; *MLT*, 261–262.
39. Ibid., 338, trans. Wilde; *MLT*, 262.
40. Ibid., 339, trans. Wilde; *MLT*, 262–263.
41. Ibid., 340, trans. Wilde, author's emphasis; *MLT*, 263–264.
42. "The cult of Sinai is true worship because the worshipping people have really met the liberating God in a praxis of liberation; it is not in any way true and sufficient by itself," ibid., 341, trans. Wilde; *MLT*, 264. The same can be said of the Catholic celebration of the eucharist. Its sacramental efficacy does not arise in a historical vacuum, as some interpretations of the concept of *ex opere operato* suggest. See Ignacio Ellacuría, "Liturgia y liberación" (1976), *CIRD*, 279–292; *FMF*, 233–246.
43. "Historicidad de la salvación cristiana" (1984) 343, trans. mine; *MLT*, 266.
44. Ibid., 343, trans. mine; *MLT*, 266. The three verbs in Spanish are *descubrir, discernir* and *realizar*. Here, *realizar* ("to realize") corresponds to the praxis-oriented dimension of the encounter with reality. Thus, it assumes its full Zubirian meaning ("to actualize," "to reach fullness"). This contrasts with the more cognitive connotations ("to perceive," "become acquainted with," "to understand") which the word assumes when referring to the noetic dimension of that encounter; see above, chapter 4, n. 7. Ellacuría's frequent reference to the *more (más)* plays on the theologal dimension of his philosophy of historical reality while evoking another central motif from Ignatian spirituality, that of the *magis*, the "greater" glory of God. The most recent General Congregation of the Society of Jesus gives a succinct description of this note. "The *magis* is not simply one among others in a list of Jesuit characteristics. It permeates them all. The entire life of Ignatius was a pilgrim search for the *magis*, the ever greater glory of God, the ever fuller service of our neighbor, the more universal good, the more effective apostolic means," *Documents of the Thirty-Fourth General Congregation of the Society of Jesus* (St. Louis: The Institute of Jesuit Sources, 1995) 243.
45. "Historicidad de la salvación cristiana" (1984) 345, trans. Wilde; *MLT*, 267.
46. Ibid., 347, trans. Wilde; *MLT*, 269.
47. "Pueblo de Dios" (1983) 843.
48. Ibid., 843. I further examine this important theme below, chapter 7, section three.
49. Ibid., 842.
50. "Historicidad de la salvación cristiana" (1984) 348, trans. mine; *MLT*, 269–270.
51. Ibid., 348, trans. mine; *MLT*, 269–270.
52. Ibid., 352, trans. mine; *MLT*, 272.
53. Ibid., 357–358, trans. mine; *MLT*, 276. In this important text, Ellacuría chooses an unusual Spanish noun, *plasmación*, to express the concept which I have translated "inscription." There is no exact English translation that communicates the nuance Ellacuría intends here, but this nonliteral choice comes close. The verb *plasmar* means to "mold, shape, form or give concrete form to something," or even "to represent" (as in "give visible form to" something), but the nominatives, "form" and "shape" are too weak to translate *plasmación*. A strong sense of "putting one's own stamp" or "leaving one's fingerprint" on something comes through this word. The idea, then, is something like "Creation can be seen bearing the very fingerprint or stamp of the trinitarian life itself." Margaret Wilde's translation takes different tack: "Creation can be seen as the grafting *[plasmación] ad extra* of the trinitarian life itself." This translation, while creative and elegant, can be taken in a neo-Platonic fashion that Ellacuría does not intend.
54. Ibid., 358, trans. mine; *MLT*, 277.

55. Ibid., 358, trans. mine; *MLT*, 277.

56. Ibid., 353, trans. Wilde; *MLT*, 273. Ellacuría comments that the Reign of God is, "in a first moment, a seed sown in the fields of the world and in history, to make it a history of God, of a God who is definitively all in all. In this first moment the field is not subjected to the seed, but the seed to the field; or, as the other evangelical parable puts it, the leavening of the Reign is modestly and effectively mixed into the dough of the world to make it ferment and rise," ibid. 353; *MLT*, 273.

57. Ibid., 353, trans. mine; *MLT*, 273.

58. Ibid., 354, trans. Wilde, emphasis mine; *MLT*, 274.

59. Ibid., 354, trans. Wilde; *MLT*, 274.

60. See above, n. 25; Ellacuría does not *reject* this distinction: "This does not mean that the classical question about the natural and the supernatural is an idle question, only that it is not the first question," ibid., 356, trans. Wilde; *MLT*, 276.

61. Ibid., 355, trans. mine; *MLT*, 274.

62. Ibid., 355, trans. Wilde; *MLT*, 275.

63. Ibid., 356, trans. Wilde, emended; *MLT* 275. Ellacuría's formulation of this fundamental dialectic clearly echoes the famous meditation on the Two Standards from the Spiritual Exercises of Ignatius Loyola, (*Spiritual Exercises*, No. 136–148). Under the same inspiration, Jon Sobrino makes a similiar distinction using the language of Reign and anti-Reign; see, for example, Sobrino, *Liberator,* 32.

64. "Sacramento histórico" (1977) 135, trans. mine; *MLT*, 549.

65. Ibid., 135, trans. mine; *MLT*, 549.

66. "Historicidad de la salvación cristiana" (1984) 357, trans. mine; *MLT*, 276.

*Chapter Seven*

# The Cross and the Church

*What have I done for Christ? What am I doing*
*for Christ? What ought I to do for Christ?*

St. Ignatius Loyola[1]

The cross on which Jesus was crucified remains the preeminent place for meditating on the Christian mystery of salvation, for living with resurrection faith in the face of the mystery, and for producing a living theology that illuminates and fosters that Christian faith. This affirmation appears obvious, perhaps even trite, a combination that suggests that it contains hidden dangers. From Ellacuría's perspective, the key dangers arise when the cross is separated from the crucified in such a way that it appears as an abstract, idealized, or dehistoricized symbol for negativity in general. More pointedly, serious problems emerge when the cross is separated from the act of crucifixion and the fact that specific persons did the crucifying. These dangers are real, not merely speculative. They can be encountered in history today, where innocent victims suffer ten thousand versions of "crucifixion" at the hands of historically real and guilty crucifiers. If theology wants to encounter the cross of Jesus, it must encounter the historical reality—the ground—beneath his cross. If theology wants to discover the Crucified Christ, it must uncover the crucified people.

## HISTORICAL NECESSITY AND THE DEATH OF JESUS

Historical salvation can be contemplated from various aspects of Jesus' life, among which the gospel accounts of his passion and death constitute the most historically and theologically dense. The basic avenues for interpreting Jesus' death appear when Ellacuría contrasts two important and related questions. Why did Jesus die? Why did his enemies kill him?[2] The first question entails a theological-historical perspective and gives priority to the soteriological meaning of Jesus' death. The second question probes the historical reality of Jesus' death from a historical-theological point of view. It attends to the fact that Jesus was the victim of the actions and intentions of others. Ellacuría argues that the former issue cannot be interpreted apart from the latter. Just as the meaning of Jesus as the Christ must flow from the historical reality of Jesus of Nazareth, so too the meaning of Jesus' death flows from the reality of that death. Any number of theological agendas can lead to an inversion of this process: seeing the crucifixion of Jesus as nothing but an expiatory sacrifice; exclusively locating the meaning of the cross in a salvation beyond history; assigning only an ascetical or moralizing function to the cross; treating the scandal of Jesus' death as a mere prelude to his resurrection. In the name of transcendence, all of these tend to dehistoricize salvation. Paradoxically, for this very reason they undermine the realization of transcendence. Moreover, they too often produce an apologetically and morally impoverished sense of God's Reign which uses the language of piety to veil a self-centered praxis. To combat this, Ellacuría grounds the salvific significance accorded the death of Jesus in the fact that he was killed by historical forces operating with a particular historical logic.

> The "why did Jesus die" cannot be explained apart from the "why did they kill him." Moreover, the historical priority must be sought in the "why did they kill him." They killed Jesus for the life that he lived and for the mission that he carried out. This "why" of his death can be posed in terms of the "for what reason" of his death. If, from a theological-historical point of view it can be said that Jesus died for our sins and for human salvation, from a historical-theological point of view it must be maintained that they killed him for the life he lived.[3]

Ellacuría's analysis of the relationship between these two questions utilizes Zubiri's central epistemological tenet that intellection precedes and grounds conceptualization. The soteriological meaning of Jesus' death flows from the historical reality of his death. The former concern does not prove unimportant or illegitimate, but it can only be adequately addressed in the context of the latter. Moreover, Jesus' death and resurrection point back to the historical reality of his life. "The Crucified One is resurrected, and he is resurrected because he was crucified. Since his life was taken away for proclaiming the Reign of God, a new life is given back to him as the fulfillment of the Reign."[4] In his interpretation of the

soteriological dimension of Jesus' death, Ellacuría consistently emphasizes the unity between the historical reality of crucifixion and the saving
reality of the cross. The circularity that surfaces in this aim parallels the
hermeneutical logic at work in the very composition of the Gospels.

> Thus, the resurrection points back to the passion and the passion to the
> life of Jesus as the one who announces the Reign. It is well-known that
> this is the very sequence followed in the construction of the Gospels: the
> necessity of historicizing the experience of the Risen One leads to a
> historical consideration of the passion, which occupies such a dispropor-
> tionately large place in the Gospel accounts, and which needs to be
> historically justified in the narration of the life of Jesus.[5]

Ellacuría imitates the gospel writers in another way. He appeals to
the historical reality of Jesus from the interpretative context of ongoing
history. In other words, he interprets revelation from history while interpreting history from revelation. He begins with an actual salvation in
history which illuminates and is illuminated by the historical-theologal
understanding of God's presence revealed in salvation history. As was
noted above, the historical place of the theologian proves crucial to this
process, for it can either foster or hinder an authentic understanding
of Jesus. This point becomes Ellacuría's hermeneutical dictum: "[A]ny
historical situation should be seen from its corresponding key in revelation, but revelation should be focused on from the history to which it
is directed, even though not every historical moment is equally valid
when it comes to providing a clear focus."[6] In line with this point, he
interprets the crucifixion of Jesus through the passion of the poor in
order to clarify "the historical character of the salvation of Jesus and the
salvific character of the history of crucified humanity, once it is accepted
that salvation is given in Jesus and the realization of that salvation must
be given in humanity."[7]

The gospel writers attribute a kind of necessity to the suffering and
death of Jesus. In Luke's account of the road to Emmaus, for example,
the risen but unrecognized Jesus asks the two disciples, "Was it not
necessary that the Messiah should suffer these things and enter into his
glory?" (Lk 24:26). A dehistoricized view of the Messiah's "necessary
suffering" might see in it a strictly theological or merely natural necessity.
Examples of the former include many sacrificial soteriologies (salvation
requires a sacrifice, therefore Jesus had to die) and some revelatory or
prophetic explanations (the prophets foretold it, therefore he had to die).
The latter might take the form of a dialectical idealism that deploys
biological images of salvation (death is required in order to reach new

life, therefore he had to die). With regard to the first example, Ellacuría argues that " 'necessity' is not based on notions of expiation and sacrifice. Even when one has recourse to Second Isaiah in order to explain the meaning of Jesus' death on the basis of the servant of Yahweh, the thread of the discourse is not 'sin-offense-victim-expiation-pardon.' This scheme, which can have a certain validity. . .can [also] be converted into an evasion of what must be done historically to take away the sin of the world."[8] Recourse to prophetic necessity, the strategy of the second example, can also prove dangerous. For one thing, the need to interpret his death as necessary only appears after he dies. At that point, "the surprised minds of the believers discovered in the designs of God, manifested in the words and deeds of the scriptures, of Moses and the prophets, the signs of the divine will which would make the death 'necessary.' "[9] To misconstrue prophecy narratives and render a literalist interpretation of prophetic causality damages both the Christian understanding of necessity and the practice of genuine propheticism. Finally, regarding the third, to see the death of Jesus as the result of merely natural necessity "would eliminate the responsibility of those who kill the prophets and those who crucify humankind, thus casting a veil over the connection between historical evil and sin; it would also imply that the new life could emerge without the activity of humans, who would not need to convert internally nor rebel against their exterior."[10]

In contrast to these approaches, Ellacuría historicizes the notion of necessity before utilizing it in the interpretation of the death of Jesus. He incorporates theological, prophetic, and natural elements in his interpretation, but does not allow that they determine the course of history. The necessity that constitutes and characterizes human history appears as a historical necessity.

[The necessity of Jesus' death] is historical, not because it had been announced by the prophets, but because the prophets prefigured the event in what had befallen them. This necessity is grounded, through what happened to the prophets, in the opposition between the proclamation of the Reign and the verifiable presence of sin in history. The resistance to oppressive powers and the struggle for historical liberation brought them persecution and death, but that resistance and struggle were nothing but the historical consequence of a life which responded to the word of God. That long experience, explicitly recalled by Jesus, leads to the conclusion that in our *historical* world it is *necessary* to pass through persecution and death in order to come to the glory of God. And the reason could not be clearer: if the Reign of God and the reign of sin are two opposing

realities, and if both have human beings of flesh and bone as their protago-
nists, then those who wield the power of oppressive domination cannot
but exercise it against those who have only the power of their word and
their life, offered for the salvation of the many.[11]

This historical necessity refers, of course, to historical-theologal reality,
the reality that historical sin proves constitutive of the very structures
of society and history, and the reality that God's salvific will and grace
likewise penetrate those same structures. Historical reality has turned
out a certain way. It could be added that it has turned out quite badly
in many respects. It did not have to turn out this way, but it did turn
out this way. Moreover, *that* it did represents a real fact which conditions
the future. Therein lies the historical necessity of the death of the Messiah.

> Historical necessity . . . obliges us to emphasize the determining causes
> of what happens. The fundamental cause, from a theological point of
> view, is expressed countless times in scripture: the passage from death
> to glory is necessary given the fact of sin, a sin which takes possession
> of the human heart, but above all, a historical sin which reigns collectively
> over the world and over peoples. There is, in Moingt's phrase, a "theologal
> and collective sin." The announcement of the death of Christ for our sins
> refers to it, rather than directly to our individual and ethical sins. It is a
> "collective reality" which grounds and makes possible individual sins.
> This theologal and collective sin destroys history and hinders the future
> which God would desire for history. This collective sin causes death to
> reign over the world, and for this reason we have the necessity of being
> freed from our collective work of death in order to form a new people
> of God.[12]

On the basis of the historical necessity of the death of Jesus, Ellacuría
probes the particular historical reasons that led to his crucifixion and
the soteriological implications that follow from it. Neither the fact nor
the way that Jesus died were accidental. He was killed by a conspiracy
of religious and political elites, powerful people who were threatened
by his preaching and his prophetic actions. Moreover, Jesus did not
speak and act as he did in order to be put to death, as if death itself
was a value, nor in order to die but then be raised again. Rather, he
spoke and acted as he did because that is what the Reign of God
demanded. Certainly he would have realized at some point that his
words and actions were causing trouble and putting him at risk. However,
this served neither as a motivation for continuing in his course nor a
reason for backing down from it. God's Reign and its implications remained his motive and focus, weaving a continuity through the various

aspects of his life and between his life and death. "It was not accidental that the life of Jesus was what it was; neither was it accidental that this life brought him to the death that he suffered. The struggle on behalf of the Reign of God necessarily presupposes a struggle in favor of the human unjustly oppressed; this struggle leads one into confrontation with those responsible for this oppression. Because of this he died and, in this death, he conquered."[13]

Ellacuría thus accents the continuity of Jesus' life with his death. His death, of course, represents a historical rupture, but not by way of imposing a new meaning on his life. The rupture of his death confirms the irruption, in and through his life, of the Reign of God. Therefore, a soteriology that puts all of the salvific weight on the death of Jesus can be reconciled neither with the historical reality of that death, nor with the life that led to it, nor with the mission that formed the central axis of that life. "The death of Jesus is the final meaning of his life only because the death toward which his life led him reveals, at the same time, what was the historical meaning and theological meaning of his life. Therefore, it is his life that gives ultimate meaning to his death, and only as a consequence is his death, which has received its initial meaning from his life, the meaning of his life."[14] Furthermore, Ellacuría stresses the concrete historical elements that accompany the saving work of Jesus so that Jesus' saving action can continue in history. Naturally, Jesus' earthly life and death are events that transpired long ago and thus belong to the historical past. However, in another sense, these events continue in history, and do so with a peculiar force. "The continuity is not purely mystical and sacramental, any more than his activity on earth was purely mystical and sacramental. In other words, cultic worship, including the celebration of the eucharist, is not the *totum* of the presence and continuity of Jesus. Rather, a historical sequel is required which continues realizing what he realized and how he realized it."[15] The christological and ecclesiological dimensions of salvation are thus interlaced, both in the unfolding of theological method (the formal level) and in the meaning of historical salvation (the level of content). In consequence, the salvation of Jesus will transcend history only if it transcends in history, that is, if it is carried on in the traditionary structures of history. This leads to an important question. Who continues the life and work of Jesus in history?

## The Crucified People

In order to take charge of history, humans must grasp the reality of their historical world. However, this reality is structured in such a way that the lives of an enormous segment of humanity epitomize a literal crucifixion. Therefore, to truly grasp the reality of the world, one must grasp the historical reality of the crucified people. This crucifixion results directly from historical decisions, actions, traditions, and structures and represents, in Ellacuría's view, the most urgent and theologically dense of all the contemporary signs of the times. "What is meant by 'crucified people' here is that collective body, which as the majority of humankind owes its situation of crucifixion to the way society is organized and maintained by a minority that exercises its dominion through a series of factors, which taken together and given their concrete impact within history, must be regarded as sin."[16] Hence, the crucified people is not merely a colorful metaphor for human suffering in general, nor does it simply represent the sum total of all individual injuries and griefs. It refers to a historical-theologal reality that embraces a communion of victims. "The joint experience that the root of individual sins abides in a supraindividual presence of sin and that the life of each one is configured by the life of the people in which each one lives, renders connatural the experience that both salvation and perdition are played out primarily in this collective dimension."[17]

Ellacuría's phrase refers not only to a suffering people but to a crucified people, a people whose suffering is unjustly inflicted, whose suffering results, directly or indirectly, from historically real and deliberate choices, that is, from historical necessity. He does not deny that natural elements exist in the unjust structures of the world, but he does not allow this to diminish the sense of responsibility for the extent to which the suffering of the crucified people results from historical necessity, "the necessity that many suffer so a few may enjoy, that many be dispossessed so that a few may possess,"[18] and the necessity that those who hunger and thirst for justice suffer persecution. These historically real and deliberate choices often betray ideological motives. Their effects are usually ideologically justified. Moreover, the image of crucifixion evokes a profound sense of complexity and hidden complicity. These victims are not picked off randomly by snipers. They are systemically ground under by the vast, dull machinery and labyrinthine workings of social, economic, political, and cultural systems. However, the systems are not imposed on history from outside of history. Human choices construct them.

Ellacuría nuances this basic view of social-historical crucifixion in order to avoid falling into a Manichean division of the world into the crucifiers and the crucified. "While maintaining the universal pattern of people crucifying others in order to live themselves, the subsystems of crucifixion that exist in both groups, oppressors and oppressed, should also be examined."[19] He does not wish to imply, of course, that an inherent tendency toward a dualism issues from the use of structural analyses. Nor does the analysis of historical structures and social dynamics lead necessarily to the minimization of personal conversion. On the contrary, it is "precisely a structural way of looking at the problem that enables us to avoid the error of seeing as good all the individuals on one side and as evil those on the other side, thus ignoring the problem of personal transformation."[20] The point is, those who are victims of systemic oppression are fully capable of acting in ways that support the very systems that oppress them, contributing to their own oppression and that of others. More importantly, the impulse to dominate or to seek revenge appears among all people, including the victims of the larger cycles of injustice. "Flight from one's own death in a continual looking out for oneself and not acknowledging that we gain life when we surrender it to others, is no doubt a temptation that is permanent and inherent in the human, one that is modulated but not abolished by historical-structural reality."[21]

From the perspective of historical transcendence, Ellacuría observes that God's history is configured by historical sin and historically salvific grace. The conflict between them represents a war over the soul of the human and the shape of historical reality. Consequently, the salvific task of history involves noticing its concrete reality and discerning there the presence of sin and grace, in order to confront and convert the sinful reality and to promote and embody the grace that leads to the fullness of life. In the final analysis, salvation in history, like the dynamism of theological method, is mediated through the attention, discernment, and response of its human subject. Moreover, in order to have a real effect on reality, this discernment and response must attend to the historically unjust poverty and oppression which afflict the crucified people. While these realities retain their empirical character, they now appear in the light of Christian historical transcendence as primary manifestations of the sin of the world and the negation of the Reign of God. However, it is not enough to reflect on crucifying poverty and oppression under the aspect of historical sin, for they also represent the place where salvific grace irrupts into history. With the eyes of faith, the believing community thus grasps that "the poor themselves, impoverished and oppressed by injustice, have become the preferred locus of benevolence and grace, of God's faithful love."[22]

The image of the crucified people obviously alludes to the death of Jesus and the theological significance of that death. However, it is not an arbitrarily or frivolously employed allusion. In concert with his fundamental method, Ellacuría examines the death of Jesus from the perspective of the ongoing crucifixion of the people and the oppression of the people from the perspective of the cross of Jesus. He observes that anyone who "reflects as a believer on the mangled reality of this crucified people must ask him- or herself what it implies regarding sin and the necessity of salvation."[23] A believer who comes face to face with this historical reality and recognizes it as that which should not be must start asking tough questions about the sin of the world. At the same time, viewing the death of Jesus in light of the oppression of the crucified people serves to safeguard against the tendency to romanticize the suffering of either.

Ellacuría raises a further point here. "What Christian faith adds to the historical confirmation of the oppressed people is the suspicion that asks whether, besides being the principle addressee of the salvific effort, this people not also be in its crucified situation a principle of salvation for the entire world."[24] The profound theological intuition behind this question emerges as a result of the fundamental operation of Ellacuría's method. He approaches the cross of salvation history from the ground of historical reality. More precisely, he correlates the salvation made manifest in the cross of Jesus with a key question that arises from this ground. Who represents the historical continuation of the saving death of Jesus? In response to this question, Ellacuría examines Jesus' death and the cross of the crucified people in the light of the biblical salvation theory represented by the servant of Yahweh in Second Isaiah. He does not present an exhaustive biblical analysis, nor a comprehensive study of the theological and historical issues involved. However, he does sketch the main features of his salvation theory, modeling it on a servant christology.

The Christian tradition has long associated Jesus with the servant of Yahweh. However, this does not preclude the association of other historical persons or groups with this Old Testament figure.[25] The dogmatic assertion that the passion of Jesus must continually be renewed in history indicates that the one servant will be embodied in a variety of historical forms. This does not mean that multiple servant figures will be generated, nor is it necessary to fall back on a univocal determination of the concrete shape that the servant will take in any given situation. All who discharge the mission of the servant are included, in some way, in the figure of the servant. On the basis of this logic, Ellacuría associates the historical communion of victims with the servant and with Jesus as the preeminent embodiment of the servant. This communion includes "anyone unjustly crucified for the sins of humans, because all the crucified form a single unit, one sole reality, even though this reality has a head and members with different functions in the unity of expiation."[26]

The theology of the servant of Yahweh involves a distinctive salvation theory which Ellacuría summarizes as follows. The servant suffers horribly at the hands of others and is eventually crushed by the sufferings inflicted upon him. However, the people nearest the servant, those who inflict and/or witness his sufferings, do not regard him as a savior figure. On the contrary, they judge that he has not only been struck down and humiliated by his human adversaries, but also rejected by God. As one thus rejected, and in line with an Old Testament understanding of divine retribution, the servant is regarded as a sinner. On the basis of this inference, he is buried among sinners. However, in the view of Isaiah, which becomes the perspective of the believer, it is not because of his own sins that the servant appears as a sinner. Rather, it is because he has taken upon himself the sins of others. Moreover, the servant willingly accepts this burden, even though it brings him to the threshold of death. "His death, far from being meaningless and inefficacious, provisionally removes the sins that were afflicting the world. His death represents expiation and intercession for sins."[27] Because he sacrifices his life for the sake of the others, the servant triumphs. For this reason "he shall be raised high and greatly exalted" (Is 52:13). Most importantly, the text indicates that God accepts this whole situation. God shoulders responsibility for human transgressions and even wills that the servant die for the expiation of those sins.

> Only in a difficult act of faith is the singer of the servant songs able to discover the very opposite of what appears to the eyes of history. Precisely because he sees one who is burdened by sins he did not commit, as well as the consequences of those sins, he dares, by reason of the very injustice of the situation, to attribute all that is happening to God. God can do no less than attribute to this act of absolute historical injustice a fully salvific value. God can make this attribution because the servant himself accepted his destiny of saving those who caused his sufferings by bearing those same sufferings.[28]

In light of this salvation theory, and drawing on an approximation of what the servant figure might look like in history, Ellacuría explores the possibility of correlating the crucified people and the crucified Jesus in terms of the figure of the servant of Yahweh. Above all, such a correlation hinges on the relationship between the servant and God. It is God who chooses the servant and designates him or her as such. It

is God who says, "I, the Lord, have called you for the victory of justice,
I have grasped you by the hand; I formed you, and set you as a covenant
of the people, a light for the nations" (Is 42:6). Moreover, from the
perspective of New Testament theology, the servant is accepted by God
through his/her likeness to Jesus, above all, his/her likeness to what
happened to Jesus in his passion and death on the cross. Hence, the
servant will be rejected, dehumanized, and crucified, not for his/her own
sins, but for the sins of others. Likewise, there will be a connection
between this servant's passion and the realization of the Reign of God.[29]
On the basis of the similarity between the passion of Jesus and the
passion of the crucified people, Ellacuría concludes that the people appear
not only as victim of the sin of the world, but as savior and judge of
the world. The crucified peoples represent the savior in history insofar
as they epitomize the crucified body of Christ which bears the sins of
the world in order to save the world. They represent the judge in history
insofar as their "judgment is salvation, insofar as it unveils the sin of
the world by opposing it, insofar as it makes possible the redoing of
what has been done badly, and insofar as it proposes a new exigency
as the unavoidable way to achieve salvation."[30]

In the life and death of Jesus, the theology of the servant reaches new
depths of integration. Like the servant, but in an even more thoroughly
historicized fashion, Jesus first struggles against sin before dying because
of it. This proves crucial. It was pointed out above that the salvific
meaning of Jesus' death flows from its connection to his life and his
mission. This same point applies to the life and death of the people. In
their suffering and collective crucifixion, they participate in the salvific
work of Jesus, but this crucifixion cries out to heaven. Like the persecution
of Jesus, the oppression of the crucified peoples represents a monstrous
evil, something to be resisted, something which the coming of God's
Reign will reverse. Like the crucifixion of Jesus, the crucifixion of the
people serves as a powerful protest against and condemnation of the
worldly powers that deal out death in the place where God wills life.
The crucifixion of the crucified people contradicts utterly the will and
the Reign of God. Therefore, while following Jesus may well lead to
persecution and martyrdom, the disciples of Jesus do not directly seek
to be crucified. In the name of Jesus, his followers seek to put an end
to crucifixion, to bring the crucified peoples down from their crosses.
Like Jesus himself, they seek the Reign of God. In this way the salvation
that Jesus mediates continues in history through the same Spirit that
raised Jesus from the dead.

## HISTORICAL SOTERIOLOGY AS ECCLESIOLOGY

At the beginning of chapter 6 I introduced Ellacuría's claim that salvation is salvation in history. Now it is time to return to this claim in order to ponder what this salvation in history involves. As was noted above, the issues of soteriology start to merge here with those of ecclesiology. However, I do not attempt to lay out a detailed summary of Ellacuría's reflections on the church, nor even to trace the extent to which he developed a systematic ecclesiology. My aim is more modest: to probe the pre-ecclesial and ecclesial dimensions of his historical soteriology in order to further observe the implications of his theological method. I also seek to address the issue of theology's relevance which lies beneath the substantive questions of historical soteriology. What difference does theology make? In particular, what difference does liberation theology make? From the perspective of historical soteriology, what is the salvific import of theology itself?

The logic implicit in Ellacuría's project provides a striking response to these questions, especially the last one. Salvation links historical reality to the Reign of God. Ecclesial praxis incarnates that link. Theology objectifies that incarnation in such a way that soteriology manifests an ecclesiological horizon, and ecclesiology exhibits a soteriological motive and foundation. Therefore, by illuminating how the human task of history participates in God's salvific plan for history, theology makes a real difference in our world. Moreover, it empowers those who follow Jesus to understand and exercise their discipleship in terms of that task. This logic can be traced in reverse, beginning with the text in which Ellacuría offers his most elaborate definition of liberation theology. I quote that text in full.

> The theology of liberation understands itself as a reflection from faith on the historical reality and action of the people of God, who follow the work of Jesus in announcing and fulfilling God's Reign. It understands itself as an action by the people of God in following the work of Jesus and, as Jesus did, it tries to establish a living connection between the world of God and the human world. Its reflective character does not keep it from being an action, and an action by the people of God, even though at times it is forced to make use of theoretical tools that seem to remove it both from immediate action and from the theoretical discourse that is popular elsewhere. It is, thus, a theology that begins with historical acts and seeks to lead to historical acts, and therefore it is not satisfied with being a purely interpretive reflection; it is nourished by faithful belief in

the presence of God within history, an operative presence that, although it must be grasped in grateful faith, remains a historical action. There is no room here for faith without works; rather, that faith draws the believers into the very force of God that operates in history, so that we are converted into new historical forms of that operative and salvific presence of God in humanity.[31]

This passage is the opening paragraph of Ellacuría's important essay, "The Church of the Poor, Historical Sacrament of Liberation." As a definition of liberation theology, it contains a number of elements characteristic of Ellacuría's theological method. Among others, one sees the overall framework of historical reality and its theologal-historical horizon. One detects the emphasis on historical praxis, on faith praxis rooted in Jesus, on theological reflection which springs from and returns to praxis, and on action-oriented discipleship which has a strong communal dimension. One also discovers here the dynamics of historical transcendence, the presence of God within history, and the presence of a transcendent salvation which transforms historical reality. However, I wish to examine Ellacuría's technical use of the notion "people of God" in this definition. Both the logic and the implications of grounding liberation theology in historical reality come to light here.

First, the meaning of people of God is not self-evident. Its meaning for Ellacuría appears when this definition is related to the larger essay which the definition introduces. Earlier, I noted that people of God corresponds primarily to Reign of God; its relationship to church derives from this primary relationship. Hence, the more narrow ecclesiological meaning of the phrase emerges from its broader pre-ecclesiological meaning. Second, it is interesting to note that none of the key terms in the title of the essay—"the church," "the poor," "historical sacrament," and "liberation"—are employed in this opening definition. These four elements represent the object of Ellacuría's theological reflections. The point of the essay is to develop a sophisticated, sacramental-ecclesial symbol, the church of the poor as the historical sacrament of liberation. The themes mentioned in the opening paragraph, including people of God, introduce the method and presuppositions by which he arrives at this sacramental-ecclesial symbol. In other words, he first establishes his method, then deploys that method to launch a theological investigation of the soteriological motive and foundation of the church. He uses people of God as a general anthropological symbol to denote the place of his reflection, the crucial second dimension of his theological method. He begins his theological investigation from this historical reality. The result is a genuine ecclesiology from below.[32] As in christology, where the designation "from below" first appears, the result is not a rejection or denigration of doctrinal affirmations. On the contrary, by starting from historical reality, Ellacuría retrieves a vision of the church that is dogmatically sound and credible. To unfold the implications of this claim, I explore further his use of the two phrases, "the true people of God" and "the historical sacrament of liberation," and the logic which links them.

**True People of God.** In the Gospel of Mark, the very first sentence uttered by Jesus proclaims the advent of God's definitive salvation. "This is the time of fulfillment. The Reign of God is at hand. Repent, and believe in the gospel" (Mk 1:15). This salvation has two aspects which are strictly and essentially connected. The one involves turning away from sin, the other, embracing the Reign of God.[33] Moreover, this proclamation of the Reign of God, with its concomitant denunciation of the anti-Reign, manifests a further correlation which proves central to Ellacuría's understanding of Christian salvation. "The Reign of God is for the people and only when the people of God has been constituted will the fullness of the Reign have arrived."[34] The first part of this proposition represents an explicit reference to the concrete salvation which the proclamation of the Reign augurs. The Reign of God is for the people. It does not point primarily to an individual salvation, but highlights the corporate nature of salvation which is gained through belonging to that people which God has chosen and constituted. Although not sufficient by itself, membership in the people operates as a necessary condition of salvation. This claim is supported by the view that salvation, in the form of the full, dynamic presence of the Reign of God, appears precisely when God acts to fashion a people that belongs to God. Furthermore, as the second part of this proposition affirms, the coming of the Reign is intrinsically linked to God's definitive foundation of the people of God. Salvation appears to those who respond to God's call and who act in cooperation with God's grace in order to form a true people of God. It appears when those who were not previously a people stand united by the Holy Spirit as a people. This view of salvation capitalizes on a trinitarian understanding of the God of salvation. At the same time, the very symbol, people of God, with its divine (God) and human (the people) poles, reflects the presence and operation of a salvation that is historically transcendent. Moreover, just as Ellacuría insists on a historically transcendent salvation, he understands the true people of God in a way that is both historical and theological.

Historical in the sense that it has to do with historical reality, with what is happening to people here and now, with their daily toils and struggles, with their real process of liberation. Theological in the sense that it speaks at the same time of something which has to do very directly with God, of something in which the historical becomes transcendent, not by leaving or escaping the social reality of history, but by probing more deeply and remaining in it in order to capture the Spirit that animates it, in order to propel it towards its future, negating the limits of the present and breaking the limitations that reveal it to be full of wounds and sins.[35]

Correlating the people of God with the Reign of God highlights the historical locus of the salvation which the latter represents. Hence, the symbol, people of God, embodies the profound link between historical liberation and salvation that characterizes Ellacuría's understanding of salvation as salvation in history. Moreover, the historical reality to which this symbol points, a people shown to be the true people of God, manifests several key historical-theological traits which Ellacuría details: it is a people of the poor, a people committed to the struggle for justice and liberation, a people whose way of struggling for justice embodies the *ethos* of Jesus, and finally, a people who are persecuted for belonging to the Reign of God. A brief word about each of these four characteristics is in order.

(1) "The people of God is preferentially a people of the poor, a people constituted on behalf of the poor, a people whose preferential option is the liberation of the poor."[36] Ellacuría notes that, according to revelation, this preferential option has nothing to do with whether or not the poor manifest superior values. It emerges instead from the truth about God and the scandal of a divine predilection. "This is what is represented by the model of the people of Israel, where the people come to be a liberated people and thus makes present the truth and the reality of God the liberator."[37] In the life of Jesus, as historicized by the New Testament, the poor, the outcast, the sick, and the victims who lie half-dead at the side of the road, appear as "his favorites, his chosen ones, those to whom he surrendered his blood and his word in a special, preferential, but not exclusive, way."[38] That the people of God is characterized by a fundamental option for the poor thus springs from the theological affirmation that God manifests, in God's own words and deeds, a special attentiveness to the oppressed, the marginalized, and those in bondage.

(2) Because the poverty and oppression of this world stem primarily from sin and injustice, a people constituted by a preferential option for

the poor must become engaged in the struggle to establish justice and freedom while overcoming injustice and bondage. The people of God is thus not only characterized by a willingness to bear the suffering caused by historical injustice, but also by the willingness to confront the evil which causes the suffering. Moreover, Ellacuría maintains that the struggle for liberation necessarily entails the use of force. For this reason, authentic discernment is needed. On the one hand, a group of people does not represent the true people of God if the use of force becomes an end in itself or if it generates the unjustified force of violence. Even the justified use of force must yield to the utopian Christian commitment to peace, represented in the Gospel of Matthew by the call to "turn the other cheek" (Mt 5:39). However, while this utopian commitment must permeate every level of the struggle for justice and liberation, it must not be employed in an idealistic fashion that undermines the struggle itself. The danger of falsifying uses of ideology looms large here. The gospel teaching to turn the other cheek can be quoted by oppressors to immunize them from the gospel's own critique. It can be used by the cowardly to coverup and justify their moral lassitude and inaction. In the end, justice, liberation, and freedom must be understood in such a way that the struggle for their historical realization reflects the dialectic of historical transcendence. "Freedom and justice will only be correctly historicized when they result from a process of liberation and justification, in which the liberating and justifying action of God and the liberating and justifying struggle of the people come together."[39]

(3) While the option for the poor and the struggle for justice and liberty can take many forms, the Christian understanding of these is rooted in the words and actions of Jesus which inaugurate the Reign of God. Moreover, the manner in which this option and struggle character-ize the true people of God manifests a trinitarian structure. First of all, Jesus' words and actions demand that the people of God *be effectively of God*, that the struggle for justice and freedom on behalf of the poor be grounded in an openness to God. Ellacuría argues that openness to the God of the Reign, far from alienating human beings from historical reality, actually places them in ever more profound contact with that reality and with the historical oppression that scars it. He bases this argument on his view of transcendence as transcendence in history. In so doing he responds to those who assert that an openness to transcendence undermines the option for the poor and paralyzes the struggle for justice and liberation. Second, the openness to historical reality which takes shape in and through an openness to God cannot be expressed in word and cult alone. Those who constitute the true people of God embody

that twofold openness in their hearts and actions, and they do so precisely *as disciples of Jesus*, "disciples of Jesus in the realization of the Reign of God, and not only in the individual configuration of its interior dispositions, disciples of Jesus in the conversion of the heart toward the things of God but also and equally in the conversion of the heart to the things of the people in order that they come to constitute themselves as the family of God."[40] While this argument must not be turned around to say that only the followers of Jesus can belong to the true people of God, it does assert that the disciples of Jesus are in a privileged position to link the action of the people of God to the hope of the coming Reign of God which Jesus inaugurated. In other words, the disciples of Jesus are in a position to demonstrate the full Christian meaning of a salvation which appears in the first place as salvation in history. Third, the option for the poor and the struggle for justice and freedom must be *of the same Holy Spirit* that animated Jesus. The spirituality of the people of God is thus characterized by a faith which is open to the manifestation of God's Reign, by an active hope which says "thy will be done" even in Gethsemane, and by a love that fights against every injustice done to God's people, yet remains love in all its projects and struggles. "Given the historical reality of individuals and peoples, compassion is very often the form in which faith, hope and love present themselves; a mercy and a compassion that is preferential towards the most weak, but which extends itself universally to all humans because all human beings are the children of sin and, at the same time, the parents of sin."[41]

(4) Because this world is dominated by sin, and because the proclamation of the Reign of God presupposes the denunciation of the anti-Reign of sin, the true people of God encounter fierce persecution. The persecution of the people as the people of God does not occur for ethical-political reasons alone. Ellacuría argues that, inasmuch as it is unleashed against the people of God for seeking to reconfigure historical reality along the lines of the Reign of God, this persecution has a theologal character. "Any persecution against the people, understood as the gathering of the poorest, above all if they are seeking liberation from their situation of poverty and oppression by just means, is in itself a persecution aimed against the people of God."[42] This does not mean that every action taken against the people necessarily represents an act of persecution in the theologal sense. The political and the theologal spheres, although they are profoundly related, remain distinct. However, the lines between them are often hard to draw, and in some instances, the struggle for justice can involve inevitabilities so fixed that no path to integral liberation can be found except that which involves direct confrontation. The perse-

cution which ensues and which seeks to brutally suppress every legitimate liberative effort contradicts the will of God and represents
persecution for the sake of the Reign.

Ellacuría's enumeration of these four characteristics of the true people
of God proves interesting for at least three reasons. First, the people
of God *qua* theological place manifests the very characteristics which
accompany a genuine, theologal option to shoulder the weight of reality:
the mercy which generates genuine faith, the labor for justice and freedom which incarnates that faith, and the persecution and martyrdom
that crowns it. Second, no group can claim to be the true people of God
on the basis of a merely extrinsic hereditary link to Israel in the Old
Testament or the disciples of Jesus in the New Testament. Rather, a
group of people can correspond to the true people of God only because it responds in the present to the God who calls it to be such a
people. It can be recognized as corresponding to the people of God only
because it manifests the same characteristics traditionally conveyed by
this biblical symbol. Ellacuría highlights this point in order to resist the
reductionistic temptation to interpret the people of God in either a purely
spiritualistic or a merely juridical sense. Both reductionisms sever the
concept of the people of God from the historical reality to which it refers.
"An excessive sacramentalization and hierarchicalization of the church
have abandoned what we might call the materiality and historicity of
the people of God."[43] In contrast to these tendencies, he approaches the
people of God in terms of the historically real characteristics that such
a people should manifest. Third, Ellacuría's enumeration of these characteristics illustrates the way his theological method impacts ecclesiology.
In his reflections on the church, he begins with the pre-ecclesiological
historical reality of the people of God. From there he moves to a more
fully elaborated depiction of the historical-theologal reality of the church
in terms of its salvific mission. In a way that parallels his understanding
of the relationship between historical praxis and ecclesial praxis, he
argues that the concept and reality of the people of God is prior to and
fuller than the concept and reality of the church taken by itself. To return
to the biblical metaphor of bread: where the people of God represent
a lump of dough, the church is salt and leaven.

Ellacuría's insistence that the people of God represents a pre-ecclesiological symbol entails a striking corollary. The church must be conceived
from the perspective of the people of God, not vice versa, even though
there are aspects of the people of God which cannot be fully understood
or realized except in terms of the revelation that has been entrusted to
the church. As a result, one must exercise not only exegetical caution

when moving from the people of God to the church, but theological restraint when speaking of the latter as the people of God.

> It is one thing, in order to overcome the "hierarchical" reduction of the church, to label that which pertains to its unified globality as people of God. It is a distinctly other thing to hold that the fullness of what revelation says about the people of God is expressed adequately in the church as the instrument of salvation or as the medium for the realization of the Reign of God, in which the people, which is humanity as a whole, is really converted into the people of God. This distinction is important, not only because it resolves important theological problems such as the salvific will of God, which neither limits its efficacy to those who visibly belong to the church, nor assures its efficacy to those who, while belonging to it "in the body," do not live in conformity to the dictates of conscience or the gospel, but above all because it puts in terms more historical and universal, more real and incarnated, what equals the will of God for this world. God's will cannot be reduced to the constitution of a minority group of saints who withdraw from the world in order to place themselves in salvific communication with God. Rather, it is extended to all of humanity, to all humans and to all the human, in order that they might have life in abundance not only in the areas of their personal interiority and of their communitarian relations, but also in the area of social-political structures and organization, in order that the world be configured not according to the dominating imperiousness of sin, but according to the liberating imperative of grace.[44]

Ellacuría contends that this interpretation of the true people of God takes nothing away from the dignity of the church. Neither does it diminish the importance of the church's mission to the world. On the contrary, it contributes to an ecclesiology which takes account of historical reality and makes use of historical salvation. Having acknowledged that ecclesial praxis is a part of the larger historical praxis, Ellacuría can now emphasize the importance of the former by outlining the way the church advances the salvation of history.

**Historical Sacrament of Liberation.** The church, viewed from the perspective of the historical reality of the true people of God, realizes its vocation by following Jesus and serving God's Reign. Of course, it does not exist for its own sake. The church exists in order to make the Reign of God present as salvation to the whole world. Furthermore, in following Jesus the church discovers that it is called, as he was called, to be a sacrament of God's salvation. Ellacuría notes that "there is nothing new about understanding the church as a sacrament, even less as a sacrament of salvation. Jesus is the primary and fundamental sacrament of salvation, and the church, in continuing and fulfilling Jesus' ministry, shares that nature at least indirectly. The relative newness appears when we speak of the church as *historical* sacrament of salvation. What is the contribution of this historicity to its sacramentality and to salvation, to the salvific sacramentality of the church?"[45]

In addressing this question, the relevance of Ellacuría's historical soteriology comes into full view. In effect, his soteriological thesis—salvation history is a salvation in history—spawns an ecclesiological correlative. The church as sacrament is a historical sacrament of liberation. The logic of this thesis can be followed through three stages that retain discernible traces of the operation of his theological method. First, to be a sacrament the church must incarnate Christ in history. It must become the historical body of Christ precisely by following the historical footsteps of Jesus. Second, the church becomes the historical body of Christ by becoming a neighbor to the people whom Jesus approached as a neighbor, by embracing their sorrows and struggles, their joys and triumphs. In other words, to be the historical body of Christ, the church must be a church of the poor. Third, the salvific praxis of a church guided by the Holy Spirit continues the life and mission of Jesus in history. This means, concretely, that the church acts as the historical body of Christ and the true church of the poor precisely when it serves as a historical sacrament of liberation. "It follows that the poor are the historical body of Christ, the historical place of his presence and the base of the ecclesial community. In other words, the church is the historical body of Christ insofar as it is the church of the poor; and it is a sacrament of liberation insofar as it is the church of the poor."[46] A brief examination of these images discloses how Ellacuría approaches ecclesiology from below, from the reality of historical salvation.

The sacramentality of the church stems from the originating and fundamental sacrament of salvation, Jesus Christ. "Christ is our great sacrament. This means, for one thing, that He is the sign par excellence of God the savior . . . , but also the efficacious sign, the sign which truly realizes what it announces: the salvation of God in history."[47] Ellacuría notes that the image of the church as sacrament emanates from the antecedent reality of the church's corporeality, a theme already present in the New Testament, especially in the thought of St. Paul. "For just as a body is one and has many members, and all the members of the body, though many, are one body, so it is with Christ" (1 Cor 12:12). He insists, however, that a merely natural understanding of this corporeality

actually deforms the image of the church as the body of Christ. The church
is the body of Christ in history. The logic of Ellacuría's historicization of
salvation impels him to evolve a historical understanding of the church
as the body of Christ.[48] "The historical corporeality of the church implies
that the reality and the action of Jesus Christ are *embodied* in the church,
so that the church will *incorporate* Jesus Christ in the reality of history."[49]
Animated by the Spirit, the church makes Christ visible in the world
and incorporates Christ as an operative presence in history.

> Seen theologically, *being embodied* corresponds to the Word, which *took*
> *flesh* so that it could be seen and touched, so that it could intervene in a
> fully historical way in the action of humanity. . . . *Incorporation* is the
> activation of being embodied; it is becoming a body with that global and
> unified body that is the material history of humanity. Incorporation is an
> indispensable condition for effectiveness in history, and thus for the full
> realization of that which is incorporated. Incorporation thus presupposes
> being embodied, but it also means adhering to the single body of history.[50]

The image of the church as the historical body of Christ echoes the
classical theme of the mystical body of Christ. These images are not
mutually exclusive, for a radical unity of the mystical and the historical
appears in the church, just as it appears in Jesus. "The church's mysticism
does not derive from something mysterious and occult, but from something that surpasses history from within history, from something that
surpasses humanity within humanity, from something that forces us to
say, 'Truly, the finger of God is hidden here.' "[51] Significantly, the accent
falls on the action of Christ's body, the action by means of which the
church picks up and continues the life and mission of Jesus in history,
the action in which the salvation made visible and operative in Christ
is once again visible and operative in history. This action thus represents
the praxis of God's Reign. The church fulfills its sacramental vocation
to mediate salvation to history when it makes concrete the demands of
God's Reign in each historical situation. It embodies Christ in the world
when it makes the life of God present to the world. Finally, as was noted
above, it incorporates Christ in history when it takes away the sin of
the world. Salvation history takes flesh as salvation in history in and
through those who comprise the body of Christ in history. However,
for Ellacuría, that includes not only those who explicitly believe in and
follow Jesus Christ. The church must recognize Jesus in all crucified
peoples, in order to appear as the true body of Christ in history. "One
can say that the true historical body of Christ, and therefore the preeminent locus of his embodiment and his incorporation, is not only the

church, but the poor and the oppressed of the world, so that the church alone is not the historical body of Christ, and it is possible to speak of a true body of Christ outside the church."[52]

In order to be the body of Christ in history, the church must extend the praxis and life of Jesus to each particular, historical situation in which it finds itself. That is, to be the body of Christ, the church must turn to Jesus, but to be his body in history, it must incarnate itself in historical reality. Ellacuría assumes, of course, that the turn to Jesus cannot be accomplished via the path of biblical fundamentalism nor by means of any purely text-driven quest for the historical Jesus. Likewise, the imposition of a literally interpreted biblical reconstruction of Jesus on diverse and discrete historical situations will not effect the continuation of the praxis of Jesus. At the same time, however, there can be no Christian discipleship in the abstract. The way in which believers follow Jesus must be normed by the way of Jesus. The church must labor and fight for the human salvation and liberation in the way that Jesus did. "Jesus does not focus on [salvation and liberation] in a generic and abstract way that leads to human promotion or the defense of human rights, etc., but in a unique way. Confronting a situation that presents a divided society, he seeks human promotion or human rights from the side of the oppressed and on their behalf, in the struggle against the side of the oppressors. In other words, his action is historical and concrete and it goes to the roots of the oppression."[53]

For Ellacuría, the ramifications of this demand are clear. If the poor represent the body of Christ in history, if the victims of history continue to suffer the historical crucifixion of Christ, then the church must turn to the poor, to the crucified people, in order to apprehend and proclaim the salvation entrusted to it. This means that the body of Christ in history, as the sacrament of a salvation which comes from God alone, must be a church of the poor. The church must live in solidarity with the crucified people. In this way, it appropriately assimilates the call to be the people of God. Likewise, this is the way, the only way, in which the church can assume its proper relationship to the Reign of God.

> The church of the poor, therefore, refers to a basic problem of salvation history, because *poor*, in this context, is neither an absolute and ahistorical concept, nor a *profane* or neutral concept. In the first place, when we speak here of the poor, we are actually speaking of a relationship between poor and rich (more generally, between dominated and oppressor), in which there are rich people because there are poor, and the rich cause the poor to be poor, or at least deprive them of a part of what belongs

to them. . . . In the second place, this relationship is not purely profane, not only because we have already rejected the sacred-profane duality in general, but more particularly, because its special dialectic is deeply rooted in what is essential to Christianity: loving God by loving humans, justice as the place in a world of sin where love is realized. From this follows the singular Christian and historical importance of a church of the poor, whose mission is to break that dialectic for the sake of love, in order to achieve the joint salvation of the two opposing sides, presently bound together by sin, not grace.[54]

Ellacuría argues that, to be true to its vocation as a church of the poor, the Christian community must proclaim its faith to poor people in their real situation and in such a way that they can really apprehend that faith as salvific. The salvation which faith proclaims must be historically real and attainable in real, historical situations. By turning to the poor, the church rediscovers its voice and its vision, its prophetic capacity and its utopian hope. The church, which becomes a true church of the poor, recovers its moral compass. Its praxis restores credibility to its faith. Its theology regains its apologetic weight. Finally, the gospel proclaimed and lived by such a church, far from being an opium of the people, becomes a genuine sacrament of historical liberation. Here, Ellacuría's vision of the church as the body of Christ in history achieves its full impact.

Because salvation history is a salvation in history, because the sacrament of salvation fulfills its vocation precisely as a sacrament of historical salvation, because liberation is the historical form of salvation, therefore the church is called to be the historical sacrament of liberation. The logic which drives this conclusion, a logic already latent in the very historicization of salvation, can be spelled out further in terms of Ellacuría's threefold method. A church that *discovers* that it is called as Jesus was to be a sacrament of salvation, a church which *discerns* its place among the poor and in this way becomes the body of Christ in history, *realizes* the depths of its sacramental identity in the praxis of historical liberation. To be a genuine sacrament of salvation, the church must be and must act as a historical sacrament of liberation.

Ellacuría argues further that "what the church contributes to the salvation of history is the constitutive sign of the history of salvation. The church belongs intrinsically to this history of salvation and carries within it the visible part that reveals and makes effective the whole of salvation."[55] While the contribution that ecclesial praxis makes to the totality of historical praxis does not represent the full extent of God's action with humanity, it represents something essential, something without which history cannot be fully realized. Moreover, as was noted above, the church seeks to transform history in the manner of leaven and salt, to exercise power in this world without becoming a worldly power. This argument does not result in reductionism. It does not equate salvation with historical-political liberation alone. However, it does insist that the salvation of historical reality be historically real. Finally, "if we consider the universality in our time of the historical cry of the peoples, social classes, and individuals for liberation from oppression, it is not hard to see that the church, as a universal sacrament of salvation, must become a sacrament of liberation."[56] The church is called to be the efficacious sign of God's universal salvific will, to respond to every form of oppression, to extend the liberating presence of grace in every age, to incarnate the salvation which Jesus brings in all places. Therefore, the church must mediate a liberating salvation that is both universal and integral.

> Certainly there are other forms of oppression besides the sociopolitical and economic, and not all forms of oppression derive exclusively and immediately from that one. Christians would be wrong, therefore, to seek only one type of social liberation. Liberation must extend to everyone who is oppressed by sin and by the roots of sin; it must accomplish liberation both from the objectification of sin and from the internal principle of sin; it must extend to both unjust structures and the people who do injustice; it must extend both to the inner life of people and to the things they do. The goal of liberation is full freedom, in which full and right relationships are possible, among people and between them and God. The way to liberation can only be the way that Jesus followed, the way which the church must follow historically, the way in which it must believe and hope as an essential element of human salvation.[57]

The shift in ecclesial self-understanding which Ellacuría champions helps the church embody an ever more prophetic faith, utopian hope, and historically real love. Conversely, as the impact of base ecclesial communities on ecclesiology testifies, when the church historicizes its faith, hope, and love in liberating pastoral practice, its self-understanding changes along with its way of understanding and relating to secular historical realities. Furthermore, although Ellacuría does not develop this point in detail, an ecclesiology rooted in historical soteriology might open the path to a more credible exercise of ecclesial authority. This in turn could make possible a wider range of approaches to issues of ecumenism and interreligious dialogue, to the vexing practical issues surrounding church order, and to the current crisis of church ministry. Correlatively, as Ellacuría's own theological praxis demonstrates, the church as historical sacrament of liberation flowers in a new image of the Christian university—with all that this implies—as well as new images of religious life and lay spirituality. But perhaps most significantly, this ecclesiology contains explosive personal and political implications for all Christians, for it leavens their historical praxis, thus proportionately transforming historical reality. Given Ellacuría's theologal understanding of historical reality and his view of the church as a historical sacrament of liberation, one might even argue that his writings on such "mundane" realities as Salvadoran politics and the civil war, national and international economics, the nature of popular movements, and the role of the university, etc., represent the ideological moment of a sacramental faith praxis.

The sacramental faith praxis that mediates salvation through historical liberation thus breathes new life into one's fundamental experience of church. Such an approach also empowers the church to theologically engage the crises and opportunities which accompany the dawn of a new century. Moreover, as was noted above, this image of the church radically colors the meaning of theology and the aim of the theological vocation. Jon Sobrino summarizes this point succinctly: "Theology becomes converted in its very task and not only in the contents which it offers, into soteriology. It becomes compassionate reason."[58] Hence, in the view of Ignacio Ellacuría, theology is not only an academic vocation. It too can be seen as a historical sacrament. It not only conceptualizes the link between historical reality and the Reign of God which ecclesial praxis incarnates, it embodies that link. And this view of theology is not only sketched in Ellacuría's writings; it can be verified in the utopian hope that shaped his life, the prophetic faith for which he was killed, and the radical love with which he died.

## Notes to Chapter 7

1. *Spiritual Exercises*, No. 53.
2. I trace the development of his reflections in terms of the article, cited earlier, which molds these two questions into its title: "Por qué muere Jesús y por qué le matan." Jon Sobrino cites this article and comments extensively on these two questions in *Jesus the Liberator*; see especially, chapter 7, "The Death of Jesus: Why Jesus Was Killed, 195–211; chapter 8, "The Death of Jesus: Why Jesus Died," 219–232. The question of why Jesus was killed "is explained in terms of Jesus' history"; the question of why he died "is not, strictly speaking, answered, but referred to the mystery of God," Sobrino, *Liberator*, 195.
3. "Por qué muere Jesús" (1977) 73–74.

4. "El pueblo crucificado" (1978) 196, trans. mine; *MLT*, 585.

5. Ibid., 196, trans. mine; *MLT*, 585–586.

6. Ibid., 190, trans. mine; *MLT*, 581. Ellacuría further clarifies this important hermeneutical principle. "The first aspect appears obvious from the angle of Christian faith, even though it conceals a difficulty: that of finding the correct equivalence, in order not to take as the key for one situation that which is key for another. The second aspect, which has a circular relationship with the prior one, is less obvious, above all if we hold that the situation enriches and actualizes the fullness of the revelation, and if we hold further that not every situation is best equipped to help revelation unfold its fullness and its authenticity," ibid., 190; *MLT*, 581.

7. Ibid., 190, trans. mine; *MLT*, 581.

8. Ibid., 198–199, trans. mine; *MLT*, 588.

9. Ibid., 198, trans. mine; *MLT*, 588.

10. Ibid., 197, trans. mine; *MLT*, 587.

11. Ibid., 197, trans. mine, emphasis mine; *MLT*, 586–587.

12. Ibid., 197–198, trans. mine; *MLT*, 587.

13. "Por que muere Jesús" (1977) 74.

14. "El pueblo crucificado" (1978) 200, trans. mine; *MLT*, 589.

15. Ibid., 201, trans. mine; *MLT*, 590.

16. Ibid., 201, trans. Berryman and Barr; *MLT*, 590. Ellacuría describes the crucified people with a sense of immediacy and urgency. "The historically crucified people, a permanent part of history whose crucifixion appears in ever distinct historical forms. . .is the historical continuation of the Servant of Yahweh, whom the sin of the world continues to disfigure down to the last human feature, whom the powerful of this world continue to strip of everything, snatching away even their life, above all their life," Ellacuría, "Discernir 'el signo' de los tiempos," *Diakonía* (No. 17, 1981) 58, trans. mine. Sobrino reflects on Ellacuría's own martyrdom in terms of this profound image, and he ponders the crucified peoples in the light of the well-known book by Jürgen Moltmann, *The Crucified God* (New York: Harper & Row, 1974) trans. by R.A. Wilson and John Bowden; see Sobrino, "The Crucified Peoples," *The Principle of Mercy*, op. cit., 49. As was noted earlier, Ellacuría's coining of this phrase should also be linked to his Ignatian mysticism; see chapter 1.

17. "El pueblo crucificado" (1978) 202, trans. mine; *MLT*, 590. Ellacuría develops this point to critique Western individualism. "The modern concern to highlight the individual dimension of human existence will prove faithful to reality only if it does not overlook the social dimension, something which does not occur in the individualistic and idealistic convulsions so characteristic of Western culture or, at the very least, of the *elites* within that culture. All of the egoism and social irresponsibility borne by this conception is but a negative proof of the dishonesty of this exaggeration. There is no need to deny the collective and structural dimension in order to give ample scope to the full development of the person," ibid., 202, author's emphasis; *MLT*, 590–591.

18. "El pueblo crucificado" (1978) 202, trans. Berryman and Barr; *MLT*, 591.

19. Ibid., 203, trans. mine; *MLT*, 592.

20. Ibid., 203, trans. mine; *MLT*, 592.

21. Ibid., 203, trans. mine; *MLT*, 592.

22. "Historicidad de la salvación cristiana" (1984) 361, trans. Wilde; *MLT*, 279.

23. "El pueblo crucificado" (1978) 202, trans. mine; *MLT*, 591.

24. Ibid., 202, trans. mine; *MLT*, 591.

25. Ellacuría prescinds from the scholarly debate on the question of whether the servant is a collective subject or an individual, a particular king or prophet. Both types of readings have a long history in the tradition and there is no reason to regard them as mutually exclusive.

26. Ibid., 210, trans. mine; *MLT*, 598.

27. Ibid., 209, trans. mine; *MLT*, 598.

28. Ibid., 209–210, trans. mine; *MLT*, 598.

29. See ibid., 213–214; *MLT*, 601–602.

30. Ibid., 215, trans. mine; *MLT*, 603.

31. "Sacramento histórico" (1977) 127, trans. Wilde, emended; *MLT*, 543.

32. The suggestion that Ellacuría develops "a genuine ecclesiology from below" is elaborated more fully in Roger Haight, "Ecclesiology From Below: Principles from Ignacio Ellacuría," in R. Lassalle-Klein and K. Burke, eds., *The Love That Produces Hope*, op. cit.

33. Ellacuría also calls this twofold aspect "the liberation from our sins and the divinization of our humanity," "Iglesia y realidad historica" (1976) 217, trans. mine. Zubiri uses the familiar Patristic image of "divinization" to give theological expression to his metaphysics of human realization. Ellacuría occasionally adopts this language, but prefers to explore the positive dimension of salvation using the biblical language of the Reign of God.

34. "Pueblo de Dios" (1983) 846.

35. "Verdadero pueblo" (1981) 530.

36. "Pueblo de Dios" (1983) 847.

37. Ibid., 849.

38. Ibid., 848.

39. Ibid., 850.

40. Ibid., 851–852.

41. Ibid., 852–853.

42. Ibid., 853.

43. Ibid., 855.

44. Ibid., 857–858.

45. "Sacramento histórico" (1977) 128, trans. Wilde, author's emphasis; *MLT*, 544.

46. Ibid., 148, trans. Wilde, emended; *MLT*, 558.

47. "Iglesia y realidad historica" (1976) 217.

48. The same logic that appears in this exercise of historicization constitutes the central theme of the Second Pastoral Letter of Archbishop Oscar Romero, which Ellacuría cites in "Sacramento histórico" (1977) 131; see *MLT*, 546. "The church is the Body of Christ in history. By this expression we understand that Christ has wished to be himself the life of the church through the ages. The church's foundation is not to be thought of in a legal or juridical sense, as if Christ gathered some persons together, entrusted them with a teaching, gave them a kind of constitution, but then himself remained apart from them. It is not like that. The church's origin is something much more profound. Christ founded the church so that he himself could go on being present in the history of humanity precisely through the group of Christians who make up his church. The church is the flesh in which Christ makes present down the ages his own life and his personal mission," Archbishop Oscar Romero, "The Church, the Body of Christ in History," *Voice of the Voiceless: The Four Pastoral Letters and Other Statements*, trans. by Michael J. Walsh, emended (Maryknoll: Orbis, 1985) 70–71.

49. "Sacramento histórico" (1977) 130, trans. Wilde, emended, author's emphasis; *MLT*, 545.
50. Ibid., 130, trans. Wilde, emended, author's emphasis; *MLT*, 545.
51. Ibid., 131, trans. Wilde; *MLT*, 546.
52. Ibid., 184, trans. Wilde; *MLT*, 546.
53. Ibid., 145, trans. mine; *MLT*, 557.
54. Ibid., 148, trans. mine, author's emphasis; *MLT*, 559.
55. Ibid., 141, trans. mine; *MLT*, 554.
56. Ibid., 144, trans. mine; *MLT*, 556.
57. Ibid., 144, trans. mine; *MLT*, 556.
58. Sobrino, "Principio liberación," 127.

# Conclusion

# The Ground Beneath Theology

*Ignacio Ellacuría often said, "Here in El Salvador life is worthless." He was wrong; his own example gives the lie to his affirmation.*

Gustavo Gutiérrez[1]

Gustavo Gutiérrez says that Ellacuría was "wrong" but does not mean it. He means, rather, that Ellacuría was "right," as right as a human being can be, and at the greatest personal cost a human being can pay. The life of Ellacuría confirms the profound Christian intuition that believers find the living God, the only true God, in and among the poor. If the affirmation that "in El Salvador life is worthless" betrays Ellacuría's biting irony, his commitment to those "worthless Salvadorans" reveals, as Gutiérrez notes, the magnitude of his love. "The life of Salvadorans had to be worth a lot to him to make him and his companions remain in El Salvador. These were people of great intellectual gifts and at the same time committed to that country to the point of risking their lives. The lives of Salvadorans had to be worth a lot in order for them to do this."[2] The power of Ellacuría's commitment and love lives on. It cannot be killed, as the history of martyrdom's effect on the life of the church testifies. It rises again and again in the faith of God's people, as Monseñor Romero prophesied it would just weeks before his own martyrdom.[3] Like Romero, Ellacuría and his companions continue to live in the faith and remembrance of their people. Moreover, one discovers in Ellacuría that the power of his love also abides in his theological vision. I believe this is so because his theology sprang from the ground of that love.

While the manner of Ellacuría's life and the dramatic circumstances of his death merit attention and perhaps even admiration, his importance to Latin American liberation theology and the value of his theological contribution beyond Latin America must be measured on their own terms. In the wake of his death, many people have taken interest in his life and have begun to study his thought with greater intentionality. Still, it remains true today that he is rarely numbered among the most influential and important advocates of Latin American liberation theology.[4] In his own lifetime he did not receive the international recognition afforded Gustavo Gutiérrez or the late Juan Luis Segundo, nor did he enjoy the popular notoriety of Leonardo Boff. His friend and colleague, Jon Sobrino, is far better known as a theologian, even though Sobrino himself speaks of Ellacuría as the most brilliant and original of all the Latin American liberation theologians.[5] In the area of philosophical ethics, the liberation thinker who comes most readily to mind is Enrique Dussel, not Ellacuría. The same obtains in relation to the formal study of theological method, where observers nearly always cite Clodovis Boff as the most influential Latin American theologian in this regard. At the very least it can be said that, prior to Ellacuría's death, the theological academy both in and beyond Latin America gave Ellacuría's thought only modest attention. A variety of factors may have contributed to that. I wish to draw attention to two of them, focusing especially on the way they might continue to affect his reception in North America.[6]

From the time that Ellacuría's theological writings first began to appear in English, his readers have been hampered by the relative inaccessibility of the philosophical vision behind them. Clearly his appropriation of Zubiri's thought led to some of his more fruitful insights. Likewise, what is most distinctive about his contributions to liberation theology can be traced largely to the creative way he developed and deployed his mentor's vision. Yet this dependence on Zubiri has a problematic side. It is important to recall that Zubiri severed his relationship to the academy and crafted his philosophical vision in relative isolation from institutions of higher learning. He preferred to form a private community of philosophers and followers. Moreover, he relied on his own idiosyncratic philosophical lexicon, developing a range of neologisms and fashioning new definitions for certain standard terms. This bestows a greater than usual degree of difficulty on the effort to wrestle with his thought. Finally, beyond Spain and Latin America, Zubiri remains virtually unknown. Therefore, at least with respect to the North American theological community, Ellacuría's reliance on Zubiri's distinctive vision and his regular use of Zubiri's highly specialized vocabulary exposes him to the risk of being stranded in an intellectual cul-de-sac where his works remain largely unread or at least misunderstood. If in fact Ellacuría has produced a theological method that springs from and mediates genuine faith both in and beyond Latin America, then the difficulties created by his reliance on Zubiri can be overcome. At the same time, a more thorough understanding of Ellacuría's theology might contribute to a revived interest in Zubiri's philosophy. But none of this is automatic. The reception of a scholar's contribution depends on the openness and hard work of a host of people. Even if Ellacuría's thought represents a theological treasure, as I have asserted, it must be tapped and appropriated by a wider community of academic theologians, social justice advocates, pastoral ministers, and other believers to be of use to the people of God.

Second, the modest initial response to Ellacuría's thought appears tied to the very nature of his writings, to the fact that he only provides an outline of his theological method, and deals with issues of systematic and moral theology only on an occasional basis. Thus, while moral and systematic theologians can find important contributions to their fields among his writings, they do not find in his corpus a fully developed moral or systematic theology. As for his contribution to fundamental theology, his essays witness to the comprehensive scope of his vision but fail to provide a fully developed account of it. The posthumous publication of *Filosofía de la realidad histórica* closes the gap to some extent, but as I noted above, it has not been translated into English. Moreover, it does not slake the theologian's thirst for a detailed statement of his *theological* method. And while everything seems to indicate that Ellacuría would have continued writing had he not been killed, it is not clear that he would have felt the need to produce a complete theological synthesis. What we do know is that his dedication to university administration, social commentary, and political activity, not to mention his interest in Ignatian spirituality and his love for pure philosophy, demanded much of his time and limited what he was able to contribute directly to academic theology. Whether the corpus he left behind carries sufficient weight to generate long-term theological interest and warrant further study remains to be seen.

Beyond these factors, which represent limitations on the accessibility of Ellacuría's thought, a further question arises. As a liberation theologian, did he primarily restate what others had already said or did he add something genuinely new? This question is confounding because of the subtlety with which specific insights and entire intellectual frameworks merge and mutually influence one another in the history of human thought. Yet it serves as a reminder that those who call themselves liberation theologians are not necessarily saying the same things, while those who think of themselves as anything but liberation theologians might be deeply implicated in its presuppositions and concerns. On the one hand liberation theologians frame their goals, elaborate their methods, and articulate their systematic insights in ways that bear definite family resemblances. On the other hand they also distinguish and develop their insights in a variety of ways, making use of different background theories to expound on common themes. Even those liberation theologians broadly grouped under the geographic rubric of Latin America write from specific contexts that manifest as many differences as similarities. Therefore, with certain qualifications, I would assert that the answer to both parts of this "confounding" question can be answered in the affirmative. Ellacuría does echo themes previously articulated by his mentors and colleagues. At the same time he does add something new. Moreover, his theological writings speak not only to the church in Latin America, but to the concerns of believers and the questions of theologians throughout the world.

I have argued throughout this book that Ellacuría's originality lies primarily in the way he links liberation theology to the philosophy of historical reality, a marriage that creatively transforms both partners. To underscore in another way the power of this synthesis, I review his contribution to liberation theology against a rapid sketch of several key issues treated by Gustavo Gutiérrez and Juan Luis Segundo.

Hardly anyone familiar with liberation theology, whether they be advocates or opponents, would fail to acknowledge the importance of Gustavo Gutiérrez for the emergence and vitality of this movement.[7] Considered by many to be the father of Latin American liberation theology, his text *A Theology of Liberation* is the closest thing to a classic yet produced by a liberation theologian. In it he makes major contributions to the method of liberation theology. He thinks about salvation and the church in breathtaking images, and crafts new frameworks for approaching ancient dilemmas in soteriology and ecclesiology. With several of his later books he became one of the first liberation theologians to reflect at length on the spirituality of liberation.[8] In his more recent meditations on the life of Bartolomé de Las Casas, he illuminates the history of conquest in Latin America and evokes the prophetic edge of the Christian gospel that Las Casas himself rediscovered.[9]

In all of his writings Gutiérrez consistently employs an understanding of theology that regards the reflective moment as a second act. Theology springs from and follows the primary act, the life of Christian faith.

> The point I want to make can be stated thus: God is first contemplated when we do God's will and allow God to reign; only after that do we think about God. To use familiar categories: contemplation and practice together make up a *first act*; theologizing is a *second act*. We must first establish ourselves on the terrain of spirituality and practice; only subsequently is it possible to formulate discourse on God in an authentic and respectful way.[10]

This view of theology does not arise arbitrarily. Rather, it springs from the spirituality of Christian discipleship and has long been operative in the Christian tradition, however new its formulation appears today. "The function of theology as critical reflection on praxis has gradually become more clearly defined in recent years, but it has its roots in the first centuries of the Church's life. The Augustinian theology of history that we find in *The City of God*, for example, is based on a true analysis of the signs of the times and the demands with which they challenge the Christian community."[11] Along with the priority of praxis, Gutiérrez was among the first theologians to argue eloquently from and for a preferential theological option for the poor. Perhaps his greatest achievement lies in the way he reinterprets both dogmatic theology and theological ethics from the perspective he dubs "the underside of history," a perspective that sheds light on both the meaning of history and the role of theology. "The theology of liberation begins from the questions asked by the poor and plundered of the world, by 'those without a history,' by those who are oppressed and marginalized precisely by the interlocutor of progressivist theology."[12]

While Gutiérrez develops a theology of liberation in the light of Christian soteriology and ecclesial spirituality, Juan Luis Segundo's well-known contribution to the "liberation of theology" unfolds within the rich, anthropological parameters of his christology and theology of grace.[13] By developing an ontology of human action, Segundo attempts to resolve the crisis that stems from an inadequate conception of the relationships of history to nature and between the action of God and human action. For this reason he attaches special importance to the ethical-hermeneutical task set before graced human freedom, which has as its object and destiny the eschatologically construed creation of a world. Similarly, he insists that a "political key" is necessary for developing a christology that frees Jesus "from all the false pretensions of human beings, of Christians certainly, to grab hold of him, box him in universal categories, and thus strip him and his cross of their bite and scandal."[14]

This political key proves crucial, in Segundo's view, to an adequate contemporary understanding of the parables, praxis, and destiny of Jesus. Without it Christians cannot fulfill their vocation to continuously write the gospel anew, but fall instead into the habit of repeating safe theological formulae that never come near the reality to which Jesus pointed. Hence, while theology can be liberating, it must also be liberated. Otherwise it tends to hide in abstractions, to remove itself from the real demands of life and daily justice, and to render itself incapable of mediating faith in an increasingly secular and pluralistic world. This liberation of theology depends in turn on the development of cogent background theories capable of addressing the relationship between "faith and ideologies." It is precisely here that Segundo emphasizes theology's need for the mediation of the social sciences.

Ellacuría does not often quote either Gutiérrez or Segundo directly, as I mentioned above. However, it takes no more than these brief sketches to indicate that numerous parallels exist among all three thinkers. As was noted earlier, Ellacuría deploys distinctions having to do with the use of concepts and ideologies that come very close to Segundo's insights into ideological mediation. Likewise, key elements in Gutiérrez's method reappear in Ellacuría's central theological concern to interpret salvation from the place of the poor as a salvation in history. Nevertheless, Ellacuría's thought is not simply a restatement of either Segundo or Gutiérrez. While he incorporates an understanding of integral liberation very close to that which Gutiérrez articulates, he develops it against the background of his philosophical explication of the dynamism by which reality is realized as historical reality. Like Segundo, he deploys the prophetic and utopian demands of liberation critically. But utilizing the background understanding of sentient intelligence that he takes from Zubiri, he is able to build the critical process of historicization into the very heart of his understanding of theology. Like Segundo, Ellacuría recognizes theology's need for liberation, and he argues for mediating ideologies like the social sciences so that theology can be liberated from its own ideological oblivion. But he consistently returns to the larger unified horizon of historical reality and philosophically articulates its character as ground. While he reads the Christian theological tradition in a way that exhibits deep resonances with the thought of Segundo and Gutiérrez, he also takes at least one crucial step beyond them. Without discounting the insights of his liberation colleagues, while in fact incorporating and utilizing them, Ellacuría recovers theology's need for a philosophical rendering of reality from the perspective of history and historical liberation. For this reason he begins articulating a Latin

American philosophy of liberation rooted in the philosophy of historical reality; he seeks to contribute to a philosophical discourse capable of moving liberation theology beyond the narrow socio-economic-political matrix that characterized its emergence; and he helps steer liberation theology into wider conversations concerned with history and metaphysics, culture and cultural pluralism, freedom and liberation, along with interpretation, historicization, and the critique of ideologies.

I have argued that Ellacuría's most important contribution to Latin American liberation theology appears in the way he generates the threefold structure of theological method on the basis of his philosophical sketch of the encounter with reality. One might be tempted to associate his proposal with the triple division which Clodovis Boff employs in his exposition of Latin American theological method.[15] For this reason, I briefly consider Ellacuría in relation to Boff.

As with Gutiérrez and Segundo, Ellacuría shares much in common with Boff. For one thing, both Ellacuría and Boff forge their respective methods in terms of liberation, the option for the poor, the primacy of praxis, and the view of theology as "second moment." It can even be sustained that the underlying logic that structures the way each conducts his analysis has a common source, namely, the world of the poor in all its historical concreteness. However, they approach this common source with different philosophical presuppositions. Boff articulates three theological mediations, the socioanalytic, hermeneutic, and practical, and relates them to the basic elements of the popular pastoral method that focuses on seeing, judging, and acting. But Boff's discussion of these three mediations is not simply a different way to say what Ellacuría is saying in his method. Nor do they define theology in exactly the same way. Boff describes his approach as a political theology.[16] He distinguishes a *first theology*, which deals with classical religious themes, from a *second theology* which deals with social-political issues. "Where a first theology is concerned, it seems clear to me that a theological practice will not necessarily have to be mediated by the social sciences. . . . On the other hand, it seems to me equally clear that in the area of a second theology— for our purposes, a political theology—the social sciences will be genuinely constitutive of the theoretical organization of a corresponding discourse."[17] Ellacuría views this separation into first and second theologies as "unacceptable" and potentially misleading.

> The book of Clodovis Boff,[18] so many chapters of which are excellent, might cause a distorted image of the theology of liberation or might lead it into theological regionalizations that are neither necessary nor desirable.

> The theology of liberation should not be understood as a political theology, but as a theology of the Reign of God, so that the material distinction between a T 1 that deals with the classical themes of God, Christ, the church, and a T 2 that deals with more specifically human and/or political themes, is not acceptable in itself, although secondary considerations may occasionally suggest methodical separations. Indeed, the theology of liberation deals primarily with everything that has to do with the Reign of God; but it focuses on every theme, even the most elevated and apparently suprahistorical, in the context of and often with special attention to its liberating dimension.[19]

Ellacuría criticizes Boff's distinction because he wants to insist on the radical unity of the realm of theological discourse and of the object of theology, that is, the unity of God's action in history and the Reign of God. In a similar way, as we saw above, he moves away from the classical separation of the natural and the supernatural. Every theological discussion, including those concerned with strictly extramundane realities, finds its validity in terms of historical reality.

This brings me to the key issue to be addressed in an assessment of Ellacuría's theology: the relationship between his thought and the ground from which it springs, the historical reality of Latin America. Does Ellacuría's contribution to liberation theology represent an integrated interpretation of the whole of the Christian faith in a way that remains faithful to the experiences of Latin Americans? This question assumes that his thought will prove valuable insofar as it remains both faithful to the total vision of Christianity and relevant to the particular reality of Latin America. But this question also provokes further questions regarding the very possibility and legitimacy of a Latin American theology and the criteria by which such a theology could be judged "Latin American." Because the entire argument of this book attempts to respond to these questions, I limit my remarks here to two themes that summarize my overall assessment of Ellacuría and how I understand the Latin American character of his theology. Accordingly, I briefly examine the general possibility and necessity of a Latin American theology, then look at the specific manner in which Ellacuría's theology actualizes this possibility and corresponds to this necessity.

(1) Questions about the general possibility and necessity of a Latin American theology implicate the very meaning of theology. Throughout its history Christian theology has concerned itself with the whole of Christian faith. Moreover, it has sought to articulate the lasting and universal truths of that faith. However, the notion of truth has a history

and the precise understanding of what constitutes truth develops and changes throughout that history. These changes profoundly affect the perception of theology and its lasting and universal qualities. Christians with a classicist world-view tend to find the idea of a distinctively Latin American theology incoherent or at least antithetical to their understanding of theology.[20] One can imagine them arguing that the modifier "Latin American" necessarily limits the scope or reduces the meaning of theology, and that insofar as theology aims to speak Latin American truths, it no longer adequately represents lasting and universal truths. However, I maintain that arguments like these easily fall prey to a form of "theological Docetism." They assume that universal truth can be apprehended in such a way that historicity and social context prove irrelevant to the content of truth. As we have seen, Ellacuría argues against this view. Christian revelation does not annul but operates precisely in terms of the dynamics of the human encounter with reality. Furthermore, those dynamics stipulate that the human apprehension of any truth occurs in terms of certain historical, socially situated, and culturally conditioned factors. Transcendent reality appears in and through historical reality. Thus, it is possible to do theology from specific historical settings. More importantly, *only* from specific historical settings does transcendent reality appear. For this reason it is necessary to do theology from a specific situation and to regard every theology as historically situated. This does not, in Ellacuría's view, result in a radical pluralism of theologies with no common center. Neither does it destroy the unity or universality of the Christian vision. On the contrary, a theology grounded in historical reality preserves the unity and universality of that vision from what in fact most perniciously and ubiquitously threatens it, the tendency towards ahistorical, reductionistic idealism.

(2) Because it is possible to do theology from concrete historical places, it is possible to do theology from Latin America. But beyond the *general* necessity that theology be done from some particular place, Ellacuría goes further and argues for a *specific* ethical-historical necessity that appears in our day: among other places, theology must be done from Latin America. Negatively, he argues that it is necessary for Christian theological reflection to occur precisely in, from, and for the crucified reality of Latin America in order that theology avoid degenerating into ideology. Positively, he contends that this historical reality of Latin America constitutes a genuine *lugar teofánico*—a place where the action and revelation of God can become manifest—and a *lugar teológico*—a place where God's people can grasp, understand, integrate, and respond to that action and revelation. His positive argument depends on the

contrast generated by the negative argument. That Latin America represents a privileged theological place hinges on the role played by the dialectic of utopia and propheticism in theological method and assumes the same logic as the affirmation that Latin America is a privileged place of utopia and propheticism.[21] The logic inherent in this step connects directly with the manner in which Ellacuría's theology corresponds to the possibility and necessity of Latin American theology. It sheds light not only on the meaning of theology but the meaning of Latin America, which is not some objectified "thing," but an intricate matrix of interconnected social, religious, and cultural migrations, political intrigues and economic pressures, liberation movements and personal stories, hurricanes, rainy seasons, cash crops, earthquakes, and more.

In summary, the critical, deideologizing force of Ellacuría's method springs from his insight into the dynamic structure of historical reality. It is not by speaking in the simple vocabulary of *campesinos* or urban slum dwellers that he can claim to have crafted a Latin American theology, but by unmasking and historicizing the forces that harass and kill them. As a Christian theologian he speaks to the particular context of El Salvador by naming and denouncing the powers of death that crucify the Salvadoran poor and by remembering the God of life who liberates and raises them to new life. Moreover, while this way of proclaiming the Christian gospel in both its prophetic and utopian moments emerges "from below," from the situated context of a particular historical reality, it does not remain there. The designation "from below" does not function ontologically, but epistemologically, in line with the way humans in fact encounter and engage historical reality.[22] For this reason Ellacuría's theology does not collapse into reductionistic relativism. On the contrary, the dynamism at work in Ellacuría's method progresses from the situated context toward ever more encompassing encounters with the whole of historical reality. To paraphrase Karl Rahner's brilliant insight into the relationship between the radical dependence of the creature on God and its genuine reality as distinct from God, Ellacuría's theological method recognizes that the historical relevance and universal character of theological truth exist in direct not inverse proportion to one another.[23] What is universal becomes manifest precisely through the intensification of particularity. In my judgment, this is why Ellacuría's theology has tremendous value and utility for theology today. This is why he should prove especially attractive to any and all contextual theologies, whether they be liberation theologies written from the elaborate interreligious contexts of Asia or the complex cultural-political realities of neocolonial Africa; whether they be feminist, *mujerista*, or womanist theologies originating in the

United States; whether they take the form of Metz's political theology or Tracy's public-hermeneutical theology. I am convinced that Ellacuría has something important to offer all of them: a theological method sufficiently flexible to be employed in a wide range of contexts and sufficiently catholic to highlight what holds them together.

In this book I set out to examine the writings of Ignacio Ellacuría with the aim of discovering the integrating core of his theology. At the start I proposed a thesis that formulates that core. *By grounding theological method in historical reality and praxis, Ellacuría seeks to establish that salvation history is salvation in and of history.* From the ground of historical reality Ellacuría engages the central mysteries of the Christian faith, including the mystery of the cross. He approaches the cross, where the reality of sin meets the revelation of God's salvation, as a historical reality. He approaches historical reality as the ground beneath the cross. The principal theme of Ellacuría's theology and the focal point of his entire life appear precisely here, where the cross penetrates the ground beneath it. In Ellacuría's view, the theology of liberation grows out of this ground and, in a variety of ways, this ground fortifies his claim that liberation theology continues to represent an important voice in the Roman Catholic Church as it enters its twenty-first century and third millennium.

The ground of historical reality houses the dynamic structure of Ellacuría's theological method and gives real weight to his theological articulation of the Christian faith. However, he does not posit this ground. Neither does he construct it conceptually it in order to build a theology upon it. Rather, theology engages historical-theologal reality in terms of the three crucial dimensions of human sentient intelligence. *Theological reflection* receives its focus from questions generated by the historical reality of the people of God. *Theological discernment* proceeds in terms of the signs of the times which appear in the places where the people of God live. *Theological praxis* addresses these questions and responds to these signs in the grammar of transformative action. Ellacuría's method thus renders explicit a central ramification of all liberation theologies and other contextual theologies, namely, that they operate as historically conscious theologies of reality. His own historicization of salvation illustrates this. He surveys the ground beneath the cross from the perspective of the victims of historical crucifixion. He concretely links the cross of Jesus to the oppression of God's people throughout history. He reenacts the primordial Christian gesture of taking the crucified peoples down from their crosses and, in so doing, retrieves the Christian task of history.

Utilizing this method, he thus approaches the salvation history revealed in the biblical tradition as a real salvation in and of history. The life, mission, and sacramentality of the church flow from and reflect this foundational soteriology, and all the other questions of theology are addressed from it.

In his examination of the ground beneath the cross, that is, in his development of a theological method grounded in historical reality and responsive to the cries of the crucified peoples, Ellacuría makes a distinctive and crucial contribution to Catholic theology at the dawn of the twenty-first century. His philosophical framework generates new ways to articulate the connection between the historical and the natural; his theological method produces a revitalized appreciation of the way human reality is encountered by divine reality; his historical soteriology recovers a Christian voice capable of announcing the astonishing Good News. But Ellacuría not only saw and spoke about these connections; he embraced and lived them. He lived at the crossroads where theory and praxis meet, where reason and compassion join hands, where prophetic love becomes one with utopian hope. The totality of his life and thought assumes its characteristic shape at the threeway crossroads of intelligence, mercy, and service. This latter characterization, which appears in Jon Sobrino's first "Letter to Ignacio Ellacuría," recapitulates Ellacuría's own theological method.

> Over and above everything else, you were a person of compassion and mercy, and . . . the inmost depths of you, your guts and your heart, wrenched at the immense pain of this people. That's what never left you in peace. That's what put your special intelligence to work and channeled your creativity and service. Your life was not just service, then; it was the specific *service* of "taking the crucified peoples down from the cross," words very much your own, the kind of words that take not only *intelligence* to invent, but intelligence moved by *mercy*.[24]

In short, Ellacuría embraced the cross of the crucified people precisely as a philosopher-theologian. In response to the exigencies to realize, shoulder, and take charge of the weight of historical reality, he delineated the internal coordinates which link the theology of salvation with the politics of liberation. But the exercise of compassionate reason not only gave rise to his theology; it invited him into the sufferings of his people. In the process, he became a living intersection between the world of power and the world of the powerless poor, between those blessed with academic promise and education, and illiterate peoples with elegant but often muted hopes. Upon the ground of historical reality he was drawn—

body and mind—into the mystery of Christian salvation. Lying face down at the end of the day, he incarnated anew the violent hope of the cross and took up the identity of a Christian martyr.

## Notes to Conclusion

1. Gustavo Gutiérrez, "John of the Cross: A Latin American View," in *Gustavo Gutiérrez: Essential Writings*, ed. and trans. by James Nickoloff (Maryknoll: Orbis, 1996) 326.
2. Ibid.
3. "I have often been threatened with death. I must tell you, as a Christian, I do not believe in death without resurrection. If I am killed, I shall arise in the Salvadoran people. I say it without boasting, with the greatest humility," quoted in Brockman, *Romero: A Life*, op. cit., 248.
4. Analyses of liberation theology written while Ellacuría was still alive generally place him among Latin American liberation theology's supporting cast. Christian Smith, for example, includes Ellacuría in his chart listing "Second Generation Liberation Theologians" and in several other charts, but mentions him only once in his text; see Smith, 41, 201; compare to McGovern, *Liberation Theology and Its Critics*, op. cit.; Robert McAfee Brown, *Theology in a New Key: Responding to Liberation Themes* (Philadelphia: Westminster, 1978); Phillip Berryman, *Liberation Theology: The Essential Facts about the Revolutionary Movement in Latin America and Beyond* (New York: Pantheon, 1987); Roger Haight, "Liberation Theology" in J. Komonchak, M. Collins, D. Lane, eds., *The New Dictionary of Theology* (Collegeville, Minn.: Liturgical Press, 1987, 1990) 570–576; Jacques Dupuis, "Liberation Theology" in R. Latourelle and R. Fisichella, eds., *Dictionary of Fundamental Theology* (New York: Crossroad, 1995) 1091–1097.
5. Sobrino makes frequent if somewhat general references to Ellacuría's extraordinary intellectual ability and accomplishments, although he vigorously warns against the temptation to celebrate his intelligence by abstracting it from his mercy and passion for justice; see Sobrino, "Ignacio Ellacuría," 132; see also "A Letter to Ignacio Ellacuría," *The Principle of Mercy*, 187–189. In a personal conversation in May 1993, Sobrino told me that he considered Ellacuría the most brilliant theological mind yet produced by liberation theology. He then added, almost in a whisper, "when we lost him, we lost our best."
6. To the extent that Teresa Whitfield's history of the UCA massacre serves as a biography of Ellacuría, it makes an important initial contribution to the study of his thought. However, a more fully articulated intellectual biography is now needed. Among other things, it could shed further light on the reasons behind his modest reception by other theologians, including Latin American liberation theologians.
7. The influence of Gutiérrez at the Latin American Bishops Conference meetings in Medellín and Puebla has been well documented. Likewise, he has demonstrated a longevity and tenacity to complement his originality and make him arguably one of his generation's most important theologians, Catholic or Protestant, in the world. This appears all the more surprising in light of the fact that he is not primarily a university professor, but considers himself a pastor first and a theologian only part-time.
8. Gustavo Gutiérrez, *We Drink from Our Own Wells: The Spiritual Journey of a People*, trans. by Matthew O'Connell (Maryknoll: Orbis, 1984); *On Job: God-Talk and the*

*Suffering of the Innocent*, trans. by Matthew O'Connell (Maryknoll: Orbis, 1987). These two works remain among the most poignant yet produced in Latin America on the theme of liberation spirituality. See also the third part of his most recent collection, *The Density of the Present: Selected Writings* (Maryknoll: Orbis, 1999), which deals with the relationship between spirituality and theology.

 9. Gustavo Gutiérrez, *Las Casas: In Search of the Poor of Jesus Christ*, trans. by Robert Barr (Maryknoll: Orbis, 1993). Gutiérrez dedicated this book "to Vicente Hondarza, to Ignacio Ellacuría and his companions, and in them to all those who, born in Spain, have come to live and to die in the Indies, in search of the poor of Jesus Christ."

10. Gutiérrez, *On Job*, op. cit. xiii.

11. Gutiérrez, *A Theology of Liberation*, op. cit., 5. Gutiérrez returns over and over to this basic understanding of the theological task, both developing it and tracing its roots in Christian spirituality. "A Christian is defined as a follower of Jesus, and reflection on the experience of following constitutes the central theme of any solid theology," Gutiérrez, *We Drink from Our Own Wells*, 1.

12. Gutiérrez, "Theology from the Underside of History," in *The Power of the Poor in History*, trans. by Robert Barr (Maryknoll: Orbis, 1983) 212.

13. See, for example, Juan Luis Segundo, *The Liberation of Theology*, op. cit.; *Grace and the Human Condition*, trans. by John Drury (Maryknoll: Orbis, 1973); *The Humanist Christology of Paul*, trans. by John Drury (Maryknoll: Orbis, 1986).

14. Juan Luis Segundo, *The Historical Jesus of the Synoptics*, trans. by John Drury (Maryknoll: Orbis, 1985) 39; see also, Frances Stefano, *The Absolute Value of Human Action in the Theology of Juan Luis Segundo* (Lanham, Md./New York/London: University Press of America, 1992).

15. See Clodovis Boff, *Theology and Praxis: Epistemological Foundations*, trans. by Robert Barr (Maryknoll: Orbis, 1987); "Epistemology and Method of the Theology of Liberation," trans. by Robert Barr, *MLT*, 57–85.

16. The English translation of the subtitle of Boff's most important book, *Theology and Praxis: Epistemological Foundations*, obscures this point. The actual Portuguese title, *Teologia e prática: Teologia do político e suas mediações*, translates literally into English as *Theology and Praxis: Political Theology and its Mediations*.

17. Boff, *Theology and Praxis*, 30.

18. Ibid., 30. In this article Ellacuría cites an edition of Boff's book published in Spain under the title, *Teología de lo político* (Salamanca, 1980).

19. "Historicidad de la salvación cristiana" (1984) 325, trans. Wilde, emended; *MLT*, 252. It should be noted that later in this same article, while addressing the central issue of the relationship between salvation history and the history of the world, Ellacuría refers in an explicit and complementary way to Boff's detailed descriptions of the socioanalytical and hermeneutical mediations, ibid., 354; *MLT*, 274.

20. I borrow the phrase "a classicist world-view" from Bernard Lonergan, who contrasts this perspective with what he calls "historical-mindedness." He notes that "the differences between the two are enormous, for they differ in their apprehension of man *[sic]*, in their account of the good, and in the role they ascribe to the Church in the world. But these differences are not immediately theological. They are differences in horizon, in total mentality. For either side really to understand the other is a major achievement and, when such understanding is lacking, the interpretation of Scripture or of other theological sources is most likely to be at cross-purposes," Bernard Lonergan, "The Transition from a Classicist World-View to Historical-

Mindedness," in *A Second Collection*, ed. by W. Ryan and B. Tyrrell (Philadelphia: Westminster Press, 1974) 2.

21. "It is not a willful or arbitrary affirmation to designate Latin America at the present time as a privileged place of utopia and propheticism. Rather, its own reality and some of its realizations demonstrate that it is. . . . Latin America is a region whose great potentiality and richness of resources contrast with the state of misery, injustice, oppression and exploitation that is imposed on a large segment of the people. This provides an objective basis for the contrast between utopia, viewed in its rich potentiality, and propheticism, previewed in the negation of that utopia by the reality of everyday life," "Utopía y profetismo" (1989) 399–400, trans. mine; *MLT*, 294–295.

22. The distinction between the epistemological and ontological meanings of the phrase, "from below," is carefully developed in several recent works by Roger Haight; see "Ecclesiology From Below," op. cit.; *Jesus Symbol of God* (Maryknoll: Orbis, 1999) xii–xiii, 29–30.

23. Karl Rahner, *Foundations of Christian Faith*, trans. by William Dych (New York: Crossroad, 1984) 79.

24. Jon Sobrino, "Letter to Ignacio Ellacuría," in *The Principle of Mercy*, op. cit., 188, emphasis mine; first read at Mass, November 10, 1990; originally published in *Carta a las Iglesias* (No. 223, 1990) 13.

# Selected Bibliography

In order to facilitate the reader's use of this bibliography of Ignacio Ellacuría's published writings, I wish to call attention to several of its more unusual features. First, because nearly all of his writings were originally published in the form of essays, I present them as essays here. Books that represent collections of previously published essays also appear here. Second, I have arranged the bibliography according to the year of publication rather than alphabetically. Because all of Ellacuría's essays presented in the list of abbreviations or cited in the notes include the year of publication, readers wishing to locate the full bibliographical reference can do so easily by year of publication. Third, because many of his essays were published in more than one journal, occasionally with different titles, bibliographical references include all the publications that I was able to locate. Fourth, I have gathered all of the English translations of Ellacuría's writings and presented them in a separate section at the end of the bibliography. To facilitate cross-references, these entries include the original Spanish title and year of publication. These also appear according to the year they were published in English.

## Published Writings of Ignacio Ellacuría

### 1956

"El despertar de la filosofía, I." *Cultura*, no. 11, 13–28. See also, *EF*, 47–74.
"Ortega y Gasset, hombre de nuestro ayer." *ECA*, no. 104, 198–203. See also, *EF*, 15–22.
"Ortega y Gasset, desde dentro." *ECA*, no. 105, 278–283. See also, *EF*, 23–33.
"¿Quién es Ortega y Gasset?" *ECA*, no. 110, 595–601. See also, *EF*, 35–45.

### 1957

"Marcelino, pan y vino." *ECA*, no. 122, 665–669. See also, *EF*, 109–115.

## 1958

"Los valores y el derecho." *ECA*, no. 124, 79–84. Also published as "Los valores y el derecho: presentación y significado," *EF*, 281–290.

"Bruselas, 1958, saldo negativo." *ECA*, no. 132, 527–535. See also, *EF*, 251–263.

"El despertar de la filosofía, II." *Cultura*, no. 13, 148–167. See also, *EF*, 74–107.

"Angel Martínez, poeta esencial." *Cultura*, no. 14, 123–164. See also, *EF*, 127–195.

## 1959

"El Doctor Zivago como forma literaria." *Cultura*, no. 17, 109–123. See also, *EF*, 305–328.

"Santo Tomás, hombre de su siglo." *ECA*, no. 135, 84–89. See also, *EF*, 217–222.

"El comunismo soviético visto desde Rusia." *ECA*, no. 141, 455–462. See also, *EF*, 291–303.

## 1960

"Religión y religiosidad en Bergson, I. La religión estática: su razón de ser." *ECA*, no. 145, 6–11. Also published as part of "Filosofía de la religión en Bergson," *EF*, 1996, 337–346.

"Tomás de Aquino, intelectual católico." *ECA*, no. 146, 79–84. See also, *EF*, 329–336.

## 1961

"El tomismo, ¿es un humanismo?" *ECA*, no. 157, 70–75. See also, *EF*, 387–395.

"Religión y religiosidad en Bergson, II. La religión estática: sus formas." *ECA*, no. 159, 205–212. Also published as part of "Filosofía de la religión en Bergson," *EF*, 1996, 346–358.

"Filosofía en Centroamérica." Review of F. Peccorini, *El ser y los seres según santo Tomás de Aquino*, in *Humanidades*, no. 2–3, 157–168. See also, *EF*, 397–409.

## 1963

"El P. Aurelio Espinosa Pólit, S.J." *ECA*, no. 178, 21–24. See also, *EF*, 525–533.

## 1964

"Antropología de Xavier Zubiri, I." *Revista de Psiquiatría y Psicología Médica de Europa y América Latina*, no. 6, 403–430.

"Antropología de Xavier Zubiri, II." *Revista de Psiquiatría y Psicología Médica de Europa y América Latina*, no. 7, 483–508.

## 1965

*La principialidad de la esencia en Xavier Zubiri*. Tesis doctoral en la Universidad Complutense, Madrid, "Introducción," vol. I, I–X; *Parte primera: Principialidad de la esencia e inteligencia*, vol. I, 1–442; *Parte segunda: Principialidad de la esencia y talidad*, vol. II, 443–841; *Parte tercera: Principialidad de la esencia y transcendentalidad*, vol. III, 842–1030; "Conclusión: caracter principial de la esencia," vol. III, 1032–1083; Apéndice bibliográfico y Indice general, vol. III, 1084–1094.

*Indices de "Sobre la esencia" de Xavier Zubiri*. Madrid, Sociedad de Estudios y Publicaciones.

"Cinco lecciones de filosofía." *Crisis*, no. 45, 109–125.

"Fundamentación de la metafísica." *Razón y Fe*, 313–315. See also, *EF*, 589–592.

## 1966

"La historicidad del hombre en Xavier Zubiri." *Estudios de Deusto*, vol. 40, no. 14, 245–285, 523–547.

"La religación, actitud radical del hombre: Apuntes para un estudio de la antropología de Zubiri." *Asclepio. Archivo iberoamericano de historia de la medicina y antropología médica*. Madrid, vol. 16, 97–155.

## 1967
"La juventud religiosa actual." *Hechos y Dichos*, no. 372, 124–134.

## 1968
"Carta a un ordenado vacilante." *Hechos y Dichos*, no. 385, 355–362.
"Existencialismo ateo," in I. Ellacuría, et al., *Dios-Ateismo. Tercera Semana de Teología*. Bilbao, Universidad de Deusto, 191–212. See also, *EF*, 625–644.

## 1969
"Seguridad social y solidaridad humana: Aproximación filosófica al fenómeno de la seguridad social." *ECA*, no. 253, 357–366.
"Los derechos humanos fundamentales y su limitación legal y política." *ECA*, no. 254–255, 435–449. See also, *ECA*, no. 267, 1970, 645–659; *VA*, vol. 1, 501–520.
"Violencia y cruz," in *¿Qué aporta el cristianismo al hombre de hoy? Cuatro Semana de Teología*. Bilbao, Universidad de Deusto, 261–307. See also, *TP*, 95–127.

## 1970
"La idea de filosofía en Xavier Zubiri," in A. Teulon, I. Ellacuría, et al., *Homenaje a Zubiri II*, vol. 1, Madrid, Editorial Moneda y Crédito, 477–485.
"Los laicos interpelan a su Iglesia." *ECA*, no. 256–257, 46–50.
"Progreso y revolución." *ECA*, no. 258, 152–154.
"Persecución." *ECA*, no. 259, 189–190.
"Girardi y Garaudy." *ECA*, no. 259, 223.
"Medallas para Cuba." *ECA*, no. 259, 228.
"Los obispos centroamericanos aceleran el paso." *ECA*, no. 262, 381–387.
"Teología de la revolución y evangelio." *ECA*, no. 265–266, 581–584.
"Los centros privados docentes y sus problemas." *ECA*, no. 265–266, 585–586.

## 1971
"Liberación: misión y carisma de la iglesia latinoamericana." *ECA*, no. 268, 61–80. See also, *TP*, 70–90.
"¿Teología política hace 400 años?" *ECA*, no. 278, 747–749.
"Estudio ético-político del proceso conflictivo ANDES-ministerio," in I. Ellacuría, et al., *Análisis de una experiencia nacional*. San Salvador, 125–154. See also, *VA*, vol. 1, 523–556.

## 1972
"Filosofía y política." *ECA*, no. 284, 373–385. See also, *VA*, vol. 1, 47–61.
"Un excelente psicodiagnóstico sobre latinoamérica." *ECA*, no. 285, 499–505. Foreward to I. Martín-Baró, *Psicodiagnóstico de América Latina*. San Salvador, UCA Editores, 1972.
"La ley orgánica de la Universidad de El Salvador: Reflexiones críticas en busca de una Universidad Latinoamericana." *ECA*, no. 290, 747–761. See also, H. Cerutto Guldberg, ed., *Universidad y cambio social: los jesuitas en El Salvador*, Mexico, Magna Terra Editores, 1990, 45–62.

## 1973

"Un marco teórico-valorativo de la reforma agraria." *ECA*, no. 297–298, 443–457. See also, *VA*, vol. 1, 567–586.

"El seglar cristiano en el tercer mundo." *Búsqueda*, no. 2, 15–20. See also, *CIRD*, 293–303.

*Teología política*. San Salvador, Ediciones del Secretariado Social Interdiocesano, 1973.

"Historia de la salvación y salvación en la historia." *TP*, 1–10.

"Carácter político de la misión de Jesús." *TP*, 11–43. See also, *Miec-Jecí*, no. 13–14, Lima, 1974. Partially reproduced as "Dimensión política del mesianismo de Jesús." *Búsqueda*, no. 3, 24–45.

"El anuncio del Evangelio y la misión de la Iglesia." *TP*, 44–69. Also published as "Anuncio del Reino y credibilidad de la Iglesia." *CIRD*, 219–263.

"Imagen ideológica de los partidos políticos en las elecciones de 1972," *in* J. Hernández-Pico, C. Jerez, E. Baltodano, I. Ellacuría, R. Mayorga, *El Salvador: año político 1971–1972*. Guatemala, Editores Piedra Santa, 319–362; San Salvador, UCA Editores, 321–362. See also, *VA*, vol. 3, 1487–1531.

## 1974

"Aspectos éticos del problema poblacional." *ECA*, no. 310–311, 565–592.

"Presentación," in *Realitas I. Seminario Xavier Zubiri*. Madrid, Sociedad de Estudios y Publicaciones, Editorial Moneda y Crédito, 5–7.

"La idea de estructura en la filosofía de Xavier Zubiri," in *Realitas I. Seminario Xavier Zubiri*. Madrid, Sociedad de Estudios y Publicaciones, Editorial Moneda y Crédito, 71–139.

"El espacio," in *Realitas I. Seminario Xavier Zubiri*. Madrid, Sociedad de Estudios y Publicaciones, Editorial Moneda y Crédito, 479–514.

## 1975

"La antropología filosófica de Xavier Zubiri," in P. Laín Entralgo, ed., *Historia universal de la medicina*, vol. 7. Baracelona, Ed. Salvat, 109–112.

"Introducción crítica a la antropología filosófica de Zubiri," in *Cuadernos Salmantinos de Filosofía*, no. 2, 157–184. Also published as "Introducción crítica a la antropología de Xavier Zubiri," in *Realitas II. Seminario Xavier Zubiri*. Sociedad de Estudios y Publicaciones, Madrid, Ed. Labor, 1976, 49–137.

"Hacia una fundamentacíon filosófica del método teológico latinoamericano," in E. Ruiz Maldonado, ed., *Liberación y cautiverio: debates en torno al metodo de la teología en América Latina*, las comunicaciones y los debates del Encuentro Latinoamericano de Teología, Mexico City (August 11–15, 1975) 609–635. See also, *ECA*, no. 322–323, 409–425.

"Tesis sobre la posibilidad, necesidad y sentido de una teología latinoamericana," in A. Vargas Machuca, ed., *Teología y mundo contemporáneo: homenaje a Karl Rahner en su 70 cumpleaños*, Madrid, Ediciones Cristiandad, 325–350.

"Misión política de la Universidad." *Abra*, no. 8, 2–7.

"Diez años después: ¿es posible una Universidad distinta?" *ECA*, no. 324–325, 605–628. See also, H. Cerutto Guldberg, ed., *Universidad y cambio social: los jesuitas en El Salvador*, Mexico, Magna Terra Editores, 1990, 131–166.

## 1976

"Filosofía ¿para qué?" *Abra*, no. 11, 42–48. Also published as a pamphlet by Universidad Centroamericana "José Simeón Cañas," San Salvador, 1987.

"Iglesia y realidad histórica." *ECA*, no. 331, 213–220.

"El primer proyecto de transformación agraria." Pronunciamiento del Consejo Superior de la Universidad Centroamericana "José Simeón Cañas," (June 1976). See also, *ECA*, no. 335–336, 419–424; *VA*, vol. 1, 559–566.

"La historización del concepto de propiedad como principio de desideologización." *ECA*, no. 335–336, 425–450. See also, *VA*, vol. 1, 587–626.

"¡A sus órdenes, mi capital!" *ECA*, no. 337, 637–643. See also, *VA*, vol. 1, 649–656.

"La transformación de la ley del Instituto Salvadoreño de Transformación Agraria (ISTA)." *ECA*, no. 338, 747–758. See also, *VA*, vol. 1, 629–648.

"En busca de la 'cuestión fundamental' de la pastoral latinoamericana." *Sal Terrae*, no. 759–760, 563–572. Also published as "La 'cuestión fundamental' de la pastoral latinoamericana." *Diakonía*, 1978, no. 6, 20–28.

## 1977

"Actualidad de la filosofía zubiriana." *Ya*, (Feb. 10, 1977) 23.

"Teorías económicas y relación entre cristianismo y socialismo." *Concilium*, no. 125, 282–290. Partially reproduced in "Función de las teorías económicas en la discusión teológico-teórica: teoría de la dependencia," in I. Ellacuría, et al., *La Teología de la Liberación*, Ediciones Cultura Hispánica, 1990, 97–100.

"Fe y justicia." *Christus* (August 1977) 26–33, and (October 1977) 19–34. See also, I. Ellacuría, et al., *Fe, justicia y opción por los oprimidos*, Bilbao, Editorial Desclée de Brouwer, 1980, 9–78. Partially reproduced as "La contemplación en la acción de la justicia." *Diakonía*, no. 2, 7–14.

"La Iglesia de los pobres, sacramento histórico de la liberación." *ECA*, no. 348–349, 707–722. See also, *Selecciones de Teología*, no. 70, 1979, 119–134; *Encuentro: Selecciones para Latinoamérica*, no. 1, 1980, 142–148; *CIRD*, 179–216; *ML*, vol. 2, 127–154.

"Notas teológicas sobre religiosidad popular." *Fomento Social*, 253–260.

"¿Por qué muere Jesús y por qué le matan?" *Misión Abierta*, no. 2, 17–26. See also, *Diakonía*, no. 8, 1978, 65–75; *Servir*, no. 75, 1978, 383–398; *ETM*, 25–38.

"El compromiso político de la iglesia en América Latina." *Corintios XIII*, no. 4, 143–162.

"El problema ético de la política." *Ya*, 37.

## 1978

"Historización del bien común y de los derechos humanos en una sociedad dividida," in E. Tamez and S. Trinidad, eds., *Capitalismo: violencia y anti-vida*, vol. 2, San José, EDUCA, 81–94. Also published as "Derechos humanos en una sociedad divida," *Christus*, Oct. 1979, 42–48.

"El pueblo crucificado, ensayo de soteriología histórica," in I. Ellacuría, et al., *Cruz y resurrección: anuncio de una Iglesia nueva*, Mexico City, CTR, 49–82. See also, *Selecciones de Teología*, no. 76, 1980, 325–341; *RLT*, no. 18, 1989, 305–333; *CIRD*, 25–63; *ML*, vol. 2, 189–216.

"Entre Medellín y Puebla." *ECA*, no. 353, 120–129.

"Una buena noticia: la Iglesia nace del pueblo latinoamericano: Contribución a Puebla, 1978." *ECA*, no. 353, 161–173.

"La teología como momento ideológico de la praxis eclesial." *Estudios Eclesiásticos*, no. 207, 457–476.

"La Iglesia y las organizaciones populares en El Salvador." *ECA*, no. 359, 692–701, under the pseudonym, "Tomás R. Campos." See also, *IPOP*, 147–161; *VA*, vol. 2, 659–677.

"El Salvador, juicio sobre el año 1978." *ECA*, no. 361–362, 865–876. See also, *VA*, vol. 1, 353–364.

"Zubiri en El Salvador." *ECA*, no. 361–362, 949–950.

"La Iglesia que nace del pueblo por el Espíritu." *Misión Abierta*, no. 1, 150–158. See also, *CIRD*, 65–79; *Servir*, 1979, 551–564; *ETM*, 131–143.

"La predicación ha de poner en contacto vivificante la palabra y la comunidad." *Sal Terrae*, no. 778, 167–176. Also published as "Palabras de Dios y comunidad cristiana." *Servir*, no. 73, 47–60. Also published as "Predicación, palabra, comunidad." *CIRD*, 265–278.

"Recuperar el Reino de Dios: des-mundanización e historización de la Iglesia." *Sal Terrae*, no. 780, 335–344. See also, *IPOP*, 79–85.

"Filósofo en España." *Ya* (Dec. 14, 1978) 3.

"El trasfondo económico-político de Puebla." *Boletín de Ciencias Económicas y Sociales*, no. 7, 54–59.

"Comentarios a la Carta Pastoral." Twenty-one radio broadcasts, *YSAX* (Aug. 30–Sept. 25, 1978). See also, *IPOP*, 163–205; *VA*, vol. 2, 679–732.

## 1979

"La OEA y los derechos humanos en El Salvador." *ECA*, no. 363–364, 53–54.

"Recuperación de la universidad de El Salvador." *ECA*, no. 363–364, 58–59.

"El concepto filosófico de tecnología apropiada." *ECA*, no. 366, 213–223.

"Fundamentación biológica de la ética." *ECA*, no. 368, 419–428.

"Biología e inteligencia," in *Realitas III-IV. Seminario Xavier Zubiri*. Madrid, Sociedad de Estudios y Publicaciones, Ed. Labor, 281–335.

"La seguridad nacional y la constitución salvadoreña." *ECA*, no. 369–370, 477–488, under the pseudonym, "Tomás R. Campos." See also, *VA*, vol. 1, 247–266.

*Iglesia de los pobres y organizaciones populares*. O. Romero, A. Rivera y Damas, I. Ellacuría, J. Sobrino, and T. Campos. San Salvador, UCA Editores.

"Las bienaventuranzas como carta fundamental de la Iglesia de los pobres." *IPOP*, 105–118. See also, *Diakonía*, no. 19, 1981, 56–59; *CIRD*, 129–151.

"Crece el enterés nacional por el cambio político." Radio broadcast, *YSAX* (Oct. 15, 1979). See also, *ESTE*, 558–559; *VA*, vol. 2, 801–802.

"Al fin, insurrección militar." Radio broadcast, *YSAX* (Oct. 16, 1979). See also, *ESTE*, 559–561; *VA*, vol. 2, 803–805.

"La proclama de la junta de gobierno: una importante toma de posición ante el país." Radio broadcast, *YSAX* (Oct. 17, 1979). See also, *ESTE*, 563–565; *VA*, vol. 2, 807–809.

"Insurrección popular y hostigamiento extremista." Radio broadcast, *YSAX* (Oct. 19, 1979). See also, *ESTE*, 571–573; *VA*, vol. 2, 811–813.

"La semana fue así (del 13 al 20 de octubre)." Radio broadcast, *YSAX* (Oct. 20, 1979). See also, *ESTE*, 579–582; *VA*, vol. 2, 815–818.

"La revolución necesaria." Six radio broadcasts, *YSAX* (Oct. 22–27, 1979). See also, *ESTE*, 583–605; *VA*, vol. 2, 819–830.

"La semana fue así (del 20 al 27 de octubre)." Radio broadcast, *YSAX* (Oct. 27, 1979). See also, *ESTE*, 605–608; *VA*, vol. 2, 831–834.

"Las organizaciones populares ante la nueva situación." Radio broadcast, *YSAX*, (Oct. 31, 1979). See also, *ESTE*, 613–615; *VA*, vol. 2, 773–775.

"Pronunciamiento del Consejo Superior Universitario de la Universidad Centroamericana 'José Simeón Cañas' sobre la nueva situación del país tras el 15 de octubre."
*ECA*, no. 372–373, 849–862. See also, *VA*, vol. 2, 835–849.
"El papel de las organizaciones populares en la actual situación del país." *ECA*, no.
372–373, 923–946, under the pseudonym, "Tomás R. Campos." See also, *VA*, vol.
2, 733–771.

## 1980

"El problema 'ecumenismo' y la promoción de la justicia." *Estudios Eclesiásticos*, no.
213, 153–155.
"En busca de un nuevo proyecto nacional." *ECA*, no. 377–378, 155–180. See also, *VA*,
vol. 2, 913–936.
"Universidad y política." *ECA*, no. 383, 807–824. See also, *VA*, vol. 1, 17–45; H. Cerutto
Guldberg, ed., *Modernizacíon educativa y universidad en América Latina*, Mexico, Magna
Terra Editores, 1990, 35–71.
"La superación de un 15 de octubre fracasado." *ECA*, no. 384–385, 929–950. See also,
*VA*, vol. 2, 851–868.
"La seguridad nacional y la crucificación salvadoreña." *ECA*, no. 384–385, 977–988.
"Monseñor Romero, un enviado de Dios para salvar a su pueblo." *Sal Terrae*, no. 811,
825–832. See also, *Diakonía*, no. 17, 1981, 2–8; *ECA*, no. 497, 1990, 141–146; *RLT*,
no. 19, 1990, 5–10.
"Zubiri, filósofo teologal." *Vida Nueva*, Madrid, no. 1249, 45.
"Zubiri, vasco universal." *El Diario Vasco* (Oct. 3, 1980) 22.
"Inteligencia sentiente. Libro actual, original y riguroso." *Ya* (Dec. 4, 1980) 37.
"Un tema filosófico capital." *ABC* (Dec. 27, 1980) 5–6.
"Una nueva obra filosófica del vasco Xavier Zubiri." *Deia* (Dec. 27, 1980) 2.

## 1981

"Un proceso de mediación para El Salvador." *ECA*, no. 387–388, 3–16. See also, *VA*,
vol. 2, 937–949.
"El testamento de Sartre." *ECA*, no. 387–388, 43–50.
"Errores y sofismas de la Sra. Kirkpatrick." *ECA*, no. 389, 192–193.
"¿Solución política o solución militar para El Salvador?" *ECA*, no. 390–391, 295–324.
See also, *VA*, vol. 2, 951–995; *SPP*, 13–42.
"La nueva política de la Administración Reagan en El Salvador." *ECA*, no. 390–391,
383–414, under the pseudonym, "Tomás R. Campos."
"La Iglesia en El Salvador: la salvación se realiza en la historia." *Aportes*, 34–35.
"Discernir 'el signo' de los tiempos." *Diakonía*, no. 17, 57–59.
"El verdadero pueblo de Dios, según Monseñor Romero." *ECA*, no. 392, 529–554. See also,
*Diakonía*, no. 18, 27–57; *Selecciones de Teología*, 1982, no. 84, 350–359; *CIRD*, 81–125.
"Un tal Jesús." *ECA*, no. 392, 566–568. Also published as "Una obra importante,"
presentación del libro de María López Vigil, *Un Tal Jesús*, vol. 1, San Salvador, UCA
Editores, 1982, 27–31, and as part of a chapter titled, "Jesús, la Iglesia y los pobres,"
in *ETM*, 168–171.
"Los pobres, lugar teológico en América Latina." *Misión Abierta*, no. 4–5, 225–240. See
also, *Diakonía*, no. 21, 1982, 41–57; *CIRD*, 153–178; *ETM*, 39–59.

"La declaración conjunta mexicano-francesa sobre El Salvador." *ECA*, no. 395, 845–866. See also, *VA*, vol. 3, 1235–1269.

"El objeto de la filosofía." *ECA*, no. 396–397, 963–980. See also, *FRH*, 15–47, 599–602; *VA*, vol. 1, 63–92; I. Ellacuría and J. C. Scannone, *Para una Filosofía desde América Latina*, Bogotá, Universidad Javeriana, 1992, 63–88.

"La nueva obra de Zubiri: *Inteligencia sentiente*." *Razón y Fé*, no. 995, 126–139. See also, X. Zubiri, *Siete ensayos de antropología filosófica*. G. Marquinez Argote, ed., Bogotá, 1982, 191–210.

## 1982

"Una Universidad para el pueblo." *Diakonía*, no. 23, 81–88.

"1982, año decisivo para El Salvador." *ECA*, no. 399–400, 3–16.

"Análisis coyuntural sobre la situación de El Salvador." *ECA*, no. 399–400, 17–58, under the pseudonym, "Tomás R. Campos." See also, *VA*, vol. 1, 365–432.

"Las elecciones en El Salvador." *Razón y Fe* (March) 285–294.

"Las elecciones y la unidad nacional: Diez tesis críticas." *ECA*, no. 402, 233–258. See also, *VA*, vol. 3, 1533–1555.

"Interpretación global del proceso histórico, 15 de Octubre de 1979—28 de Marzo de 1982." *ECA*, no. 403–404, 599–622, under the pseudonym, "Tomás R. Campos." See also, *VA*, vol. 2, 869–909.

"Juan Pablo II y el conflicto salvadoreño." *ECA* no. 405, 633–650.

"Regionalizar la paz, no la guerra." *ECA*, no. 406, 767–780. See also, *VA*, vol. 2, 1009–1023.

"Universidad, derechos humanos y mayorías populares." *ECA*, no. 406, 791–800. See also, H. Cerutti Guldberg, ed., *Universidad y cambio social: los jesuitas en El Salvador*, Mexico, Magna Terra Editores, 1990, 45–62.

"La independencia nacional en 1982." *ECA*, no. 407–408, 855–864. See also, *VA*, vol. 3, 1731–1740.

"El Pacto de Apaneca: un proyecto político para la transición." *ECA*, no. 407–408, 865–878, under the pseudonym, "Tomás R. Campos."

"El diálogo en El Salvador como principio de solución política." *ECA*, no. 409, 981–992. See also, *VA*, vol. 2, 997–1007; *SPP*, 43–54.

"Conflicto entre trabajo y capital en la presente fase histórica: Un análisis de la encíclica de Juan Pablo II sobre el trabajo humano." *ECA*, no. 409, 1008–1024. Also published as "Conflicto entre trabajo y capital en la presente fase histórica: Un punto clave de la 'Laborem Exercens.' " *Diakonía*, no. 24, 19–42.

"El Reino de Dios y el paro en el tercer mundo." *Concilium*, no. 180, 588–596.

"Las iglesias latinoamericanas interpelan a la iglesia de España." *Sal Terrae*, no. 826, 219–230.

"El auténtico lugar social de la Iglesia." *Misión Abierta*, no. 1, 98–106. See also, *Diakonía*, 1983, no. 25, 24–36; *ETM*, 145–156.

"Contraportada" of Jon Sobrino, "*Jesús en América Latina: Su significado para la fe y la cristología*." San Salvador, UCA Editores.

*El Salvador: Entre el terror y la esperanza. Los sucesos de 1979 y su impacto en el drama salvadoreño de los años siguientes*. I. Ellacuría et al., San Salvador, UCA Editores.

## 1983

"Luces y sombras de la Iglesia en Centroamérica." *Razón y Fe*, no. 1020, 16–26. See also, *Diakonía*, no. 26, 111–121; *Pastoral Popular*, no. 34, 50–56; *Encuentro. Selecciones para Latinoamérica*, no. 31–32, 1984, 317–320; *VA*, vol. 1, 293–302.

"El viaje del Papa a Centroamérica." *ECA*, no. 413–414, 225–234.
"Mensaje ético-político de Juan Pablo II al pueblo de Centro América." *ECA*, no. 413–414, 255–272. See also, *Diakonía*, no. 26, 144–166.
"La obra de Xavier Zubiri sobre la inteligencia humana: *Inteligencia y Razón*." *El Pais* (Mar.13, 1983) 4, book review.
"La estrategia del FMLN-FDR tras el proceso electoral de marzo de 1982." *ECA*, no. 415–416, 479–490, under the pseudonym, "Tomás R. Campos." See also, *VA*, vol. 3, 1557–1573.
"Análisis global de la intervención norteamericana actual en El Salvador." *ECA*, no. 415–416, 543–556, under the pseudonym, "Ernesto Cruz Alfaro." See also, *VA*, vol. 1, 209–229.
"Diez tesis sobre un proceso de negociación." *ECA*, no. 417–418, 601–628. See also, *VA*, vol. 3, 1271–1297.
"La cooperación iberoamericana a la paz en Centroamérica." *ECA*, no. 417–418, 629–640. See also, *VA*, vol. 2, 1025–1040. Paper presented at the Congress "Iberoamérica, encuentro en la democracia," Madrid (Apr. 26–30, 1983).
"Zubiri sigue vivo." *Vida Nueva*, no. 1396, 55. See also, *ECA*, no. 420, 895–896; *Cuadernos de Filosofía Latinoamericana*, no. 17, 34–36.
"La desmitificación del marxismo." *ECA*, no. 421–422, 921–930. See also, *VA*, vol. 1, 282–291.
"Aproximación a la obra completa de Xavier Zubiri." *ECA*, no. 421–422, 965–983. See also, *Encuentro. Selecciones para Latinoamérica*, no. 29, 1984, 137–145; I. Tellechea, ed., *Zubiri (1898–1983)*, Victoria, Edita Departamento de Cultura del Gobierno Vasco, 1984, 37–66.
"Dios, el gran tema de Zubiri." *Ya* (Sept. 23, 1983) 3.
"Espiritualidad," in C. Floristán and J. J. Tomayo, eds., *Conceptos fundamentales de pastoral.* Madrid, Trotta, 304–309. See also, C. Floristán and J. J. Tomayo, eds., *Conceptos fundamentales del cristianismo*. Madrid, Trotta, 1993, 413–420. Also published as "La espititualidad cristiana." *Diakonía*, no. 30, 1984, 123–132.
"Pobres," in C. Floristán and J. J. Tomayo, eds., *Conceptos fundamentales de pastoral.* Madrid, Trotta, 786–802. See also, C. Floristán and J. J. Tomayo, eds., *Conceptos fundamentales del cristianismo*. Madrid, Trotta, 1993, 1043–1057.
"Pueblo de Dios," in C. Floristán and J. J. Tomayo, eds., *Conceptos fundamentales de pastoral*. Madrid, Trotta, 840–859. See also, C. Floristán and J. J. Tomayo, eds., *Conceptos fundamentales del cristianismo*. Madrid, Trotta, 1993, 1094–1112.
"La paz mundial vista desde el Tercer Mundo." *Sal Terrae*, no. 6, 433–443.

*1984*

"Presentación" of Xavier Zubiri, *El Hombre y Dios*. Madrid, Alianza Editorial, i–x.
"Zubiri y los vascos." *El Correo Español - El Pueblo Vasco* (Jan. 22, 1984) 43.
*Conversión de la Iglesia al Reino de Dios: Para anunciarlo y realizarlo en la historia*. Santander, Editorial Sal Terrae. Also published in San Salvador, UCA Editores.
"Recuperación del Reino de Dios." *CIRD*, 7–19.
"Liturgia y liberación." *CIRD*, 279–292.
"Historicidad de la salvación cristiana." *RLT*, no. 1, 5–45. See also, *Selecciones de Teología*, no. 101, 1987, 59–80; *ML*, vol. 1, 323–372.
"Estudio teológico-pastoral de la 'Instrucción sobre algunos aspectos de la teología de la liberación.' " *RLT*, no. 2, 145–178. See also, *Misión Abierta*, no. 1, 1985, 79–99; *ETM*, 173–202.

"Agonía de un pueblo: urgencia de soluciones." *ECA*, no. 423–424, 1–12. See also, *VA*, vol. 1, 433–444.

"El FDR-FMLN ante las elecciones de 1984." *ECA*, no. 426–427, 277–287, under the pseudonym, "Tomás R. Campos." See also, *VA*, vol. 3, 1575–1590.

"Visión de conjunto de las elecciones de 1984." *ECA*, no. 426–427, 301–324. See also, *VA*, vol. 3, 1591–1628.

"¿Tiene solución El Salvador con el presidente Duarte?" *ECA*, no. 428, 373–396. See also, *VA*, vol. 3, 1775–1797.

"Los militares y la paz social." *ECA*, no. 429–430, 475–490. See also, *VA*, vol. 1, 231–243; *VA*, vol. 2, 1041–1053.

"El aporte del diálogo al problema nacional." *ECA*, no. 432–433, 729–756. See also, *VA*, vol. 3, 1327–1358.

"Las primeras vicisitudes del diálogo entre el gobierno y el FMLN-FDR." *ECA*, no. 434, 885–903, under the pseudonym, "Tomás R. Campos." See also, *VA*, vol. 3, 1299–1326.

### 1985

"Seis tareas urgentes para 1985." *ECA*, no. 435–436, 1–16. See also, *VA*, vol. 2, 1055–1069.

"Función liberadora de la filosofía." *ECA*, no. 435–436, 45–64. See also, *VA*, vol. 1, 93–121.

"La UCA ante el doctorado concedido a Monseñor Romero." *ECA*, no. 437, 167–176.

"Las elecciones de 1985, ¿un paso adelante en el proceso de democratización?" *ECA*, no. 438, 205–214. See also, *VA*, vol. 3, 1629–1637.

"Grave preocupación tras el primer año de la presidencia de Duarte." *ECA*, no. 439–440, 325–344. See also, *VA*, vol. 3, 1799–1817.

"El diálogo del gobierno con el FMLN-FDR: un proceso paralizado." *ECA*, no. 439–440, 389–400, under the pseudonym, "Tomás R. Campos." See also, *VA*, vol. 3, 1359–1376.

"El ejemplo de Nicaragua en Centroamérica." *ECA*, no. 441–442, 475–494. See also, *VA*, vol. 2, 1071–1089.

"Perspectiva política de la situación centroamericana." *ECA*, no. 443–444, 625–637. See also, *VA*, vol. 1, 333–351.

"Lectura política de los secuestros." *ECA*, no. 443–444, 684–700, under the pseudonym, "Tomás R. Campos."

"Causas de la actual situación de país y principios de solución." Pronunciamiento del Consejo Superior Universitario de la Universidad Centroamericana "José Simeón Cañas," *ECA*, no. 445, 773–786. See also, *VA*, vol. 2, 1091–1104.

"El Salvador 1985: peor que 1984, mejor que 1986." *ECA*, no. 446, 883–889. See also, *VA*, vol. 1, 445–451.

"FMLN, el límite insuperable." *ECA*, no. 446, 890–897. See also, *VA*, vol. 1, 197–208.

"Presentación" of Rafael Rodríguez, *Oráculos Para mi Raza*. San Salvador, UCA Editores.

### 1986

"Presentación" of Xavier Zubiri: *Sobre el Hombre*. Madrid, Alianza Editorial, ix–xxiii.

"Beitrag Zum Dialog mit dem Marxismus," in P. Rottländer, ed., *Theologie der Befreiung und Marxismus*, Münster, West, 77–108.

"La teología de la liberación es más necesaria que nunca." *Diakonía*, no. 38, 186–189. See also, *Vida Nueva*, no. 3, 1987, 24–25.

"Voluntad de fundamentalidad y voluntad de verdad: Conocimiento-fe y su configuración histórica." *RLT*, no. 8, 113–132.

"Pedro Arrupe, renovador de la vida religiosa," in M. Alcala, ed., *Pedro Arrupe: Así lo vieron*, Santander, Sal Terrae, 141–172. See also, *RLT*, no. 22, 1991, 5–23.

"La teología de la liberación, rehabilitada." *Proceso*, no. 234, 10–11.

"Hacer la paz en El Salvador." *ECA*, no. 447–448, 5–17. See also, *VA*, vol. 2, 1139–1150; *SPP*, 79–91.

"Replanteamiento de soluciones para el problema de El Salvador." *ECA*, no. 447–448, 54–75. See also, *VA*, vol. 2, 1105–1138; *SPP*, 55–77.

"Estados Unidos y la democratización de Centroamérica." *ECA*, no. 450, 255–274. See also, *VA*, vol. 3, 1741–1759.

"Dos años más de gobierno de Duarte." *ECA*, no. 451–452, 375–387. See also, *VA*, vol. 3, 1819–1830.

"El Salvador en estado de diálogo." *ECA*, no. 453, 525–533. See also, *VA*, vol. 3, 1417–1424.

"Análisis ético-político del proceso de diálogo en El Salvador." *ECA*, no. 454–455, 727–751. See also, *VA*, vol. 3, 1377–1416; *SPP*, 93–117.

"Centroamérica como problema." *ECA*, no. 456, 821–833. See also, *VA*, vol. 1, 123–131.

"Factores endógenos del conflicto centroamericano: crisis económica y desequilibrios sociales." *ECA*, no. 456, 856–878. See also, *CINAS Cuadernos de Trabajo*, 1987, no. 9, 9–38; *VA*, vol. 1, 139–172.

## 1987

"Aporte de la teología de la liberación a las religiones Abrahámicas en la superación del individualismo y del positivismo." *RLT*, no. 10, 3–27.

"La teología de la liberación frente al cambio socio-histórico de América Latina." *RLT*, no. 12, 241–264. See also, *Diakonía*, no. 46, 1988, 131–166; I. Ellacuría, et al., *Implicaciones sociales y políticas de la teología de la liberación*, Madrid, Escuela de Estudios Hispanoamericanos y Instituto de Filosofía, Consejo Superior de Investigaciones Científicas, 1989, 69–90; I. Ellacuría, et al., *La Teología de la Liberación*, Ediciones de Cultura Hispánica, 1990, 79–86; *ETM*, 61–89; *VA*, vol. 1, 303–330.

"Zubiri, cuatro años después." *Diario 16* (Sept. 21, 1987) 2.

"¿Por qué no avanza El Salvador?" *ECA*, no. 461, 167–189. See also, *VA*, vol. 1, 175–196.

"Lecciones del Irán-Contras para El Salvador." *ECA*, no. 462, 289–299. See also, *VA*, vol. 3, 1761–1771.

"Caminos de solución para la actual crisis del país." *ECA*, no. 462, 301–311. See also, *Mensaje*, 3–19; *VA*, vol. 2, 1151–1169.

"La cuestión de las masas." *ECA*, no. 465, 415–434. See also, *VA*, vol. 2, 777–798.

"Nueva propuesta de diálogo del FMLN-FDR: los dieciocho puntos." *ECA*, no. 465, 435–447. See also, *VA*, vol. 3, 1425–1448.

"Análisis ético-político de Esquipulas dos." *ECA*, no. 466–467, 599–610. See also, *VA*, vol. 3, 1681–1701.

"Los noventa días de Esquipulas dos." *ECA*, no. 468, 665–673. See also, *VA*, vol. 3, 1703–1711.

"El proceso de pacificación en Centroamérica." *ECA*, no. 469–470, 803–816. See also, *VA*, vol. 3, 1713–1727.

"Propuestas de solución en el marco de Esquipulas dos." *ECA*, no. 469–470, 865–889. See also, *VA*, vol. 2, 1171–1215.

## 1988

"La superación del reduccionismo idealista en Zubiri." *ECA*, no. 477, 633–650. See also, X. Palacios y F. Jarauta, eds., *Razón, ética y política. El conflicto de las sociedades modernas,*

Colección pensamiento crítico—pensamiento utópico 37, Barcelona, Ed. Anthropos, 1989, 169–195; *Congresso de filosofía, ética y religión*, vol. 4, San Sabastián.

"Trabajo no violento por la paz y violencia liberadora." *Concilium*, no. 215, 85–94. See also, *ETM*, 91–102; *Reflexión y Liberación*, no. 4, 1990, 4–11.

"1988: un año de transición para El Salvador." *ECA*, no. 471–472, 5–20. See also, *VA*, vol. 1, 453–466.

"Elecciones aleccionadoras." *ECA*, no. 473–474, 151–174. See also, *VA*, vol. 3, 1639–1661.

"El desmoronamiento de la fachada democrática." *ECA*, no. 475, 311–327. See also, *VA*, vol. 1, 267–281.

"Duarte, el final de una presidencia." *ECA*, no. 476, 461–485. See also, *VA*, vol. 3, 1831–1851.

"Recrudecimiento de la violencia en El Salvador." *ECA*, no. 480, 861–871. See also, *VA*, vol. 1, 467–483.

"El significado del debate nacional." *ECA*, no. 478–479, 713–729. See also, *VA*, vol. 3, 1469–1483; *SPP*, 119–135.

"Ambigüedad de las nuevas elecciones presidenciales." *ECA*, no. 481–482, 995–1012. See also, *VA*, vol. 3, 1663–1678.

"Los partidos políticos y la finalización de la guerra." *ECA*, no. 481–482, 1037–1051. See also, *VA*, vol. 3, 1449–1468.

"Nuevo orden mundial propuesto por Gorbachev." *ECA*, no. 481–482, 1099–1101.

"Presencia sacerdotal en la guerrilla." *Cartas a las Iglesias* (no. 168) 7–10; (no. 169) 11–13; (no. 170) 5–7. First published as the preface for the Italian edition of María Lopez Vigil, *Muerte y vida en Morazán: Testimonio de un sacerdote*, San Salvador, UCA editores, 1987. See *Morto e vita in Morazán: Un sacerdote nella guerriglia in Salvador*, Bologna, Italy, EMI della Coop. SERMIS, 1989.

## 1989

"Utopía y profetismo desde América Latina: Un ensayo concreto de soteriología histórica." *RLT*, no. 17, 141–184. See also, I. Ellacuría, et al., *Utopía y Profetismo*, Madrid, Centro Evangelio y Liberación, 1989, 81–101; *Christus*, 1990, no. 632, 49–55; *ETM*, 103–129. Also published as "Utopía y profetismo," *ML*, vol. 1, 393–442.

"En torno al concepto y la idea de liberación." I. Ellacuría, et al., *Implicaciones sociales y políticas de la teología de la liberación*, Madrid, Escuela de Estudios Hispanoamericanos y Instituto de Filosofía, Consejo Superior de Investigaciones Científicas, 91–109. Also published as "Liberación," in C. Floristán and J. J. Tomayo, eds., *Conceptos fundamentales del cristianismo*. Madrid, Trotta, 1993, 690–710; *RLT*, no. 30, 1993, 213–232.

"Diez afirmaciones sobre 'Utopía' y 'Profetismo.' " *Sal Terrae*, no. 917, 889–893.

"Una nueva fase en el proceso salvadoreño." *ECA*, no. 485, 167–197. See also, *VA*, vol. 3, 1855–1897.

"Vísperas violentas." *ECA*, no. 486–487, 279–284. See also, *VA*, vol. 1, 485–498.

"¿Resolverá el gobierno de ARENA la crisis del país?" *ECA*, no. 488, 413–428. See also, *VA*, vol. 2, 1217–1231.

"El diálogo en los primeros cien días de Cristiani." *ECA*, no. 490–491, 683–694.

"El desafío de las mayorías pobres." *ECA*, no. 493–494, 1075–1080.

## 1990

*Filosofía de la realidad histórica*. A. González, ed. San Salvador, UCA Editores. Also published by Madrid, Editorial Trotta.

"Historización de los derechos humanos desde los pueblos oprimidos y las mayorías populares," in J. Aguirre and X. Insauti, eds., *Pensamiento crítico, ética y absoluto. Homenaje a José Manzana*, Ed. Eset, 147–158. See also, *ECA*, no. 502, 589–596.

"Teología de la liberación y marxismo." *RLT*, no. 20, 109–136.

"Quinto centenario de América Latina ¿descubrimiento o encubrimiento?" *Cuadernos Cristianisme i justicia*, Barcelona. See also, *RLT*, no. 21, 271–282; *Christus*, no. 638, 7–13. Also published as "El quinto centenario del 'descubrimiento' visto desde América Latina," *Diakonía*, no. 56, 15–32.

I. Ellacuría and J. Sobrino, eds., *Mysterium Liberationis: Conceptos Fundamentales de la Teología de la Liberación*. 2 vols. Madrid, Editorial Trotta. Also published in San Salvador, UCA Editores, 1991.

*Ignacio Ellacuría: Teólogo mártir por la liberación del pueblo*. Madrid, Editorial Nueva Utopía.

"Iglesia en Centroamérica." *ETM*, 159–167, as part of a chapter titled, "Jesús, la Iglesia y los pobres."

"La Iglesia y la UCA en el golpe del 15 de Octubre de 1979." *Presencia*, no. 7–8, 132–138.

## 1991

*Veinte años de historia en El Salvador (1969–1989): Escritos políticos*. 3 vols. San Salvador, UCA Editores.

"Lectura latinoamericana de los Ejercicios Espirituales de San Ignacio." *RLT*, no. 23, 111–147. Based on previously unpublished notes from a course given in 1974 at the UCA.

## 1992

"Subdesarrollo y derechos humanos." *RLT*, no. 25, 3–22. Transcript of a talk given to the 3rd International Congress of Youth in Venice, 1987.

"El desafío cristiano de la teología de la liberación." *Cartas a las Iglesias* (no. 263) 12–15; (no. 264) 11–13; (no. 265) 14–16. Transcript of a paper given at the *Seminario*, "Lo temporal y lo religioso en el mundo actual," organized by la Fundación Banco Exterior, Madrid, 1987.

## 1993

"Salvación en la historia," in C. Floristán and J. J. Tomayo, eds., *Conceptos fundamentales del cristianisimo*. Madrid, Trotta, 1993, 1252–1274. Also published as "Historia de la salvación," in *RLT*, no.28, 3–25. From a previously unpublished manuscript dated 1987.

"Misión actual de la Compañía de Jesús." *RLT*, no. 29, 115–126. See also, *Diakonía*, no. 68, 33–42. Written in preparation for the 33rd General Congregation of the Society of Jesus, 1983.

## 1994

"Esquema de interpretación de la Iglesia en Centroamérica." *RLT*, no. 31, 3–29. See also, *Diakonía*, no. 72, 4–27. From a previously unpublished manuscript dated 1981.

"Escatología e historia." *RLT*, no. 32, 113–128. Edited from course notes dated 1974.

I. Ellacuría, J. Sobrino, R. Cardenal. *Ignacio Ellacuría: el hombre, el pensador, el cristiano*. Bilbao, Editiones EGA.

*Seis pistas para la paz*. Bogotá, Centro de Investigación y Educación Popular.

## 1996

*Escritos filosóficos.* Vol 1. R. Valdés and H. Vargas, eds. San Salvador, UCA Editores.
"Angel Martínez Baigorri, S.J." *EF*, 117–125. Previously unpublished (1956).
"Correspondencia con Angel Martínez." *EF*, 197–213. Previously unpublished (1954–1956).
"Posibilidad y modo de aproximación entre la filosofía escolástica y la filosofía vitalista moderna: Reflexiones ante el libro de Ramírez, *La filosofía de Ortega y Gasset.*" *EF*, 223–250. Previously unpublished (1958).
"Ortega, existencia desligada." *EF*, 265–270. Previously unpublished (1958).
"Sobre la irreligiosidad." *EF*, 271–280. Previously unpublished (1958–1959).
"Filosofía de la religión en Bergson." *EF*, 1996, 337–385. Partially published as "Religión y religiosidad en Bergson, I & II" (1960, 1961); partially previously unpublished (1960).
"Suárez y la neoescolástica." *EF*, 411–413. Previously unpublished (1960).
"Técnica y vida humana en Ortega y Gasset: Estudio de *Meditación de la técnica.*" *EF*, 415–518. Previously unpublished (1961).
"Carta abierta al autor de *Viridiana.*" *EF*, 519–523. Publication unknown (1962).
"Religiosidad pluriforme: Carducci, Maragall, Rilke." *EF*, 535–543. Previously unpublished (1963).
"Introducción al problema del milagro en Blondel." *EF*, 545–558. Previously unpublished (1963–1964).
"Reflexiones sobre la lógica estoica." *EF*, 559–587. Previously unpublished (1965).
"*Verum est declarativum aut manifestativum esse:* Sobre una cita de santo Tomás." *EF*, 593–596. Previously unpublished (1966).
"Introducción a la filosofía." *EF*, 597–624. Previously unpublished (1966).

## Writings of Ellacuría Published in English Translation

## 1976

*Freedom Made Flesh: The Mission of Christ and His Church.* Maryknoll, Orbis. Trans. by John Drury from *Teología política* (1973).
"Salvation History and Salvation in History." *FMF*, 3–19. Trans. from "Historia de la salvación y salvación en la historia" (1973).
"The Political Character of Jesus' Mission." *FMF*, 23–79. Part of this article can be found in "The Political Nature of Jesus' Mission," in J. Miguez Boniño, ed., *Faces of Jesus: Latin American Christologies.* Maryknoll, Orbis, 1984, 79–92; *FMF*, 23–51. Trans. from "Carácter político de la misión de Jesús" (1973).
"The Church's Mission: Signs of Its Credibility." *FMF*, 82–126. Trans from "El anuncio del Evangelio y la misión de la Iglesia" (1973).
"Liberation: Mission and Charism of the Latin American Church." *FMF*, 127–163. Trans. from "Liberación: misión y carisma de la iglesia latinoamericana" (1971).
"Violence and the Cross." *FMF*, 167–231. Trans. from "Violencia y cruz" (1969).
"Liturgy and Liberation." *FMF*, 233–246, from a previously unpublished manuscript; later published as "Liturgia y liberación," CIRD (1984), 279–292.

## 1977

"The Function of Economic Theories in Theological-Theoretical Discussion on the Relationship between Christianity and Socialism," in J. Metz and J. Jossua, eds., *Christian-*

*ity and Socialism*, New York, Seabury, 125–131. Trans. from "Teorías económicas y relación entre cristianismo y socialismo" (1977).

### 1982

"Human Rights in a Divided Society," in A. Hennelly and J. Langan, eds., *Human Rights in the Americas: The Struggle for Consensus*, Washington D.C., Georgetown University Press, 52–65. Trans. from "Historización del bien común y de los derechos humanos en una sociedad dividida" (1978).

"The Kingdom of God and Unemployment in the Third World," in J. Pohier and D. Mieth, eds., *Unemployment and the Right to Work*, New York, Seabury, 91–96. Trans. from "El Reino de Dios y el paro en el tercer mundo" (1982).

### 1988

"Violence and Non-violence in the Struggle for Peace and Liberation," in H. Küng and J. Moltmann, eds., *A Council for Peace*, London, T & T Clark. Trans. from "Trabajo no violento por la paz y violencia liberadora" (1988).

### 1990

I. Ellacuría, J. Sobrino, et al. *Companions of Jesus: The Jesuit Martyrs of El Salvador*. Maryknoll, Orbis.

"Persecution for the Sake of the Reign of God." *Companions of Jesus*, 64–75. Trans. from the conclusion to "El verdadero pueblo de Dios, según Monseñor Romero" (1981).

"The Task of a Christian University." *Companions of Jesus*, 147–151. Trans. from "Una universidad para el pueblo" (1982).

"The UCA Regarding the Doctorate Given to Monseñor Romero." *Envío 9*, 15–18. Trans. from "La UCA ante el doctorado concedido a Monseñor Romero" (1985).

"The Writings of Ellacuría, Martín-Baró, and Segundo Montes," in *The Jesuit Assassinations*, Kansas City, Sheed and Ward, 1–26. Trans. from brief extracts of various writings.

### 1991

*Towards a Society That Serves Its People: The Intellectual Contribution of El Salvador's Murdered Jesuits*. J. Hassett and H. Lacey, eds. Washington, D.C., Georgetown University Press.

"Liberation Theology and Socio-Historical Change in Latin America." *TSSP*, 19–43. Trans. by James Brockman from "La teología de la liberación frente al cambio socio-histórico de América Latina" (1987).

"Utopia and Prophecy in Latin America." *TSSP*, 44–88. Trans. by James R. Brockman from "Utopía y profetismo desde América Latina: Un ensayo concreto de soteriología historíca" (1989). Also in *MLT*, 289–328.

"Fundamental Human Rights and the Legal and Political Restrictions Placed on Them." *TSSP*, 91–104. Trans. by Phillip Berryman from "Los derechos humanos fundamentales y su limitación legal y política" (1969).

"The Historicization of the Concept of Property." *TSSP*, 105–137. Trans. by Phillip Berryman from "La historización del concepto de propiedad como principio de desideologización" (1976).

"The Challenge of the Poor Majority." *TSSP*, 171–176. Trans. by Phillip Berryman from "El desafío de las mayorías pobres" (1989).

"Is a Different Kind of University Possible?" *TSSP*, 177–207. Trans. by Phillip Berryman from "¿Diez años después: es posible una universidad distinta?" (1975).

"The University, Human Rights, and the Poor Majority." *TSSP*, 208–219. Trans. by Phillip Berryman from "Universidad, derechos humanos y mayorías populares" (1982).

"The True Social Place of the Church." *TSSP*, 283–292. Trans. by Phillip Berryman from "El auténtico lugar social de la Iglesia" (1982).

### 1994

I. Ellacuria and J. Sobrino, eds., *Mysterium Liberationis: Fundamental Concepts of Liberation Theology*. Maryknoll, Orbis. Trans. of *Mysterium liberationis: Conceptos fundamentales de la teología de la liberación*, 1990.

"The Historicity of Christian Salvation." *MLT*, 251–289. Trans. by Margaret D. Wilde from "Historicidad de la salvación cristiana" (1984).

"The Church of the Poor, Historical Sacrament of Liberation." *MLT*, 543–564. Trans. by Margaret D. Wilde from "La Iglesia de los pobres, sacramento histórico de la liberación" (1977).

"The Crucified People." *MLT*, 580–603. Trans. by Phillip Berryman and Robert R. Barr from "El pueblo crucificado" (1978). Also in I. Ellacuría and J. Sobrino, eds. *Systematic Theology: Perspectives from Liberation Theology*. Maryknoll, Orbis, 257–278.

### 1996

I. Ellacuria, J. Sobrino, I. Martín-Baró, *A Different Kind of University: Ignatian Voices from El Salvador*. O. Morgan and F. Homer, eds. Scranton, Pa., Center for Mission Reflection.

I. Ellacuria and J. Sobrino, eds. *Systematic Theology: Perspectives from Liberation Theology*. Readings from *Mysterium Liberationis*. Maryknoll, Orbis.

### 1998

"What Is the Point of Philosophy?" *Philosophy & Theology*, vol. 10, no. 1, 3–18. Trans. by T. Michael McNulty from "Filosofía ¿para qué?" (1976).

# Index